THE FATHER I HAD

Martin Townsend

CORGI BOOKS

TRANSWORLD PUBLISHERS
61-63 Uxbridge Road, London W5 5SA
A Random House Group Company
www.rbooks.co.uk

**THE FATHER I HAD
A CORGI BOOK: 9780552155199**

First published in Great Britain
in 2007 by Bantam Press
a division of Transworld Publishers
Corgi edition published 2008

Addresses for Random House Group Ltd companies outside the UK
can be found at: www.randomhouse.co.uk
The Random House Group Ltd Reg. No. 954009

The Random House Group Limited supports The Forest Stewardship
Council (FSC), the leading international forest certification organisation. All our
titles that are printed on Greenpeace approved FSC certified paper carry
the FSC logo.

Our paper procurement policy can be found at
www.rbooks.co.uk/environment

Typeset in 12/16pt Granjon by
Falcon Oast Graphic Art Ltd.

Printed in the UK by CPI Cox & Wyman, Reading, RG1 8EX.

2 4 6 8 10 9 7 5 3 1

To my family

There is no limit to the number of times
Your father can come to life, and he is as tender as he
    ever was
And as poor, his overcoat buttoned to the throat,
His face blue from the wind that always blows in the
    outer darkness
He comes towards you, hesitant,
Unwilling to intrude and yet driven at the point of love
To this encounter.

You may think
That love is all that is left of him, but when he comes
He comes with all his winters and all his wounds.
He stands shivering in the empty street,
Cold and worn like a tramp at the end of a journey
And yet a shape of unquestioning love that you
Uneasy and hesitant of the cold touch of death
Must embrace.

Then, before you can touch him
He is gone, leaving on your fingers
A little more of his weariness
A little more of his love.

                    Emyr Humphreys, *From Father to Son*

1

Missing

Dad left the house early that Saturday morning, his old cane fishing-rods in their canvas bag tied with string to the handlebar of his bike. He had kissed Mum and me goodbye – that familiar cold, rough cheek against mine; the whiff of Silvikrin and Embassy cigarettes – then wheeled his bike out through the back gateway and up the sloping path to the road.

Mum had stayed in the kitchen. I'd dawdled up the path after him, watched as he heaved himself up onto the bike, pushed down heavily on the pedals to get going, then wobbled away slowly up the street. He turned back to glance at me and gave a half-smile, but the eyes, through the thick, plastic frames of his black and cream glasses, were dead.

He had not said a word: not where he was going, not when he'd be back. He was very 'high' – not quite as 'high as a kite' (the phrase he'd use, with a heart-breaking cheerfulness, when he was so high that no one could reason with him and he was in the grip of a sort of terrible arrogance), but almost. High enough, anyway, that all communications with us had been closed down and he had sunk into a dead silence.

I watched him until he had pedalled to the end of the Close, and swayed, almost in slow motion, round the corner, a feeling of dread in my stomach as he did it. It was like watching one of those little planes at an air-show as it disappears behind the inevitable line of bluey-grey trees and you know that it's going to crash.

There were only two possible destinations: the three little ponds at Stanmore Common, where I often fished myself, or the 'boot pond' at Bentley Priory. Neither was more than a couple of miles away, an easy cycling distance. But I didn't want him to go anywhere. I never wanted him to go anywhere when he was high. I wanted him to stay at home and sit quietly in a chair, smoking a cigarette or one of his small cigars and getting through it. But it was never like that.

Now it was after 9 p.m. and he still hadn't come home. The rain lashed our bay windows, forming long, water-mark patterns behind our net curtains. The television was off. Mum sat in the armchair, leaning forward, her hands gripped together between her knees. She was in her nightie and dressing-gown. Her wavy brown hair

10

was neatly styled as ever, but beneath it her face – her pale, open, innocent face with its startling blue eyes – looked careworn. There were big blotches of red in a 'V', either side of her neck: worry.

I was furious. Furious with myself for not running round the back that morning, grabbing my little bike – the one he'd salvaged from the 'tip' at the end of our street – and begging to go with him. Angry with him for not suggesting it.

How could he be out there on his own in this rain? How could he survive on that old bike, in that black donkey-jacket he always wore, which offered no protection against the wet but just sucked it in, like a blanket? And his shoes! He was wearing those Dunlop Green Flash plimsolls that he always put on when he was high (plimsolls that my mum hated, hated, hated, because their appearance was always the first indicator of the illness coming on).

I had visions of his bike lying somewhere, rain splashing and dripping off the chain and the pedals. And my dad – where? Somewhere, but certainly dead.

I'd never see him again. The tears welled up in my eyes. 'Oh, Mum.' It was more a complaining tone than a helpless one, my tears, for the moment, dammed back by frustration: why was he like this? Why couldn't he be like everyone else's daddy – working nine to five in a bank, then sitting nicely with us, speaking in a deep, posh voice like our doctor – Dr Hicks – who was the poshest man I knew. Why couldn't he be steady and reliable like that?

Now there was thunder and lightning. The rain accelerated against the windows, grew thicker, whipped across by the white flashes. It hammered on the black roof of our semicircular bay – the roof that 'sweated' in summer, so that when my brother and I climbed up there in our shorts we'd have streaks of tar all over our legs. It hammered too on the little porch over our front door – the one we'd climb to reach the easily openable window of the box-room if we ever forgot our keys.

How I longed to hear the click and scratch of his keys in the front door now. The rain just grew more heavy. This was ridiculous. This was God playing with us. Dad was missing and He not only didn't care but was determined to make it worse. My mum just said, 'tch', and sighed. I couldn't define, and had never really understood, my mother's concerns for my father. She had lived with his illness for much longer than I had, of course, and, as I later discovered, thought she understood the cause of it. But my concerns for him, I felt, were more realistic and more serious because I had been out in the world with my dad when he was high. I had seen, first hand, how in that condition he greeted the world, and how the world regarded him.

I had walked around with him – 'bowled' around, as he always said – or gone out for a 'blow' with him. 'Just

12

going out for a blow,' he'd say to my mum, pulling on his coat, the plimsolls flashing on his feet like warnings. 'You comin' with me, tiddler?' It was always me. We never went out as a family when he was high, and my brother – then in bed upstairs, unaware of our crisis – was two years younger than I was: too young to be his walking partner.

My father and I walked for miles. Once, when Dad had breezed away alone, all afternoon, he came in with his plimsolls clogged with blood: he had walked the skin off his feet.

But we didn't just go walking aimlessly. When he was high he would often be filled with a vast, unreasonable and often terrifying anger at the sedentary life he supposed my mother had got us used to. He would insist, then, that we 'got out' to various events. 'You keep 'em stuck in!' he'd accuse my mother. 'In front of that bloody telly! They've gotta get out, they've gotta ... meet people!'

Then he would take my brother and me to the museums – always the Science Museum or the Natural History Museum – or to Hampstead Heath to watch the radio-controlled boats on the ponds. 'You've gotta get in there, talk to people,' he'd insist – and I would be embarrassed. I was shy, I didn't want to meet people – well, not complete strangers out of the blue.

'It's interesting,' he'd say, whatever 'it' was – a dinosaur in the museum, a boat, temporarily dry-docked at the side of a pond, being tended to with small and mysterious tools by grown men who breathed noisily through their noses. He would attempt to launch into conversations with such people, asking Janet and John questions that made me squirm with embarrassment. 'What sort of boat is it?' 'How does it work?'

And he wouldn't listen to their answers. Not really listen. Because he was miles away, his eyes glazed, and – if he'd been persuaded to start taking the medication that would eventually slow his racing mind back down again – his lips pursing and re-pursing. It looked like an attitude of concentration but it wasn't: it was just a side-effect of the drugs.

When he was high he would keep pushing other versions of himself forward to make the contact, do the talking. The real dad would then drop back and look on, uncomprehending: locked in his illness, the dry, sore lips working, working . . .

It was after 10 p.m. now. I should have been in bed, like any other ten-year-old, leaving my mother to her lone vigil. We probably also should have called the police. But it never occurred to my mother to call them. Her assumption was always that they'd be far too busy with important matters to interest themselves in our problems. Our first instinct, living on a council estate where we knew most of our immediate neighbours, was to knock and ask them for help – or at least for advice. They knew about Dad.

They knew about the illness and its consequences.

But it was too late at night to do that. My mum wouldn't call anybody, even a member of the family, after 9 p.m. 'They'll be in bed,' she'd say. 'I can't disturb them this time of night.' And she'd look at me disapprovingly for even suggesting it.

So we started a half-hearted game of Scrabble in silence, and drank tea, my mum looking up every now and then to sigh at the bay windows, where the rain still knocked, or to frown and sigh at me. Then we heard 'the gate go' – the family's phrase for the lifting of the little latch on our front gate, and the soft crash as it was pushed back against the privet hedge.

My mum stood, and I saw her mouth open and shut. I knew what she was thinking. She was thinking, *Here come the two policemen to deliver the bad news* (one with his helmet already tucked deferentially under his arm, the other frowning up at the rain as he followed suit). She was thinking of when she was living at home with her mum and dad at Moorhouse Road and Mrs Portsmouth's son Peter was killed in an explosion at Colchester barracks; how the whole road saw those two coppers arrive ... But then we both heard the click-click of Dad's bike chain on the path and, seconds later, the scrape of his key in the door.

'Ron!'

He was soaked to the skin. He was smiling. He held the central stock of his bicycle handlebars as if his bike was a horse. In his right hand, at his side, was some sort of elliptical-shaped tin. I'd seen it on many occasions in the bottom of his wardrobe. It was a strange, drab, military green.

'Open the back gate, Peg.'

My mum took her coat from the peg in the hall and hurried to the kitchen. I heard her open the back door, the rush and swish of the rain, then the metallic rasp as she shot open the bolt on the gate into the garden. Dad propped his bike against the dark-creosoted back-garden fence. He unscrewed the front light from it – the bright beam picking out slow-motion globules of rain – and then, picking up the green tin box, ushered Mum and me down to our garden pond. I was in my anorak over my pyjamas. I could feel the bottoms of my pyjama trousers clinging coldly to my ankles. Mum had pulled an old coat on over her nightie.

'Come on, son.'

He knelt by the pond, a blue plastic-moulded model with 'shelves' at each end for plants, which he'd salvaged from the local dump. The green tin had flap-openings at each end. He opened one now and shone the bicycle light into the murky water. I peered in and there were three or four fish, six or seven inches long, their dark-grey backs breaking through the muddy surface. He would never have put them in so little water, I thought: some must have slopped out as he carried the tin home, swinging under his handlebar.

'Rudd,' he said, and he was so proud. 'For the pond.' He pulled back a corner of the netting that we used to thwart the cats, lowered the tin into the water and tipped out the fish gently. We watched them dart down to the bottom.

Dad straightened up and smiled, his hands dangling at his sides. 'Cup of tea?' he said to my mum.

We had one map in the house: a map of the London borough of Harrow, where we lived. I would lay it out on the green- and yellow-patterned carpet in our front room and study it for areas of blue – the ponds, lakes, streams and reservoirs, some of which I knew and a few of which, intriguingly, I did not.

Sometimes my dad would join me down on the carpet, poring over those little irregular patches. Water, fish, fishing: the sight, the smell, the feel of ponds, of pondweed, of the thick, black, acrid mud at the edges – there was a deep yearning in both of us for all this: perhaps the deepest yearning we shared.

As he crouched down to look, I'd feel his breath on my neck and the top of my arm, then catch its slightly sour smell, which was always, always, mixed up with that of Silvikrin and the sweet smell of summer sweat underneath that was so much him. Even now, decades later, a single whiff of that hair cream can conjure him up – a genie from a plastic tub.

Ronald Norman Townsend (how I hated the dreary

toll of that 'Norman' with its echoes of 'normal') was just over six feet tall, with broad shoulders, jet-black hair and an almost permanent, inquisitive smile. He had a broad head, slightly tapered towards the top, so that when he was in the army doing his ill-fated national service his mates called him 'bullet head'. He liked the sobriquet. He liked anything that conferred 'character' on himself, and was admiring of anyone else who in any way embodied that quality.

When I spoke to him, he had a way of tipping his head back ever so slightly, then opening his mouth a little, in wonder, as if everything I told him was going to be new and surprising.

Every route we traced, with our fingers, on that map, every route we mapped out for our bikes (because my father never learned to drive, and neither have I), began at a three-quarter-inch oblong towards the middle of the sheet at the left. This oblong – out in a comparatively blank area of the map, bordered by railway lines and adjacent, gloriously in my youthful opinion, to the municipal dump – was Cullington Close, our street.

(Years later, pausing at the top of Stamford Street, near Waterloo station, on my way home from work, I saw that blessed oblong, five or six feet wide, on a 'Transport for London' advertising poster promoting the Mayor's push for more buses in London. I thought it almost miraculous that, of all the squares from the *London A to Z* Mayor Livingstone could have used, he chose the one with my small, isolated street, and not much else, in it. A place where, ironically, no bus ever visits.)

Cullington Close. It's still there. Shrunken, somehow, these days – the fate of every place we cherish from our youth – but still best seen from the eastern end, either under a lowering winter sky of watery yellow and heavy grey, or in brilliant sunshine.

It was, and still largely is, a council estate: two parallel rows of grey houses, set back at the eastern end behind an oblong grass verge either side, and, at the far, western end, round a wide circle, inevitably full of vans and trailers and cars on bricks or under ancient tarpaulins. This was what we thought of as the 'rough' end, though the families, in truth, were no more or less rough than those at any other point along the road.

Each house had a small front garden, in most cases set behind a low brick wall and privet hedge. Each front door had an identical porch over it and, in summer, when my brother and I sat on top of the porch, picking at the melting black surface and watching the world go by, there were other children, all along the road, doing the same thing. In fact, from our porch we could jump onto the roof of our bay window and then over to the roof of our neighbour's one too.

At the back, most of the gardens were close on a hundred feet long. Ours, laid almost completely to lawn, was always full of children.

My father, my mother told me, had gone through 'hell' to get this house. He and my mum, Margaret – or 'Peggy' – had married in 1956 and moved in with Peg's mother, Winnie. I had been born in 1960, my brother Ian in 1962, and in that same year we had been given the house in Cullington Close. To secure it, Mum had told us, Dad had been forced to move into lodgings for quite a long while and had been very unhappy. It was only one of a few periods of unexplained 'unhappiness' to which my brother and I, probably wrongly, later attached some of the blame for our dad's illness.

Dad had laboriously moved all our stuff from our nan's house in the side-car of his motorbike. We couldn't afford a removals van.

The back garden, when we moved in, was just a sea of mud, so Dad and his old man, Albert – or 'Elb' – set to work to lay a lawn and build at one end a square of crazy-paving that we wouldn't have dreamed of calling a 'patio'.

The garden was the most important thing to our dad. He had inherited Elb's love of gardening and couldn't wait to put in flower-beds, plant his favourite rose bushes and – of course – install the pond that he found, one Saturday afternoon, at the dump. He dug the hole for it – involving hours of back-breaking work shovelling through the heavy, yellow clay – then crouched on his haunches watching it slowly fill with water from the garden hose. When he took off his spectacles and swept the sleeve of his jumper across his face I wasn't sure whether it was sweat or tears he was wiping away.

'All right, son?' he said.

2

Cullington Close

My dad left school at fourteen and went to work at a jeweller's, Caulfields, in Golders Green, north London, as a clock- and watch-repairer. He loved the job and his employers trusted him enough to allow him to carry valuable items to other places in London.

Dad was called up for national service in the REME (Royal Electrical and Mechanical Engineers) and sent to Bielefeld in Germany. When it was over, in 1951, he went to work with one of his uncles in a printing firm, but he ran into problems that had something to do, my mother told me, with the company allowing only fathers and sons to join. He tried his hand repairing electricity meters and got a job at the London Electricity Board – which also, at differing times, employed his father. At around this time he met my mother. She was twenty-one. They lived at either end of the same street in Harrow, and had gone to the same junior school, but had never spoken before.

They met on a bus. My mother was in a back seat, my father at the front. 'He got off at the stop before me,' my mother told me years later, 'and I looked back at him. He told me he knew I was going to do that so he turned round as well. He told his sister, Jean, he wanted to ask me out and she teased him and said I was married.'

In June 1952 Dad went to Mum's house and asked her to go to a show with him. It was called *London Laughs*. They were engaged in 1954 on 6 November on Hammersmith Broadway. They had gone out to choose an engagement ring together and my dad, impatient as ever, had handed it to her there and then. They were married on 15 September 1956.

Like most small boys, I adored my mum but only dared to think of her as 'beautiful' when she was safely enshrined in an old photograph. There were dozens of black-and-white pictures of her, and the rest of my family, crammed into an old blue biscuit-tin at the bottom of my dad's wardrobe. In these neat little prints, as a teenager and, later, on holidays and dates with my dad – in pedal-pusher trousers, for instance, with a sweater draped across her shoulders – my mother was, indeed, strikingly good-looking.

Mum had inherited her mother's fussiness about her hair. Scrupulously styled and brushed back from her forehead, it framed a face that was open, smiling and innocent. Her eyes were of the palest grey-blue and they too seemed impossibly wide open and happy, as if child-hood, adolescence and marriage at twenty-five had blended into one continuous happy dream.

A decade on, she cut a more practical and down-to-earth figure. Her face and hair were still very beautiful but she seemed slightly shorter than in those old pictures, and tougher. When she cuddled me, or sat me on her lap, I could see the first few worry-lines on her forehead and round her mouth.

My mother had a wonderful sense of humour and a great ability to laugh at herself, but her nimble wit was tempered by a quickness, a nervousness, in her movements that reflected deep anxieties about my dad. She could have a certain brittleness in her tongue, too – a trait inherited from her mother – and would allow no serious comment or criticism to pass without the sharpest of retorts. She always seemed to be in a hurry and on the verge of forgetting something at the same time, so that she bustled along, slim but strong-shouldered, her big handbag held rigid in the crook of her arm.

Cullington Close, my mother told me, with a hint of self-mocking laughter in her tone, was where the council put the miscreants: 'problem families' – I always liked that description – and those who had persistently failed to pay their rent elsewhere.

It all went over my dad's head. 'They seem all right, though, don't they, Peg? None of them seem like bad people, do they?' He always spoke like this – in rhetorical questions to my mum – but, in truth, he was keen to see the best in people, a characteristic that would get us all into a lot of trouble in the years to come.

Dad was working, at this time, as an electrician's mate at Edgware General Hospital. It was to be the first of a series of manual jobs in which, to a greater or lesser degree, my dad found himself trapped rather than employed. He always made the best of it – usually going way beyond what was required of him in order to keep the job interesting – but as the years went by it often struck me that the father I spoke to, walked with, played with, deserved something more creative than it was his lot to get.

On Saturdays, when my dad was working a weekend shift at Edgware, my mum would take my brother and me to meet him at the hospital. It was a gloomy place – and, back then, very strict about how people behaved on the wards and in the corridors. We all had to talk in whispers – but I was impressed by the way everyone seemed to know my dad, and by the way he greeted them. Afterwards, on our walk to the bus stop, we would see the big red-and-white drum on top of the nearby Boosey & Hawkes musical instrument factory: a sight that never failed to thrill me. Sometimes, when we were on our own, my dad would take me off into different little paths and lanes around Edgware just to see the drum from different angles: between the chimneys, over a roof, partly obscured by a tree. He did it to amuse me, but it was clear he loved to 'bowl' around the streets, peering and pointing into people's gardens, especially if they had ponds. We knew every pond on all our walks.

In later years, seated in his armchair in our 'back room', pursing his lips, chattering through the curling blue smoke from his little cigar, my dad would refer to Edgware Hospital as 'the best job I ever had' – and I think it was. Certainly some terrible ones would follow. But it was also the beginning of a problem.

I was too young, back then, to know that my father had already been diagnosed as manic-depressive, so when he began to chatter incessantly about the doctors at Edgware – how he could *help* them, how they *needed* his help, how, really, he was a doctor – I took very little notice. As far as I was concerned, this was Dad being his usual sociable self, wanting to give others a bit of a hand.

But my mum could recognize the fearful dichotomy: that the more he – the hospital electrician – claimed to be involved with the doctors, the more he was moving into the 'high' phase of his illness. This was the phase that put the greatest pressure on us, his family, not only because, eventually – and sometimes twice annually – he became impossible, literally, to live with, but because his over-arching cheerfulness, his willingness to help, seemed almost a positive thing to people outside the family, including, in some cases, the doctors we were appealing to for help.

All of this, back then, in those early years of the 1960s, my mum had to deal with alone. My brother and I were too young to understand fully, and my father's parents were of a generation that simply couldn't, or wouldn't, deal with it, so the weight of responsibility fell, almost palpably, across my mother's shoulders.

One afternoon, during the summer of the World Cup – 1966 – my dad summoned me into the back garden. He was out on the crazy-paving, making something or other. He had two long planks of wood he had rescued from somewhere – the dump, perhaps, or a skip along the road. He had one of the planks lying across an old padded stool he had also salvaged and, kneeling on one end to steady it, he was sawing away at the other.

'What are you doing, Dad?' I could sense my mum pausing in the kitchen behind us, waiting to hear the answer.

'I'm making something for the hospital. Me and you'll take it up there.'

I didn't want to go up there. Whatever it was he was making, I didn't want to be seen with it. I was six years old by then, I had started school, and I was beginning to recognize the changing atmospheres and temperatures in the house during the year as Dad soared slowly upwards into a high, then came spiralling, slumping down. I was beginning to feel depressed myself by his moods. It was wearying to come home from school not knowing what he might do or say, and I had begun to recognize that there was a thin line, a very thin line, between the outer edges of one of these 'happy' highs and an explosion of sudden, ferocious temper.

It was the knowledge of this line, more than anything else, that left me exhausted and frustrated by the attitude of outsiders to him when he was like this. 'Oh, Ron's in a good mood,' they'd say; 'what a lovely bloke.' And I'd want to kill them, literally kill them, for their ignorance of what was really going on at number 32.

My dad picked up the shorter of the two pieces of wood and, after carefully positioning it about two-thirds of the way up the longer piece, took up his hammer and began nailing the planks together.

Oh God, I thought, please tell me he isn't making what I think he's making – and God was, indeed, the right person to ask.

Dad took up the cross and, slinging it over his shoulder, reached out for my hand. 'Come on, tiddler.'

I saw my mum's face through the window. She was staring at me hard, her mouth gaping open, as if there was something I could do. Her mouth closed and she shook her head. But Dad was striding off, tugging me along behind. Through the back gateway, up the path, the cross over his shoulder – Dad and me off on the road to Calvary.

I knew we were going to Edgware Hospital. It didn't seem odd to be going there – I had realized, by then, that Dad had grown obsessed with the place, with the way

they 'helped people'. As ever, when he was high, it was
to the concept of universal goodness he was drawn. But
it seemed odd, to me, to be going to a hospital on such a
sweltering day. As we walked up to Belmont Circle,
about a mile away, to catch the bus, Dad chattered in
short bursts, then fell silent, his mouth working, working. He was trying to buy me a bike but he had only
thirty shillings. He'd shown me the one-pound note and
the ten-shilling note in a plastic zip-up purse. It was to
replace the little Raleigh Pavemaster he'd pulled off the
dump about a year ago, its punctured tyres hanging limp
from the buckled rims. He'd 'done it up' for me and it
had served for a while. But now he had his eye on something better. Dad never had much money but he liked
spending it – especially on my brother and me.

'We'll see if we can get a racer, eh? Get a racer,' he
said, half to himself.

I watched the other people on the 183 bus. Dad had
propped the cross next to our seats, but no one seemed to
be taking much notice. Dad couldn't have cared less anyway – he was in a world of his own.

At Edgware Hospital, Dad was master of the
situation. He stuck his head in at the little lodge by
the gate, where an affable old watchman sat and read the
paper, occasionally putting it down and nipping out to
lift the red-and-white metal barrier for a visiting car.

'I'm popping by to put something up for 'em,' Dad
said. This was always the case when he was high – the

strange and unusual things he did were always at some-one else's bidding.

We walked up the wide drive, then turned off to the tennis courts. Dad lifted the cross up high and began tying it, with string, to the plastic mesh boundary fence. I had a headache from the bus ride, the sun and, now, the anxiety: I didn't want Dad to be 'caught', to be humiliated.

He had just finished hanging the cross and we were both tilting our heads to admire it, when a youngish doctor, good-looking, with jet-black hair like my dad's, came over from the gate. He wore a white coat and was carrying books of some sort. He was accompanied by a small woman in a coat too heavy for the day, who looked like his mother. They both smiled warily.

'Hello, Ron – what you up to?' He glanced at me.

'Putting this up for the chief. The chief wanted it up. When people are playing, they can see it.'

The doctor was smiling and nodding. The woman was looking at the cross.

'I brought the tiddler with me, if that's OK,' Dad added, touching my head. He obviously thought my presence on hospital property was more serious than hanging an enormous cross in their tennis courts.

The doctor and the woman both smiled at me. 'OK, good,' he said. 'You gonna pop by next week?'

'What for?' My dad was immediately on the alert.

'Have a chat.'

Dad worked his lips and nodded. 'Yeah, yeah, I'll have a chat with you.'

On the way back home, Dad was silent. He was out of his trance now and was merely distracted, his lips working, working. He kept smiling at me: 'All right, tiddler?'

He knew he was going to be sectioned.

My dad went away a few days later. I didn't know where they had sent him. My mum was a bit tearful the first evening he was gone, shaking her head and wiping her red-rimmed eyes with the back of her hand. I didn't fully comprehend, until a few years later, the powerful combination of relief and sorrow that always shuddered through my mum when Dad was eventually taken into hospital. She would weep openly, at the same time wiping her streaming eyes and running nose and protesting: 'I'm not crying, I'm fine,' as if willing her sense of relief to be the more dominant emotion.

I would kneel on the floor in front of her, my hands in her lap, begging her not to cry. 'He'll be all right, Mum. He really will.'

How many times would I end up saying that over the years?

Life went on. On the kitchen shelf, the little transistor radio in its leather case, splattered with paint from the time Dad had painted the ceiling, played 'Penny Lane'. With its busy barbers and rushing firemen and general air of wistfulness, the song lodged in my head as a tale of the life led by people with dads who didn't get ill and have to keep going away. I sat on the kitchen floor making crude Thunderbird models with my Lego.

When he came back, about two weeks later, Dad went straight to bed and stayed there. Venturing into my mum and dad's bedroom, which smelled of his sweat and hair cream, all I could see was his black hair on the pillow, all sticking up. I slipped onto the bed and cuddled his shape under the eiderdown.

A day or so afterwards, late in the morning, he was sitting in his underpants and vest on the edge of the bed, his head in his hands, just staring at the floor. His knee jumped up and down, the heel of his foot tapping out an incessant thumpety-thump beat on the carpet. This, I found out a few years later, was a side-effect of the drugs he'd been given. The jerking had worked his balls out from the side of his pants and I was fascinated by them.

He looked up. 'All right, tiddler?' His eyes were dark-rimmed and red from crying, but at least the light was back in them. He had returned to the world, at the very least.

I went to put an arm round his shoulder.

'I'm getting up in a minute,' he breathed. 'I'll come downstairs and watch the telly.'

As soon as the drugs and his willpower and the passing of time had got him – this time – through the depression, he was out and about. He played football with me in the garden. He chalked a wicket on the back wall of the house and we played cricket with a tennis ball. The weekends became exciting again.

The weight lifted off my mother's shoulders almost visibly. The tightly wound, determined woman in a raincoat hurrying up to whatever hospital he was in became bright and girlish again. She would sit, arms folded, at our kitchen table and quietly fill in the crossword in her paper, while Dad moved around, inspecting the garden, oiling his bike, catching up with the world once more.

One afternoon, wheeling his bike through nearby Kenton Park, Dad spotted a brand-new park bench. That evening, after dark, he took our old green-and-white Silver Cross pram and strolled back over there with it, returning about a half-hour later, puffing and sweating, with the bench slung across the chassis. It was amazing that the springs held up.

Mum appeared to be angry with him, but the anger did not seem entirely genuine: it had a watchful edge to it. She was trying to work out whether this was a straightforward theft or an indicator that he was becoming high again.

'Look, Peg . . .' and he was spreading his arms, pleading and laughing, and winking at me, 'the kids'll just smash it up if you leave it over there. They break up every bench along the path.'

He painted it white 'in case anyone comes round'.

'Edna', who, according to the brass plaque screwed to the back of it, 'always loved this spot', was now going to have to get used to a different view.

Dad was popular in Cullington Close, especially with the wilder teenagers. He had organized some of them into a rudimentary youth football team, and there were matches against other groups of lads. They were always arranged at the last minute and, always, it seemed to me, teetered on the edge of becoming mass punch-ups.

As with many streets on council estates, Cullington Close revolved round the activities – nefarious or other-wise – of one or two key families, and it was the scions of these clans that Dad paraded, in a raggle-taggle of long hair, shared fags and mismatching socks and shirts, to whatever pitch in whatever local park he had managed to book.

He would drag me along from time to time to watch, but I shook my head and looked away if he asked me to play. On his side he seemed oblivious to the fact that I was only seven – a good eight to ten years younger than any of the other players. For my part I was too shy, and in a quiet way didn't like being criticized or told what to do.

I'd stand, hopping from foot to foot to keep warm, on

the touch-line, embarrassed even that my catalogue-bought parka was blue and not the green that you were supposed to have. Nothing about me was 'laddish' or dangerous at all – not like the boys he had in the team. I felt over-educated and 'girly', even at my young age, compared with these tearaways.

None of the boys themselves seemed bothered that I wasn't playing: it was only my dad who cared and his degree of caring would increase as his mood cranked up yet again to a 'high'. His obsession with the fact that I and, to a lesser extent, my brother 'didn't get out enough' had turned into a preoccupation with trying to get us to be sporty, and each time he grew ill this preoccupation would become more and more uncomfortable for me.

One of the groups of teenagers in Dad's team lived a few doors away from us. They were four brothers, the Browns, ranging in age from twelve to twenty. In the evenings all but the eldest, Steven, would sit on the wall outside their house, smoking and playing kerb-ball. They were the sort of boys who could look after themselves and who got into occasional fights, but they didn't make trouble or go looking for it.

The youngest boy, Roger, was a big favourite of my dad's. He had sandy hair, an honest face and a great sense of humour.

One evening I was hanging around, chatting to the Browns, when Roger spotted an old man who had just entered the street at the far end. This was Mr Saville.

Mr Saville was a small, pale, painfully thin man, always very well dressed. Above his over-large collar and tie reared a white, wrinkled throat that I could never quite avoid staring at. It seemed paper-thin, like the stretched neck of a turkey, and his voice, which was a reedy gurgle, seemed to be produced right down there, in that tight fold of collar, and never to attain any volume or power as a result.

Mr Saville was always moaning at the Browns when their ball bounced near his car. He had a terminally ill wife and guarded her peace and quiet, and his own peace of mind, rapaciously.

'Mr Saville,' muttered Roger to the others and, as the old man approached on the other side of the street, he began humming the theme from *Steptoe & Son*.

I was utterly horrified and deeply impressed at one and the same time. Here was I, so well-behaved that I disgusted myself, right at the epicentre of trouble. Unable to stop myself, I burst into laughter.

Mr Saville stopped in his tracks. 'Oi!'

The Browns melted away, over the wall, into their house – gone. But I just stood there, my mouth dry, the blood rushing in my ears. Mr Saville came over. He leant down to me. I could smell, for some reason, Spam – and the Spam smell combined with the twitching turkey-neck made me imagine Mr Saville, somehow, as old, dying meat. He put his hand on my shoulder.

'I know you didn't mean it,' he said. 'But you mustn't

hang around with those boys, because they'll get you into trouble – all right?' He had very fair eyelashes, like the feathers of a chick, and cloudy little eyes.

I just nodded. I was frozen. What if my mum and dad were looking out of the window?

He straightened up and walked away, checking his old, lime-green Cortina as he passed it. I walked home, so stiff-legged I felt as if I was learning to walk all over again.

3

Breaking Down

At Easter 1968 I found myself in Edgware Hospital as a patient. I had been practising at school for a spring concert, kneeling for long periods on a hard wooden stage. Perhaps it was a splinter, perhaps it was just the pressure on the joint, but one morning I woke up to find I was unable to bend my left knee. There was a hot pain under the kneecap and, as it started to swell up, a tiny pimple of yellow appeared.

Our family GP was on holiday and the locum could not be convinced to visit. I limped up the road to the bus stop, clinging on to my mum, feeling more hot and faint with every step.

I felt sick in the surgery, the walls beginning to dance a bit in my vision. When the doctor eventually saw me, he called an ambulance. He was shaking his head and muttering. My temperature was just over 105°.

I felt like I knew Edgware Hospital and I couldn't

wait to see Dad. As soon as we arrived, my mum found him buried away down in the little subterranean workshop he and the other electricians used.

He turned up in his brown overalls, looking more worried than I'd ever seen him. 'You all right, son? Is there anything you need?' He sat down at the side of the bed and held my wrist.

Dad seemed to know everyone who passed by or came up. A doctor, a chubby-faced fellow with receding curly hair, told me I had an abscess under my left kneecap that had filled with pus. Next day I would have an operation to drain it.

I was in hospital for three weeks. There was a record in the charts that I liked called 'Rainbow Valley' by The Love Affair – and the day after my operation my dad brought me the sheet music for it. He'd bought it from Mr Clipp's, the TV and record shop where my mum did some cleaning. 'Now you can sing along when it comes on the radio,' Dad explained. I opened the four-page song sheet on my chest and read the first few words:

> *I'm heading home again*
> *'Cos it seems I don't fit in . . .*

I looked up at my dad and he leant down and kissed me.

'Love you, son.'

He disappeared to talk to somebody and my mum came over.

'He's very excitable at the moment,' she said.

I noticed her neck was red and her mouth was tensed the way it always was when Dad was starting to get high again.

'It'll be all right,' she said. She sighed. 'It's just what we always have to put up with, isn't it?'

Within weeks, Dad was high again. The process always followed the same pattern. Some event or other – a problem in the family, a disaster out in the world some-where, or perhaps simply the impact that a film or stage play had on him – would cause my dad to stop taking his tablets.

These tablets were a cause of continual resentment to my dad. They triggered side-effects that he found embarrassing: the involuntary pulling and pursing of his mouth, and, when he was sitting down, the staccato drumming of one or other of his feet on the floor. But they maintained, as far as they could, his mental equilibrium.

When he was provoked to stop taking them, he would first of all become irritated and critical of those around him, with my mum and me bearing the brunt. Then he would begin his pacing – up and down, up and down the carpeted floor of our front room – all the while clench-ing and unclenching his fists.

He was adept at hiding his tablets away, so we would not always be aware he had come off them. But as the years went on, and we all became more familiar with the warning signs, my mum would squirrel away stocks of his tablets so that she could crush up his daily dose in his cup of tea. Sometimes it worked, but at other times he stopped drinking tea altogether; then, after the initial pacing had finished, he'd begin to slip away from us completely. Tea would go cold, untouched, in front of him. He'd sit for hours, staring into space, occasionally snapping back to ask me or my brother, not unkindly, what we were doing or what we'd been up to that day. We could tell him anything, because he never really heard a single word. He'd nod – 'Sure, sure' – and carry on smoking and staring, a look of beatific peace on his face.

Then he would begin doing odd things: playing the same record again and again all night, with the windows of the house wide open so that everyone could hear. He was obsessed with Frank Sinatra and that obsession would turn into a fixation on one or two songs: once it was 'Love and Marriage'; another time 'I Will Drink the Wine'. From Sinatra, at various times, he moved on to Dean Martin, Jerry Lewis, Topol, Johnny Mathis . . . He would write letters to the artistes, or scribble messages of encouragement all over their record sleeves, telling them where they were going wrong and suggesting they come to him for help.

At these times we always faced the same problem: how to convince first Dad's GP, then various doctors, that Dad was ill enough to be taken into hospital and forced back onto his medication. If we were lucky, he would do something silly – like putting the cross up at Edgware – so that the doctor would have no alternative but to take him in.

The whole process of trying to get Dad sectioned was painful and wearying – not least because my mum and I would be racked by guilt at how terrible it was for my dad. We knew that he came off the tablets because they made him twitch and thump and feel humiliated. We knew that he avoided, at all costs, being put back on them because the required initial dose of lithium plunged him into the blackest of black depressions. Knowing all this, the temptation was to let him be – but then our lives would be utterly miserable and his just a blank, a trance.

Dad went back into hospital that summer of 1968 and when he came out the depression seemed endless.

At Christmas, he tried to go back to work. It was bitterly cold and the short days of semi-darkness closed in on him. One afternoon, feeling particularly down, he got permission to leave work early. By the time he reached home, he was in tears.

My mum sat him down at the dinner table, he still in his works donkey-jacket and scarf, and Dad told his story. He'd been walking out past the hospital gatehouse when he noticed a water hydrant that had burst and begun to freeze as it spurted up, fountain-like, from the road. As he glanced at it, he'd seen in the ice the figure of a veiled woman, about three feet high. The water was still running from the top of the sculpted ice, so that it appeared to Dad that the figure was crying.

'I looked away,' he said, 'and when I looked back I couldn't see the woman any more. I walked round and round it, but she had gone.' He put his thumb and forefinger up to his eyes. 'Oh, Peg, I feel so low. I feel so low.' And he wept.

My mum put her arm round him as the sobs shuddered through his big shoulders. She looked up at me and rolled her eyes.

Her response seemed inappropriate, then, considering the profundity of the experience my father had just claimed to have had. But my mum could not always afford the luxury of sentiment, and as I got older I came to see this eye-rolling as a defensive gesture. I would feel, over the years – and with varying degrees of shame – embarrassment, irritation and anger both at my dad's illness and what I perceived, in my young mind, to be his willingness to succumb to it. But Mum never stopped supporting him. The roll of the eyes was for her own benefit: 'Here I go again,' she seemed to say; 'what toll will it take on me this time?' For the truth was that Dad's illness was unpredictable: it could go, as we grew used to saying, 'either way'.

It could strike so hard and so deep that his true character was simply erased for weeks on end. He would rail against going into hospital and 'blame' my mother bitterly when he was eventually admitted. Or it could simply deal Dad a sort of glancing blow. He would become high but not so deranged that he wouldn't co-operate in getting well.

My mother never knew which course it would take and this uncertainty, more than anything, aged her. It made her fretful and often frightened. There were times, when Dad was becoming ill, that my mum would be dry-mouthed and shaking with apprehension.

The depression that followed the 'fountain' incident lasted for weeks. When Dad finally emerged from it he was filled with renewed vigour to make a 'man' of me. I was enrolled into the local Cub Scouts, whose weekly ritual would make me dread Tuesdays more than any other day. Each time we had to turn up with a diary, a pencil, a piece of string and a shilling 'subscription'. The 'Akela' was very strict and accepted no excuses for forgetting any of these items, so that it was not unusual, while we waited for her arrival in the hall, to see boys ripping lengths of thread from the old mats that were stored in a heap in one corner. These were the ones who had forgotten their string. I gave up on the cubs after a month. I told Mum but I didn't dare tell Dad. I polished my lace-ups, put on my uniform and left the house every

Tuesday on my bike. Then I cycled round the streets for two hours.

That year Dad took me to my first 'proper' football match – Watford v Queen's Park Rangers. I didn't really want to go all the way to Watford – a place that was off the corner of my map of 'Harrow & District'. I didn't want to mix with real football fans. I'd seen pictures of them scowling and fighting in the *Sunday Mirror*. I was happy to watch football on the TV, or on Saturday afternoons a mile up the road at Wealdstone, where large areas of the ground were near-deserted and you stood between clumps of weeds that had pushed their way up through the cracks in the tired concrete terracing.

But Dad was thrilled by the huge crowd at the Watford match. He swelled up in the face of it, full of confidence, laughing low and quietly to himself as the fans swelled forward en masse on the terraces and were then eased back by those in front, holding me tightly in front of him as I struggled not to be pushed over. 'Don't worry, son,' he whispered. 'I've got you.'

We stood behind one of those metal barriers – like miniature goal posts – that dotted the terraces. He had his long arms looped round my shoulders, holding me inside his big donkey-jacket.

My nose and fingertips grew numb on the cross-piece of the barrier as I strained, on tiptoes, to see any action. I was trying to make out the familiar features of QPR's star player Rodney Marsh and was delighted – certainly more delighted than Marsh must have been – when he was bundled off the ball and over the touch-line at 'our' end of the ground. An impossibly glamorous figure with tousled blond hair, he sat in touch, rubbing his right calf. I grinned up at Dad and he smiled broadly and nodded, confirming, 'Rodney Marsh,' as if handing me a figurine of the man on a plinth. I loved this about Dad. He took pleasure in showing me things – things and people.

After the match – a 2–1 victory for Rangers – we joined the jostling throng pushing their way out and winding along the narrow streets down to Watford Junction station. Clutching Dad's hand tightly, I felt relieved to have left the ground in one piece.

The streets were unlit and a light rain was falling. Puffs of cigarette smoke wafted across the heads of the people in front. I felt sorry for all the residents of the houses along the street, who had to put up with this route march of fans every week. Suddenly, up ahead, there was the sound that I was dreading, that I would dread all through my youth; it was that raised, hiccuping half-laugh, half-shout, which silences every other voice around: the sound of 'trouble'.

A scuffle had broken out round a car ahead of us. I gripped my dad's hand more tightly. I wanted to turn round and walk the other way, but he just kept walking, walking. Years later, I thought I recognized that emotion in myself with my own kids when trouble seemed to

loom: *just keep going, don't show them you're frightened*.
But I don't think Dad was frightened.

Some fans were rocking a car – a car which, I was
sure, must belong to one of the residents with whom I'd
just been sympathizing. Two of the fans stood, straddle-
legged, their hands gripping the lip around the roof of
the vehicle, trying to push it over. I could hear water or
petrol swirling and swashing around inside the car as it
lurched up, like a grotesque child's cradle, then bumped
and hissed back down on its dusty wheels.

I wanted Dad to hurry me past, but he never altered
his easy pace. There were lads all about us, hands on
hips, scarves tied at the waist or round their wrists,
watching the fun. I wanted to rush away from whatever
was going to happen next. Dad looked straight ahead
and kept walking calmly. He hadn't even glanced down
at me. He seemed not to notice what was going on.

At the station, large numbers of fans were milling
down towards the platforms. I could hear shouts and
yells echoing round the old roof timbers. We followed a
throng down a steep stone staircase and I felt my heart-
beat quicken and my mouth dry as I saw the mêlée of
QPR and Watford supporters engaged in a battle strung
out the length of the platform. The train was already in.
Every carriage door had been flung open and these too
were now playing their own part in the fray, as stray
shins and shoulders struck and sent them flapping back
and forth.

For the first time Dad tightened his grip on my left hand, guiding me into the bulk of the more peaceful supporters as we all hurried along the outside edge of the platform, ducked behind the train doors and stepped into the carriages.

This was a 'football special': old rolling stock whose elegant wall lights, mirrors and net luggage racks were, ironically, deemed more suitable to be wrecked by football thugs than the bland new stock with its absence of such antiquated comforts.

Dad thrust me into a corner seat and sat close beside me, his bulk providing immediate protection from the raving mob that was already flooding in after us. One young fan in skinny jeans, scarf tied round his wrist, immediately placed a booted foot on the seat beside my dad and pulled himself up to sit in the luggage rack, his legs dangling. At that point – and I could barely believe it was happening, let alone how fast – my dad bellowed, 'Oi! That's enough,' reached up, seized hold of the lad's ankles and yanked him back down.

I closed my eyes and wished to be anywhere else – anywhere far from this carriage, far from this station, and away, away, over some fields somewhere; on the back of my eyelids I could see a picture of Dad and me running through wet grass that soaked our knees.

The lad turned angrily. His eyes were raw and red-rimmed, his face throbbed with energy, and his mouth was quivering and working on an insult or retort that just wouldn't form itself. He said nothing. Dad just glared into his face. There was a bark of laughter from someone else in the carriage, then more laughter and a burst of chatter that rushed into the silence that followed. The boy turned away – halfway to crying, or did I imagine that? – and in that moment the mood of threat that had flared, briefly, just a few seconds before lifted and evaporated. Outside, just a few stray shouts lifted above the sound of hundreds more fans spilling onto the platform and trying to find space on the train. Our door opened and shut six, seven, times: we were just commuters now, waiting to move.

My dad put his arm round my shoulder. 'Don't worry, son,' he said – and I wasn't worried. I didn't see how I could ever be worried with Dad at my side. A few months later he had his first real breakdown.

4

Two Secrets

My world was a triangle consisting of our house in Cullington Close, Moorhouse Road, where my three surviving grandparents lived, and my school, Priestmead.

We pinballed between these places, walking, cycling, sometimes taking the bus – though none of my family, who hated just to hang around, had much time for the sluggish, staring ritual of waiting for one. My dad would stand, literally, for ten seconds, squinting up the road, before turning with a wave of his arm: 'C'mon, Mart. We'll walk.'

Occasionally we also ventured out to my Auntie Jean's house, so that our territory extended north to the splendidly named Canon's Park.

My mum and dad had grown up at opposite ends of Moorhouse Road, a couple of miles from Cullington

Close. They had attended the same little school, Kenmore Park, which crouched behind a wire fence at one end of it. Moorhouse Road was, and is, the very model of a pre-war council street, its neat red-brick houses set back from the narrow, quiet road by little, squared-off front gardens and, in a couple of places, wider grass verges.

My mum had lived at number 72 with her father, George Pattrick, a lifelong railway worker, with a clock for twenty-five years' service on his mantelpiece, and her mum, Winifred, known to everyone as 'Win'. I called her 'Nana'. Mum had an older brother and sister, Ernie and Joy.

Dad lived at number 17 with his father, Albert Townsend – or 'Elb' – who worked for the London Electricity Board, and mother Liz, who did not work. They also had a daughter, Jean.

These homes, and the people in them – my family, my flesh and blood – had been through the war and subsequent National Service and as I grew up this became more and more significant to me, particularly in relation to my father, who, I was eventually to learn, had been literally shaped by it.

I never knew Granddad Pattrick – he collapsed and died of a heart attack on Stanmore station a few months after I was born in 1960 – but his memory was frequently evoked by my mum and Nana.

No one casts as long a shadow as the suddenly absent.

My mum and Nana had been robbed abruptly of the finest man they had ever known and so their adoration went on, quietly: beautiful music heard through a wall.

I would hear so much about this grandfather I had never known – how I looked so much like him, how he would have loved to see me now – that his photograph, solid and immovable on Nana's mantelpiece, seemed to vibrate with life. In the picture he stands, in his shirt-sleeves, in a garden that I knew – Nana's garden, unchanged, with its roses and its old Anderson shelter overgrown with brambles – and it seemed extraordinary that I wasn't out there on the little lawn with him.

Granddad Pattrick had a large head and a big, beaky nose and I would read more into his expression as I grew older: at first it seemed blank to me, just an empty glance into my mother's Brownie box camera, but then as I saw it under different circumstances – my mum, perhaps, taking refuge at Nana's from one of my dad's furies – his large, pale face would appear regretful, pitying. I imagined him touching my dad's shoulder – just that: the tiniest pat of the fingers – and saying nothing. I did not know what sort of relationship he had with my dad but the clear message of the picture – conveyed, apparently, by Nana on more than one angry occasion – was that my dad could never be as good as he was, could not match up.

With his long years of service on the railway, his uniform, his – I imagined – measured walk, his stolid patience over the crates of transported racing pigeons that, my mother said, was the only part of the job he didn't like, Granddad Pattrick was undeniably solid and good. He would not raise a hand, or even his voice, to a woman. He scooped up all the magazines and newspapers left on the seats of the trains and brought them home to number 72 for the children to read. Selfless acts from an unselfish man.

My nana, Win, had had an interesting early life. Her mother had been a milliner all her working life and one day her boss – 'a big, ugly foreign man' – had caught Win in the shop drawing on one of her mother's sketchpads. The young girl thought she was 'for it', but the ugly man had a kind side: he immediately engaged Win to travel up to the big stores in London's West End and copy the most expensive hat designs displayed in the windows.

It was a job Win loved and it brought a little more money into what was a grindingly poor household: her father – my mum's grandfather – was almost always out of work. He had been a 'gentleman's gentleman' and had travelled twice to America at the expense of various toffs, then took bit parts in silent movies – 'having', as Nana would gleefully tell me, 'things thrown at him' – to pay for his passage back. But he had eventually taken to drink.

The unpredictability of her youth – interrupted by two world wars (in the first of which Granddad Pattrick had served with the Grenadier Guards and been gassed twice) – had left my nan with an unshakeable sense of humour. But it lay a little deeper now: early widowhood had rubbed away some of her playfulness. She was always ready to laugh but when conversations, of any sort, lapsed she'd raise her head slightly and look off and up to the right with a deep sigh, wrinkling her nose once or twice to straighten her spectacles.

What I remember most vividly about her house at number 72 was its brooding silence. The immaculately polished lino, the nets at the sash windows, Granddad's clock with its slow tick. She would stand up awkwardly from her armchair, sighing once as she straightened up, touching her bad back with her fingertips. Then she'd open the hinged glass on the clock, take a small key from its hiding place under the base, insert it into the little brass keyhole in the face and turn it once, twice.

Nana had taken on my late grandfather's solidity. Her life was ordered, and orderly. She cleaned, she polished, she did the garden, pouring the old tea-leaves on her roses, bending in rubber gloves to wash a leaf with soapy water or squint at a new bud. She moved slowly, deliberately, because she always had a bad back and bad hips. Her whole family, with the exception, thank God, of my mum, were tormented by their bad joints.

Nana had a succession of budgerigars – all yellow and green, all called Joey – whom she loved but pretended merely to tolerate. My brother and I, who were always foraging through her old button-box, with its salvaged zips and fastenings and strange little sewing gadgets, would be sitting on her floor, sifting through these items, when the budgie would squawk, just once, shattering the silence.

'Oh, shut up,' Nana would snap unsmilingly.

And the budgie would come back with the phrase, in the same strangled cockney, 'Oh, shut up!'

When Nana said, 'You're a lovely boy, aintcha?' Joey replied with the single, joyful 'aintcha', as if pouring scorn on my nan's accent.

This bird, and its many successors, was a bond with my dad. He would go straight to the cage and offer his lips for the bird to peck. He loved all animals apart from dogs, which he mistrusted on sight, and cats, whose selfishness irritated him. He did not like to be taken advantage of.

Dad and Nana circled each other at number 72. He rarely took his coat off. I never saw him go upstairs. As soon as he arrived he seemed anxious to leave. Even when he stood at Nana's back door and looked down over her immaculate garden – a prospect that, in any other place, would excite him into action – he kept his hands in his pockets.

She never seemed sure about him. He, in his turn – dry-lipped, nervous, asking questions to which he already knew the answer – always seemed apprehensive about what she might do or say: the power she might have. I loved Nana and could not understand any of this, but I tried to put it all together in my mind, as I toyed with the button-box or rearranged the jangling brushes and shovels on their chrome stand in the fireplace.

George Pattrick stared across the silence. I decided that one day, finally growing tired of my dad's illness and the toll it took on her daughter, Nana would keep my mum at number 72 for ever – and refuse him permission to see her.

Years later, after the house was burgled and she moved into a warden-controlled flat, my father visited her much more regularly. I realized then that it had never been Nana that he disliked: it had been Nana in that particular house.

If life at number 72 was orderly and civilized, if a little lonely, the atmosphere at number 17 was more intriguing.

Encouraged by Mum, my brother and I always considered Granddad Townsend – 'Elb' – to be a bit of a rogue. He was a hard-working man, but he liked to drink and to gamble and there were often nights out with his mates at the Victoria sporting club in London watching boxing or wrestling, both of which he loved.

Underlying it all, too, there was a slight suspicion, just the merest hint, of dishonesty and, some years later, unfaithfulness. Dad could never quite make up his mind how much of this amused him and how much left him annoyed. In later years, after Granddad had left his job at the London Electricity Board, he would do odd-jobs as an electrician, taking his son along from time to time to help out. My dad would come home ranting and raving about the 'death-traps' his old man had unwittingly left in old ladies' houses. 'That poor cow'll touch that switch and the whole bloody lot will go up, boof!' he'd tell Mum.

Nevertheless there was a strong bond between my dad and his father even if it seemed more like love on my dad's side. It was only when he was very old, widowed and tormented by glaucoma, in his early eighties, that my granddad seemed to give in to it. During those late years of the 1960s, when illness was a constant shadow loping along at his son's side, Elb appeared to replace love with practicality – taking things to Dad when he was in hospital, running him home in the car. He turned his gaze away from the illness itself, sometimes literally. When Dad was high, and acting up, my granddad would suck his teeth and rattle his change in his pocket, the tiniest tear of embarrassment or shame in the corner of his eye, or stare blankly at my mum, as if his son was some sort of modern art that he refused to countenance. I felt very sorry for him.

But my dad loved his father deeply – more deeply, I think, than he ever found himself in a position to say. For much of the time, there was something in Elb's briskness, his cockiness, his hands-in-pockets sense of purpose, that would have made expressions of affection seem ridiculous. Dad saw in him a certain knowing charm, a casual style, that, mistakenly, he didn't feel he himself had ever quite pulled off. There was something of the wartime spiv about Elb. He was a man with certain methods and particular secrets.

My gran and granddad would come over every other Sunday night to chat and play cards, cribbage or sometimes Scrabble. Often they'd bring my nana with them. At the end of the evening Granddad would always silently hand my brother and me two bob each, merely nodding his wide little head when the coin was accepted.

Their arrival was an event. Granddad would 'park up' his pale-green Ford Popular in front of our house and they'd emerge from it with an uprightness and gravity that always seemed a cut above Cullington Close. Granddad would have his hands in his pockets; my gran, a few steps behind, her hands clasped in front.

When he was well, my dad would look forward to these visits all week, fussing over having beer in the fridge, for shandies – we barely drank anything much as a family usually – and what sandwiches we'd have in front of the telly. As soon as his dad appeared he'd become boyish and playful again – and I loved him like that. It was the dad I convinced myself that I knew best.

Granddad would sit, small and low in his chair, in his blue-grey or charcoal suit, always with the tiny knot of a tie spilling out of his V-neck jumper. He'd lean forward over a tin of Old Holborn tobacco and painstakingly build himself exquisitely slim roll-ups, sealing the paper with the barest tip of his pink tongue. The whole process fascinated me, as did the construction of the little boxes of Rizla papers.

'Oi, don't mess 'em up!' he'd say with a smile, as I plucked one or two of the papers out. 'Cheeky bugger!'

'Cheeky bugger' was his catch-phrase. Everyone was a cheeky bugger.

Then he'd sit, nodding through the smoke, flexing his lips over his very straight, very sharp teeth, listening to his son's plans for the house and garden: Dad always had some project on the go. They'd discuss places to find wood or stone, or bits of carpeting, but everything, eventually, was acquired or got passed around; very little was straightforwardly bought.

'I can get you *plywood*,' Granddad would say, always as if the particular material was his stock-in-trade and it was foolish to even consider paying for it. '*Lino*? I can get you lino.' Alternatively he'd be offering up his car for something: 'I'll run ya there. Let me run ya, Ron.'

Once, in our teens, when my brother and I found ourselves stranded at the Lyceum ballroom in London – there'd been a stabbing and the police held everyone there until they'd written down our names – I called Granddad in desperation to come and collect us. It was only when we were getting out of his car later that I noticed his pyjama bottoms showing just below his suit trouser-legs.

He was a generous man above all, but there was a slightly resigned look in his eyes when he did favours for us, as if he knew that generosity was his saving grace and was rather ashamed of the fact.

The extent of Granddad's involvement in any of my dad's work around the house was dependent on his 'shifts' at the LEB. Sometimes he'd work nights and then would sleep all day. Other times he would work odd hours of the day, so that it was never certain whether he'd be awake or what sort of mood he'd be in if he was. Sometimes, when we went over to Gran and Granddad's for a visit, Gran would open the door slowly and usher us in with a finger pressed to her mouth. 'Dad's asleep,' she'd whisper – she always called Elb 'Dad' – and she'd point her finger upwards. My brother and I would be disappointed. All the toys she kept for our visits – the little tin garage, the clockwork fireman that could clamber up her mesh fire-guard – were stored at the top of the house, but when Granddad was asleep up there we were strictly forbidden even to play in the hall or on the stairs.

Gran seemed so different from Elb that I often wondered how they'd ended up together. Where he was roguish, she was disarmingly sensible; where he was slightly flash, almost dandyish in his suits and hats, she was so colourless and plain that you were barely aware of her clothes. Gran had frizzy grey hair and small eyes set wide in a pale, almost yellowish face. She always wore a pinafore and she'd either have some cooking on the go or be preparing sliced bread and butter – or, as she called it for our benefit, 'bread and buppy'. On Sundays, sometimes, when we visited them, she would bring round a tray of hot roast potatoes in advance of the main dinner. My brother and I would salt these, then suck and blow over them, trying desperately to cool them down.

The key to Gran's personality lay in her sense of humour, which was sudden, unexpected and raucous. In many ways she seemed like an austere woman, almost dried up and severe. But when something tickled her she would throw her head back and rock with laughter, the tears springing almost immediately to her little pale eyes and turning them a mouse-like pink. 'Oh, that's *good*,' she'd weep, as Granddad smiled his lewd, straight-toothed smile and chuckled low under his breath. 'That's really, really good.'

As I grew older, though, I realized that this laughter was largely for my granddad's benefit. It was a defence, above all, because she had an almost Victorian attitude towards sex and to anything she considered 'private' or shameful. This included Dad's illness.

When Dad was first taken into a mental hospital, Gran instructed my mum: 'Tell people he has got appendicitis, Peg, and don't, for God's sake, take the kids to see him.' As a result my mother did not really get on with her and would express her dislike by referring to her always as 'Liz', as if she was a friend of the family rather than her mother-in-law. It always amused my mother that she had the same name as the Queen, because Mum considered her to be overly grand, bossy and demanding, particularly concerning such matters as how to bring children up 'properly'.

Gran didn't think it was healthy for children to sleep for too long and, when my brother and I were babies, she would think nothing, if my mother's back was turned, of scooping us up out of our cots and waking us up 'for a cuddle'. This would send my mum into such a rage that all my dad could do was hop from foot to foot, trying to sympathize with both parties. 'She only wants to cuddle him, Peg.' 'You didn't have to wake him up, Mum.'

Her daughter, Jean – my dad's only sibling – had two children, Gary and Linda, who Gran would wake up constantly. 'She'll make them bad-tempered,' my mum would tell my dad, 'you'll see. But she's not doing it with my two.'

There were two mysteries, the two abiding mysteries of my childhood, attached to Moorhouse Road. The first, which I linked in my mind to number 17 – and which, I knew, had something to do with the army – was, my mum believed, the precise reason for my father's mental illness. The second was an incident that supposedly occurred at number 72 and which brooded in the relationship between my mum and Nan for many years.

These things were barely mentioned when I was a boy. If they came up at all, they were quickly ushered away again by a conspiracy of whispering and the shaking of heads. We children – my brother and I and our cousins Gary and Linda, Jean's children – were not to be told anything of these episodes for years and years. The one person who would have told me, clearly and honestly, I'm sure, was the one person that I could never bring myself to ask.

5

Priestmead

My brother and I followed each other through the same primary and secondary schools. Then we went on to the same sixth-form college. I became a journalist, Ian a teacher. We were only two years apart but vastly different characters. Where I took after my mother and was a worrier, my brother was like my father: he appeared, most of the time, to let nothing on earth trouble him.

Ian was prettier than I was as a child and grew up to be taller, stronger and more handsome. Back then in the mid-Sixties he had dimpled cheeks and blond, curly hair, which prompted aunts and uncles to say that he must be the sort of child who 'ate his crusts'. But he ate no crusts. He ate, in fact, hardly anything at all. For the first few years of his life he lived on minced meat, fish-fingers and slices of white bread with sugar sprinkled on them. He ate no vegetables at all until he was about twelve. He also ate cardboard. He would rip off the backs of books, stuff the hard material into his mouth and chew it into pale string; then he'd either swallow it or drop it, in a damp wad, into the bin.

Our GP, Dr Hicks – of whom much more later – said that it was a childhood craving and perfectly normal. It could do my brother no harm, he insisted. Some of his young patients, he said, chewed coal. This comforted my mother to a degree because, when pregnant with Ian, she had nibbled sticks of white chalk. Yet my brother's limited diet became a worry for her, on top of everything else – especially when, at five or six, he also began to develop eczema on his hands and face and appeared to be anaemic.

None of this troubled my father in the least. He loved my brother, praised him for his achievements, encouraged him at every turn and was careful to treat us both exactly the same at Christmas and on our birthdays. But he disregarded Ian, almost completely, as a subject for ongoing 'improvement'. All his effort, to promote the idea of 'manliness' and of the efficacy of an outdoor life of sport and exercise, was directed towards me, particularly when he was high.

This didn't exactly 'let Ian off', but it allowed him, I thought, to have a different attitude towards Dad's illness: to witness it much more as a spectator than as would-be protagonist or collaborator. I resented this. In my young mind he appeared to be largely carefree – at least in that area of our family life – while I felt as if I was constantly in danger of being drawn in. As a result the fights we had all through our childhood became more spiteful as we got older.

What did I really know, though? Night after night from about the age of three or four until a year after he started at secondary school, my so-called happy-go-lucky brother would wet the bed. I considered it to be one more childish habit of a pesky younger brother. Dad, in his usual way, waved it aside – 'He'll get over it.' Mum, perhaps guessing at deeper-lying problems, blamed anxiety over school. This puzzled my brother even more than it did me, because we couldn't have been happier at our junior school.

Priestmead stood about a mile from where we lived, a handsome, if rather austere, 1930s building rendered in brown, with rusting ribbon-windows through which points of weak yellow light could just about be seen as my brother and I plodded up from the main gate.

Our mum would walk us up to the school every morning, wheeling her bike so that she could cycle back. She'd balance one of us on the crossbar while the other walked along by the side, holding the saddle.

Our school was an imposing two or three storeys high at the front but much more friendly-looking at the back, where it was built around the playground, in a single, flat-roofed level. Some wooden, Nissen-style huts with a continuous veranda in front of them had been added at one side of the playground, and in the playing fields at the back a series of long, concrete air-raid shelters still remained.

Mum had put our names down for this school as soon as we had moved into Cullington Close. She knew that a brand-new school, Elmgrove, was about to be built at the end of our road – one that would have been less than a minute's walk from our house – but Mum didn't want us to go there. Priestmead had a reputation for good teaching and results. It was worth the extra journey.

Priestmead was also a very strict school. With his well-cut grey suits and squarish head with cropped grey hair, the headmaster, Mr Hart, looked like an American. He had a presidential air: hard but polished and urbane. Every child held him in awe. He made no threats; he barely spoke at all, and so his power was absolute. To be sent to the headmaster's office, for any reason, was like a death sentence.

Mr Hart employed similarly tough teachers. There were two ruddy-faced, middle-aged spinsters in crisply cut suits with the hint of wartime service about them: Miss Glennie and Miss Ashcroft. Miss Ashcroft would be my final teacher at Priestmead, steering me off to grammar school, but at the time of which I write, when I was about eight or nine years old, I was in the charge of Mr Rawlins.

Rawlins was small and pugnacious, like James Cagney, and the effect was helped along by his pronounced limp – the result, it was rumoured, of having a false leg. He had piercing blue eyes, made slightly watery and tinged by the clouds of smoke from his omnipresent pipe, and dispensed practical advice with a fearless lack of embarrassment: 'It is important that you go to the toilet when you need to,' he'd tell us. 'Do *not* hold it in. In the end it will kill you.' He stomped up and down the veranda outside the huts, puffing at his pipe, his false leg making a fearsome racket.

Both my dad and I loved Mr Rawlins and love really was not too strong a word: he was wise, he was funny, he was fair. He also knew, and understood, about Dad. At the end of a lesson, sometimes, he would take me aside, on the creaky veranda, and ask me, in his practical way, how he was. 'Do they treat him well in hospital? What did you think of it?' Then he'd cock his head towards me and half-close one yellowing blue eye for the answer. His face would be very close to mine and I'd see the little pink, child-like, lips working on the stem of his pipe.

I always found it hard to talk about Dad at that age without my eyes beginning to tickle and burn with tears. I was grateful that he asked about him, though, because I was always collecting allies. One day, I thought, something will happen – Dad will do something that is really beyond the pale – and then the whole family will need a place to go and trustworthy folk to turn to. I made lists of these people in my head.

One or two of the children also were aware of my

dad's illness, and they knew that he had been in mental hospitals. 'Mental' was a word that had some currency among us nine-year-olds, but not very much: a few of the rougher boys in the school bandied it around a bit but with little idea of what it meant – or of how hurtful it might be. It was like 'tits' or 'penis': it was there at the edge of their understanding but its full meaning remained unknown.

All of this came as a relief to me. I was not ashamed of my dad's illness but I didn't want to have to explain it. I had a reputation for telling long stories and jokes in the playground but I couldn't be anything but truthful about my dad – and the bland details of his illness would have disappointed them. There was no dribbling or bulging eyes or running around with no trousers – no sign at all, in fact, of the cartoon 'loony' – just a long process of wearing us, his family, down. It would have bored my friends and made them suspect I was being 'over-sensitive' and 'cissy'. I kept my mouth firmly shut.

My mother and father were both conscious of what they saw as their lack of education, and so they were quite nervous of Priestmead. My mum would march up to open evenings in her best coat, her handbag held tight in the crook of her arm, with my dad bowling along at her side in his best green tweed 'sports jacket'. 'Sports jacket' was a phrase he liked: it suggested, I think, a free-wheeling life, a devil-may-care attitude.

I was desperately ashamed, and it shamed me, of my

dad's lack of a 'proper' job, and this emotion would eventually get me into trouble. The other parents at the school all seemed to have professions. The father of my best friend Richard Hoare was a bank manager and his house – with its phone and its central heating; its fitted carpets and the shiny car in the drive – seemed to sit at the polar opposite of ours. The Hoares had books, too: proper, bought books, not ones that had to be taken back to a library.

Mr Rawlins, I knew, was well aware of my discomfort. He said nothing but he was a man from whom nothing could be concealed. If you had not tried, had not worked hard enough at an essay or learning a times table, his hard, yellowing eyes would blaze and he'd bring his pointer-stick down – crack! – across his desk. But anger was not at the heart of his power: his authority rested in those painful, limping walks up and down the veranda, the few words he exchanged with his pupils and the watching and listening that he did. I have never encountered such a good listener: Mr Rawlins had hungry ears.

We had precisely three books in our house: a volume about aquarium fishes, the *Reader's Digest Complete Do-it-yourself Manual* – which fascinated me because it was bound up in a little vinyl attaché case – and an old encyclopaedia. This was known as our 'red book'.

I was very proud of this encyclopaedia. It was losing its spine, and some of its pages, tissue-thin and yellowing, had been mended with sticky tape. I took it into school one day. We had to give a talk and I gave mine about budgerigars. I wanted to quote from the book and, rather than copy out the passage, I wrote my talk and took the book with me.

After the lesson, as I was walking out, Mr Rawlins summoned me over to his desk. 'Let me see this,' he said, and he cradled the book gently, so gently, in his broad hands and opened it carefully, smoothing the fragile pages. 'Is this your dad's?' he said.

'Yes.'

He nodded slowly, pursing his lips. 'It's a beautiful book.' He looked up at me, his eyes boring into mine: 'You're very, very lucky,' he said, 'that your dad is clever enough to keep a book like this in the house.'

I didn't know what to say. I looked out of the window. I wanted to cry so badly and I could feel the salt rimming under my eyelids, but he was looking back down at the book.

He handed it back. 'Yes. You're very lucky indeed.'

At weekends, when he was well – and, even more often, when he was high – my dad would pull on his wind-cheater, put some change in his pocket and then usher me out of the house and up to Harrow-on-the-Hill. The move from Moorhouse Road to Cullington Close was, in my dad's mind, a process of improvement because it brought us slightly closer to the Hill. We would thread through Harrow-on-the-Hill station, then walk up the grassy slope from Lowland's Road to join a little winding path up to St Mary's church and its famous graveyard. Here was the 'Peachy stone' in its rusty iron cage, where the boy Byron, a bored pupil at the nearby Harrow School, would sit and compose his early poetry. Here, too, was to be found every variety of grotesque epitaph carved into the old, stained stones. My dad's and my own favourite was for an early Victorian unfortunate who had had both legs sliced neatly off by a train.

'He'd have bled to death,' my dad would say, leaning on the corner of the ugly slate stone and stroking his chin. 'He'd have laid there and bled to death.'

There was, and is, a little viewing promontory on the Hill, neatly lined by privet and furnished with a cold stone backless bench where a gap had been made in the trees. We'd stand there sometimes for a half-hour or more, gazing across to the west, where a huge gasometer pronounced NO to passing aircraft. 'It's lovely, Mart, isn't it?' my dad would say. 'Beautiful.' He stood, always, with his hands clasped together behind his back, like Prince Philip. Inevitably, I find myself doing it now. This view, somehow, was a big part of the repayment my dad had earned for his struggle to get us into Cullington Close.

To every question that I asked, particularly about Harrow but on almost anything else too, my dad had the same answer: 'Let's go to the library and look it up.

Come on.' Sometimes we would walk straight down from the Hill and into the reference section of Gayton Library – one of four or five in Harrow that I'd later become very familiar with – to find out some piece of information or other.

Dad was not one to delay over such things and this same urgency, this obsessiveness, was one of the consistent parts of his personality whether he was well or as high as a kite. 'Let's do it now, let's go. Come on, Peg.'

6

Nice 'n' Easy

There had been a few little signs, in the early summer of 1969, that something had triggered one of Dad's highs. The Green Flash plimsolls had made their first, dreaded appearance for over a year, and he had taken to wearing a medallion – a carved, silver-plated depiction of Taurus the bull: his star sign. He had bought a similar one for my mum, with her zodiac sign, Libra, on it, so in my young mind, where I was already learning to file the positives and negatives that may or may not have added up to the misery of a new 'high', I wasn't sure whether the medallion was a good or bad thing.

Then, one Saturday morning around Easter-time, Dad went up to Curry's electrical shop on Wealdstone High Street and bought, on hire purchase, a new record-player for twenty-four pounds and eleven shillings. It was lime-green with a hinged lid and had the sort of spindle that could be loaded with three or four single records at a time. It also had a flip-over stylus so that 78s could be played.

Dad brought it home on the bus, wrapped in polythene. He set it down on the floor in the corner of our front room and stood gazing at it as if it was a baby in a cot. Crouching down, he opened the lid so gently with his forefingers and with such a look of concentration I barely dared to breathe.

My mum fretted over that record-player. Her neck flushed red and she chewed her bottom lip. She wouldn't touch or even go near it. We didn't have the money for the monthly repayments on twenty-four pounds and eleven shillings. Ever since I could remember we had bought everything 'off the boards' – secondhand – or on what my granddad called the 'never-never'. Even the little Thunderbird 2 I'd once had for my birthday had been 'put by' at the sweet-shop, then paid off by my mum at sixpence a week.

But this record-player wasn't the 'never-never', it was the never. My mum held her chest and shook her head, breathing hard. 'It's got to go back, Ron.'

We were in the front room. I was crouched down by the record-player, still in my pyjamas, dying to hear it. The Saturday morning sun was flooding in, lighting up whirling motes of dust around my dad's head.

'No, no, no, no, it's not going back.' He was brisk, on the edge of being annoyed. My mum pulled a face. 'It's not going back,' he repeated, with slightly less certainty.

He looked at me – 'All right, tiddler?' – and winked. I shrugged.

Ian came down from upstairs. 'Oh, brilliant – a record-player!' He knelt down and fingered the silver dials. His knee stuck through a hole in his brown-patterned pyjamas. His clothes seemed to wear out overnight.

'*Ian* . . .' I hissed. He was only seven but I resented his artlessness. Didn't he realize the unease the record-player was causing?

He pursed his lips. 'Well, I like it,' he said, as if this was the debate we'd been having. 'Can we play something on it?'

I didn't know whose side I should take. I had fallen in love with the record-player on sight too. It had a speaker at the front and silver knobs. Nothing this new and modern had ever come into our house before.

'It *is* very nice,' I said to my mum.

She pulled another face, and I felt sick: obviously we had something that we shouldn't have; something that was somehow 'beyond' us. Years later I'd feel the same way when I bought my first house.

I saw my dad clench and unclench his fists, bouncing once, twice, on the balls of his feet. He was excited with his new purchase, but my mother wasn't. He licked his lips and began to form up his mouth to argue, but no argument would come and by then, anyway, my mother was in the kitchen, clattering out her irritation among the cups and saucers.

Dad subsided into a chair, swallowing hard, but was immediately leaning forward on his knees. He winked at me again.

I didn't like any of this stuff – the twitching, the bouncing: it all had a familiar rhythm to it. Suddenly I hated Dad for buying the record-player. I got up and went out into the kitchen.

Mum had been crying and now she was swallowing and sniffing and making too much effort to wash things that didn't need washing. She scratched her forehead. 'Oh, Mart.'

I was angry now. 'You can just take it back,' I whispered. 'Why not?'

She shook her head. 'No. It's up to him. If they come knocking for it back, I'll be upstairs.'

The idea of various mysterious people coming 'knocking' for things had followed me all through childhood. If I ever took a day off school, for instance, ill but still able to play in the garden, my mum warned that the 'school board man' would come knocking and haul me back to Priestmead by the ear.

Ian took me out into the hall. 'Perhaps *we* can pay for it,' he said. 'You know, save up.' He was constantly coming out with schemes like this: every problem had a practical solution if you looked hard enough. Years later, teaching in a tough Milton Keynes school and faced with a boy in his class who would not behave himself or take any notice in lessons, my brother, who had taken evening classes in tailoring, taught the lad how to cut and stitch together a shirt. 'He thought it was a miracle when he put it on,' said Ian, laughing. 'He'd never made anything before.'

We went back into the front room as the first chords of Frank Sinatra's 'Nice 'n' Easy' crackled from the speaker. It was a record my mum had grown to loathe.

> *Nice and easy does it*
> *Nice and easy does it*
> *Every time . . .*

My dad shook his head in wonder. 'Beautiful, innit?'

On fine summer evenings in Cullington Close, for as many years as I could remember, my mother and various neighbours would gather on the long, low brick wall in front of our house.

Our neighbour to the left, Ellen Ludbrook, was always there. I called her 'Auntie Ellen' and she was the kindest and most patient of our neighbours. She sat out together with her skinny husband Reg, who worked for the GPO, and one or more of their five sons and daughters. They'd be joined by Tom and Elsie Herbert, our neighbours from number 34, whose children had long since left home.

There was another, and much larger, family of Herberts, completely unrelated to the first, at number

28. Lou and Albert Herbert, who were the senior members of the clan, were probably in their early fifties but seemed easily the most 'elderly' of our immediate neighbours. They would come out with their son-in-law Fred. He was a short, smiley, practical man who owned a brand-new greenhouse. He and his wife, Win, still lived with Lou and Albert, her parents, and would never move out. Win chain-smoked. She had very long, very black hair, of which she was inordinately proud, and a permanently mournful expression.

The Herberts also had a much younger daughter, Ann, who brought out a series of ancient, angry-looking, clay-faced dolls. She would sit them in a line on the wall. These dolls terrified my brother and me.

The neighbours would sit and gossip, and Mrs Ludbrook and old Mrs Herbert would knit seemingly endless piles of baby clothes without ever glancing at their dancing needles. They'd also add the 'awkward' arms or necks to garments for other, less-accomplished knitters in the street.

My dad would not come out to the wall very often. Although he got on well with the younger people in the street, and with everyone when he was high, he treated the older ones with a certain degree of suspicion when he was back to normal, as if somehow the wall ritual had a sinister purpose. If he ever came out at all it was only to fetch my mum back in again. On these red-letter visits Mrs Herbert and Auntie Ellen would applaud him up

the path – 'Here's Ron!' 'Come on, Ron!' – and pat the
wall so that he'd be embarrassed into sitting with us for
a while.

Our front garden sloped down from behind this wall,
so that you looked back and down at the bay windows of
our house. These windows, in the summer, would be
flung open dramatically by my father – '*Wheeew*, let
some air in, Peg.' Then he'd lie on the sofa, fully clothed,
and watch the television. If the television went off and
the sounds of Frank Sinatra suddenly came floating out
of the window, Dad was high. It was like the Pope's
smoke.

Our neighbours on the wall never took much notice at
times like this. Auntie Ellen's older daughters, Anita and
Jackie, who shared an obsession with boys on motor-
bikes, had a habit of playing terrible, tragic records about
teenage road deaths at high volume from their windows
– 'Terry' by Twinkle or 'Leader of the Pack' by the
Shangri La's. This would set various neighbours, and
their own mother, growling on the wall, half looking
back and using language, under their breaths, that I
always found quite surprising. But Dad's records never
raised any comment at all, not even from old Mrs
Herbert, who looked, and behaved at times, a bit like my
dad's mum.

There was a respect for my mother, I think, that pre-
vented comment. On this particular Saturday evening
there was no television and no music either. The front

windows, as ever, were wide open but number 32 was eerily quiet. I was out on the wall with my mum and one or two of the neighbours. Mum had already shared news of the 'bloody record-player' with Mrs Herbert.

Mrs Herbert had fierce, dark eyes under a strong brow and a frown that only disappeared if something struck her as outrageously funny, which was normally a joke or comment made by her jovial, round-faced son Fred.

She greeted the news of Dad's latest venture as she greeted all news, good and bad: by shaking her head very slowly and looking at the ground.

At her side, Auntie Ellen carried on knitting. She was a plump woman who sat very upright with her varicose-veined, clay-coloured legs – which I never dared look at because they made me feel queasy – disappearing into ancient, fluffy slippers. 'Twenty-four pounds!' said Auntie Ellen. She breathed in through her nose, significantly. Mrs Herbert shook her head again.

I was thinking about Dad. I knew exactly where he'd be: sitting in his armchair in the back room, drawing on a cigarette and exhaling the smoke slowly through his nose.

Out on the wall my mum crossed her arms and shivered. 'I'm going in, Ellen . . .'

Ellen looked up from her knitting. 'OK, Peg. Don't worry.'

My mum shuddered. 'Tch.'

Old Mrs Herbert put down her knitting and stared at the ground, her woolly grey head shaking slowly back and forth.

The next few days should have been glorious ones. That was the thought I always had in my head during those years, when the sun was shining, our newly mown back lawn was blazing green, and my friends from the street dashed up and down our side alley with machine-guns made of wooden off-cuts or with towels pinned round their necks in imitation of TV's Batman.

But the record-player had grown. It had swollen up; it had become an issue, a problem, a trigger – set, immovably, in the corner of our front room like some sort of vengeful demon. I knew, I knew from the first moment it entered the house, that it was the 'thing' – the entity, solid or otherwise – that would, in my mum's words, 'set Ron off'. And so from loving it I hated it and that spoiled the feeling of those days as well. Why couldn't we just have a record-player, in the middle of all this summer sunshine, like other people, even if we couldn't really afford it? Why did it have to represent something so terrible?

A few days after the record-player arrived, the rows began. I was upstairs with my brother, playing in the big back bedroom that we shared, when we heard the raised voices from the front room.

'I know you don't fucking want it.'

'I *do* want it, Ron, but . . .'

'Why do you have to spoil everything? Eh? What's wrong with you?'

'There's nothing wrong with me. I—'

'You're *ill*, Peg, d'you know that . . . ?' There was a pause and I knew my dad's mouth would be working, working. 'I'm trying to do something for the kiddies . . .' Oh no, I thought, please don't drag us into it . . . 'I'm trying to do something for them and you don't fucking like it . . .' He was shaking his head now, sarcastically. I could see it in my mind's eye. 'You and your fucking mother.'

Here we go . . .

'Well, take it fucking back, then. Go on, take it back!'

I heard his heavy footsteps stalk across the floor and then the front door slam – *bang!*

Ian shook his head: 'Here we go again.' But he didn't move. He was lying across the carpet in our bedroom, drawing and colouring.

I ran downstairs. 'Where's he gone?'

Mum was shaking her head. She looked exhausted. 'I don't know, Mart.'

These were the situations I hated the most, at that time: when Dad was beginning to go high and Mum looked as if she'd given up.

'Oh, he's probably just gone over to Granddad's,' my brother Ian said as he came skipping down the stairs behind me, two at a time. 'Can I have a cup of tea, Mum?' He flopped himself down on an armchair in the front room. 'Come on, Mart,' he said. 'He won't have gone far away.' He rolled up his trouser-leg and scratched the eczema on his knee. He was very pale and Mum always worried that he was, as she put it, 'slightly anaemic'.

I shook my head. I saw Dad's LPs stacked against the wall next to the cursed record-player: 'Topol 68', 'The Flower Drum Song', 'South Pacific'. Old records he'd had for years; a few, like Topol, he'd acquired over the last few months from Woolworths. I felt, suddenly, very sorry for him. He had so little, I thought. So little to show for all the early mornings moving around down-stairs getting ready for work. The smell of Silvikrin. The three inches of soapy, shaving water I'd find in our washing-up bowl when I got up for school and came down to make tea.

My mum had gone next door to use Auntie Ellen's phone. I watched her walk round the bay window, squeezing past the big yellow shrub that Dad had grown from a cutting he took from the park.

'He'll be at Granddad's, you watch,' said my brother, between mouthfuls of biscuit. 'Let's put the telly on.'

A few minutes later Mum was back. 'He's at his dad's.'

I couldn't concentrate now. I couldn't watch the tele-vision. The evening, like so many evenings, was spoiled. The front room seemed to close in on us at these times. The green- and brown-squared wallpaper with its two dim wall lights, the curtains drawn around the bay windows: suddenly everything was dull and hopeless.

My mum sat down and crossed her arms, her lips pursed tight. I knew she was already waiting for the front gate to swing back against the hedge and something new to start.

It was just before eleven when Dad returned. We were all in our pyjamas and having a last cup of tea before bed. He walked straight in, breathing heavily through his nose. He smelled of sweat, and there were big saddle-bags of damp under his shirt-sleeves. It was two miles to my granddad's house and he'd marched there and back.

He didn't say anything at all. His eyes were glazed. He went over to the record-player, slipped 'Topol 68' out of its sleeve and put on a song called 'Shoshana'. It was some sort of Israeli folk-song.

'*Shoshana, shoshana, shoshana – you're sweet as the grapes on the vine.*'

Dad took off his shirt and sat, in his vest, in the arm-chair, the Taurus medallion catching the light. There was a frown of intense concentration on his face as he stared at the bay curtains.

I poked my head in at the door. 'Night, Dad.'

He looked wildly round. 'Oh, yeah.' He smiled. 'Night, son.'

'Everything all right, Dad?'

He smiled. 'Yeah . . . yeah, I'm OK. You OK?'

I nodded. I didn't really want to go upstairs. I wanted to stay and watch until Dad took the record off, put it back in its sleeve, and climbed the stairs with us. I wanted all that because I knew there was no hope at all that it would happen.

'Night, then,' I said.

But Dad was lost again, staring, staring at the curtains.

I met Mum at the top of the stairs. She looked very small and vulnerable in her nightie. Her neck was flushed. Her face was all shiny from taking her make-up off.

'What's he doing?' she asked.

'He's just sitting there,' I said. 'Don't go down.' I didn't want another row.

Mum chewed on her bottom lip. Topol was singing his heart out in our front room. 'Listen to it,' she said, and sighed.

Dad played Topol again and again very loudly. Upstairs, in the room I shared with my brother, I lay awake, cringing at the volume, hoping that I'd hear the record go off, the soft click of the lid and then the sound of his footsteps on the stairs. But all of that happened hours later. The choruses of 'Shoshana' followed me into sleep.

The next Saturday Dad left the house early and brought home a picture of a bullfight. It was a print, glazed and lined to look like an oil painting, of a matador, seen from the back, swinging his red and gold cape at an improbably huge bull. It was about four foot by two foot in a cheap and flimsy wooden frame.

My dad propped it against our back-room wall and called my mum out from the kitchen. 'It's *fantastic*, isn't it, Peg? Taurus the bull, see?'

I wished my mum could pretend at times like this but she never could. In all the years of my dad's illness, through all of the pain and chaos it caused, she never once failed to tell him what she really thought. 'I'm not going along with it,' she'd say to me – 'it' being, inevitably, some new and ridiculous purchase or project – 'I'm just not.'

At the time I thought she did this for our sake – to keep him in his place, to stop his schemes spiralling out of control and embroiling us. Now I'm more convinced it was for her own sanity – to keep firmly at the front of her mind that whatever he was doing when he was high, it was the illness and not the man she married that was responsible.

Now she just stared at the bullfighter and shrugged. 'It's all right.' She crossed her arms.

Anger flashed across my dad's face. 'Well, what do you fucking know?'

My mum shrugged again and turned away. She looked irritated herself now. My dad, instantly picking up her change of mood, said no more. He snatched up the picture and carried it up to our 'spare' room: the little box-room above the porch at the front of the house.

That afternoon Dad went out and bought some small tins of paint and a large sheet of white board. I thought the board must be a proper oil-painting 'canvas' because the surface of it was slightly hairy, but since I'd never seen a canvas before I didn't really know. He propped the board up against the wall, on top of a little chest of drawers in the box-room. He put the bullfighting picture against the wall next to it. Then he went out to our little stone-built council shed in the back garden and started rummaging around for something. I could hear him swearing and cursing out there.

In his sudden absence my mum crept up to the box-room. 'What's he doing?' she said. Her face was flushed red at the neck.

'He's going to try to copy that picture,' my brother reported cheerfully. 'He said I could do the stirring.'

'Paint?' said my mum. 'What's he want to *paint* for?'

I sympathized with her. Dad had never shown any interest in painting before. This was something new, and 'something new' was always a problem. She suddenly looked very tired: it was one thing after another for her, and everything caused upset. Out in the garden now, Reg – Auntie Ellen's tall, thin, nosy husband – had come out to see what Dad was doing and had already disappeared into his own shed, at the end of his garden, to find brushes.

When Dad was well, the very appearance of Reg in the garden set his teeth on edge. Always eager, bless him, for a chat, Reg would appear the moment my dad settled down in his old deckchair or started doing some gardening and I'd see Dad's shoulders stiffen as he heard his voice. 'You can't get five minutes' peace out there with that bloody bloke,' my dad would moan, though he'd never dream of saying anything to Reg himself.

Now, though, Dad was standing at the sagging fence between our garden and the Ludbrooks', shouting encouragement to him.

'Anything you got, Reg. Anything at all. It's only a bit of painting. I'm doing a picture for her wall.'

Mum watched from the window of our bedroom. 'For *my* wall!' said my mum. 'For *my* wall. Listen to him.'

Reg came swishing back up through the long grass in his untidy garden, brandishing brushes. My dad was hopping and fizzing with excitement the other side of the fence.

I started laughing. 'You've got to admit it's funny, Mum . . .' I said.

But she was shaking her head. 'I don't know whether I'm coming or going,' she said. 'I really don't. First the record-player, now this . . .' She flapped her hands at Dad's pots of paint. 'I really have had enough.'

Dad came thumping back up the stairs. 'Reg gave me some brushes.'

My mum stood back as he reached the top landing. 'What do you want those for?' she said.

'Oh, don't worry about it,' he said, as he bustled past –

and he didn't even look at her. 'You just carry on in your own fucking boring way. I've got things to do. Me and the little 'uns are going to paint, aren't we, kids?' He looked at me, licking his lips.

I shrugged. Out of loyalty to my mum I couldn't look even vaguely enthusiastic.

'That's it,' he said. 'That's it. Stick with your fucking mother.' He slammed the box-room door shut.

I crept in to have a look a few evenings later. Dad, who had sunk back into glazed-eye silence, had cycled up to the library, as he did most weeks, to change his books. Mum was downstairs in the kitchen.

In the tiny box-room, Dad's little tins of paint stood on sheets of newspaper on the carpet. The spillages down the sides half obscured names that had nothing to do with oil-painting, as far as I knew: Dulux, Crown, Woolworths. Some of them, I guessed, had come from my granddad's shed.

Dad's half-finished copy of the painting was still propped on the chest of drawers. There were flecks of red paint on the wallpaper above the top edge where it leant against the wall.

I was enormously impressed. He had carefully copied and brushed-in the same areas of colour as on the original painting, and had begun to work on the intricate patterns on the matador's cape. Even the fact that the paint – designed for decorating walls not paintings – had

a breed of intelligent, interested shopkeepers that was rare even then.

Later, Mum worked as a dinner-lady at the newly built school at the end of our road and would bring us home trays of left-over puddings. The bready and metallic smell of these always reminded me of old people.

Mum did not earn very much, but as long as she and Dad were sensible in their spending it was enough to get us by, and it brought her into constant contact with people with whom she felt comfortable about sharing her problems. Whereas, over time, my dad pinballed between bosses – 'foremen', 'supervisors', the whole panoply of niggling middle-management – who displayed wildly differing tolerances of his illness, my mum's little network of friends were always there for her.

Dr Hicks, in particular, was a hero to our family. He was an unshakeable figure of sanity and good sense as the shape of Dad's moods began to change. Dark-skinned and with thin lips set in a permanent half-smile of understanding, Dr Hicks would sit almost motionless in his beautiful oak chair, his heavy, gold fountain pen poised over my mother's 'notes', and just listen. He barely ever spoke, and when he did it wasn't to express an opinion or sympathize – he rarely sympathized – but to confirm, in a tone of half-regret, what my mother had already told him.

Then he would act. I would watch, in fascination, as the nib of his pen danced minute little spirals across his pad, prescribing something to get my mother through the worst of whatever was to come, but, more importantly, noting, like a Victorian diarist, the details of my dad's behaviour. For here was the irony: Dr Hicks was never, in any capacity, at any time, my father's doctor. He was, instead, the nemesis of Dad's illness: the figure who, charged with the responsibility of looking after my mother's health, would make the calls, forge the connections, move around in the shadows as Dad's depression took hold. His job, at a certain stage – always unspoken, never confirmed or explained – was to do his best to get my dad into a hospital, for my mother's sake, in the face of whatever doctor my dad was using to try to keep himself out.

A few days after the bullfight painting appeared in the house, my mum made an appointment to see Dr Hicks. It was easy to do this without my dad knowing, because she was going there three or four times a week, anyway, as his cleaner.

Dr Hicks's surgery occupied the ground and first floor of a large house at the bottom of a long hill called Honeypot Lane in Stanmore, about two minutes' walk from my nana's house at the bottom end of Moorhouse Road.

Next door to the surgery, squat in the centre of a large car park, was The Queen of Hearts, a big, grand old pub in the classic, brick-built 'railway' style. Elb was a regular drinker and cribbage-player here and sometimes, when I was sitting in Dr Hicks's neat little white-painted waiting-room, I'd stare across at the pub's elaborate portico of an entrance and imagine him half-stumbling down the steps, his hat askew, waving goodbye to his mates.

In contrast, Dr Hicks's surgery was a place of quiet calm and authority. Patients, who were handed little wooden squares of hardboard with numbers on them to determine their place in line, sat serenely, waiting to be admitted to the great man. To me and my mum it felt like the most precious place of refuge.

It was early evening before Mum could tell me what Dr Hicks had told her. His name could not be uttered in front of my dad at times like this, and so she had to wait until he'd gone upstairs to the box-room to carry on with his painting.

I had come in from playing in the garden. Mum cleared some cups away and ushered me up onto the draining board to wash my muddy knees to be ready for school the next day. She tied a pinafore around her middle. Like Nana, even around the house my mum always dressed well, usually in twin-sets and skirts and only very occasionally in trousers. Lately she'd taken to wearing the Libra medallion Dad had bought her. The sculpted scales and the little silver-bevelled edge of this fascinated me. I wondered if it had been expensive. She would eventually lose it, bizarrely, in the old walrus pool at London Zoo. The chain caught and broke in the metal fence round the rim of the pool as she was peering in.

'He's going to have a word, Mart,' she said. 'See if he can get someone to see him.'

'From the hospital?'

'No: his own doctor.'

I tutted. Dad's 'own doctor' was elderly and blessed with such infinite tolerance that my dad could have run amok for years without being referred.

'It's not his normal doctor,' said my mum, 'it's a locum: some Indian bloke. I think it might be all right.'

'They want me up the doctor's, Peg,' Dad announced a few evenings later. He had just come in from work and delivered this news in such a matter-of-fact way that I thought, for a moment, he'd quietly come through his wobbly period and that everything might be OK after all.

'What's that for, then, Ron?' said my mum, feigning ignorance of the process she'd unleashed, I thought, rather too obviously.

Dad pursed his lips. 'Oh, I think he's new and probably needs to talk to me. I can *help* these blokes, you see.'

I had a strange, sick feeling in my stomach when I heard my dad talk like this.

'I think he probably wants some advice.' He sniffed and stretched, hanging his old duffel bag up on the coat hook. 'I think I'll go out for a blow,' he said. 'You coming with me, tiddler?'

'Don't you want your tea?' said Mum.

'No, I'll, er . . .' He looked blankly at Mum as if he'd suddenly forgotten the question. His right heel was off the ground and his lower leg was shaking, quivering uncontrollably. He had suddenly, almost instantly, become more distant.

He blew out air through his lips and nose. 'Whew! Hot in here.' He stood for a moment, his leg bouncing, just staring into space. 'I'll see you later,' he said. And he was gone, closing the front door behind him with elaborate care. All thought of my going with him – all thought of anything – had been lost in an instant.

Mum sighed and glanced across at me. 'I think I'll have another word with Dr Hicks.'

Dad saw the locum at his surgery a couple of mornings later. He went straight from there to work. When he came home in the evening he had little to say about the meeting. 'He was all right. Nice bloke.'

Mum folded her arms and pursed her lips. 'What did he want to see you about?'

Dad shook his head. 'Nothing, really. We just 'ad a nice chat about this and that.' He rubbed his chin.

He was still wearing his Green Flashes. He smiled at me. 'You all right, tiddler?' I nodded. He reached into his donkey-jacket pocket and pulled out a 'Lucky Bag'.

'Brilliant,' I said, and it almost was: Dad buying us Lucky Bags was part of the 'normal' ritual, like him lying on the sofa in his pyjamas to watch television, and the games of cribbage he played with Granddad on a Sunday night.

'I got one for Ian too. Where is he?'

My mum looked at me and I could see she was as confused as I was. But there was nothing more she could ask him, not without giving the game away.

The next day, after cleaning Dr Hicks's surgery my mum went to see Dad's locum herself. She took me with her, having rung Priestmead to say that I had a doctor's appointment, which, in a strange and roundabout way, was true.

The surgery my dad used was even closer to Moorhouse Road than Dr Hicks's. It sat behind a high hedge right by the 140 bus stop. Traffic thundered past the waiting-room constantly. The locum was a young Indian man of thirty or thirty-five who sat sideways in his swivel chair, his arm across the blotter on his desk.

'Your husband is a very interesting man, very interesting,' he said, lifting and dropping the corner of the blotter, 'and very intelligent.'

'We're really worried about him,' my mum said. 'He's behaving very peculiarly. As you know, he's a manic-depressive . . .'

The locum nodded. 'Yes. I see that on his records.' He flapped his hand at some papers on his desk.

Mum told him about the record-player and about the painting.

He shook his head. 'This man, you see, he has many, many interests. He is an intelligent man.' He spread his hands. 'I can't put him in hospital for that.'

'I'll be honest,' my mum said, and her expression now was tight and anxious, her lips clamped tensely together. 'He is not behaving normally and he's only going to get worse, and if we can get him into hospital *before* he gets worse . . .'

The locum seemed unimpressed.

'You know,' said my mum, 'he starts doing stuff at work and . . .'

Now the locum was shaking his head. 'This man . . .' he said, and he was smiling almost dreamily. 'We sat here and for an hour, an hour and a half, we talked very sensibly together about the war.'

'The war?' My mum looked at me.

'The war,' said the locum. 'The First World War. Ron, as you know, is very, very anti-war and so the First World War for him is very painful . . . He talked about some pictures in the Imperial War Museum. He was telling me about those.' The locum swivelled in his chair. 'He is very interesting – and you,' he jabbed a finger at me, 'you have a very, very interesting father. Perhaps you should talk to him more.'

Mum shook her head. 'You don't understand.'

'No,' he said, 'no, no, no. It is you two, I think, who do

not understand. There are no grounds for this man to be taken away. None. He is fine. Perhaps if you tried a little harder to communicate with him . . .'

My mum put her hand to her forehead. Her eyes glittered with tears. 'Oh,' she said, 'we do, don't we, Mart?'

The doctor shook his head. He pushed the blotter away, pushed back in his seat. 'OK,' he said, and offered his hand. 'Good to meet you anyway.'

My mum took his hand. He held onto it for a long moment – so long, in fact, that when I looked back from his surgery door he and my mum were still standing there.

His voice became lower, more sympathetic. 'Perhaps I can help *you*,' he said to my mother. 'Perhaps I can put you in touch with someone *you* can talk to.'

She shook her head. 'No.'

'Well, I'm sorry,' he said. 'I really am. But you have a good man there. A very good man.'

The record-player disappeared about a week later. My mum was on the phone when I came in from school and waved me away when I tried to interrupt her. I put my bag down in the hall and went into the front room to turn the television on. Dad was nowhere to be seen. In the corner, where the record-player had stood, Dad's records had flopped over and lay on the floor. I propped them back up carefully against the wall.

'Nan's offered to pay for it,' my mum announced.

'Yes, but, where's it gone?'

Mum spread her hands. 'He's taken it somewhere.'

'Taken it somewhere?'

'He gives stuff away, doesn't he? I don't know.' My mum flopped down on the sofa, her hands between her knees. I could see she'd had hours of this. 'He went out with it this morning,' she said.

I stared at the space where the record-player had been and tried to imagine him picking it up, unplugging it, in the hope this would lead me to imagine its destination. 'Perhaps he's taken it over to Granddad's.'

Mum shook her head. She'd made all the calls. 'He's taken the painting as well.' She flicked her head upwards.

I laughed. 'Oh dear.'

Mum was laughing now, too, for the first time in weeks. 'Some poor sod's going to get that bloody thing,' she said. Then: 'Nan said she'll lend me the money for the record-player and I'll pay Curry's off. So,' she sighed, 'that's a relief.'

'Where is he now?'

My mum sniffed. 'I don't know and don't care, Mart, to be honest. He's a bloody nuisance.'

For all the worry it had caused that day it was obvious Mum was pleased to see the back of the record-player. But it was equally obvious that she dreaded him coming home. I knew that I did.

'Perhaps he'll bring it back with him,' I said.

* * *

I saw Dad march along our wall a couple of hours later. He was moving very quickly, his body leaning forward. He had on no jacket or jumper. I tried to work out how to greet him.

He opened the door with his key. Another bad sign.

Mum met him in the hall. 'Where have you been, Ron?'

Mum's courage in confronting him at times like this always astounded me. Perhaps her desire always to know instantly what was going on prevailed over her fear. Nine times out of ten it disarmed him.

'Hospital,' he said.

'Did you take the record-player up there?'

He'd brushed past her now and was on his way into the kitchen. He took a pint of milk out of the fridge, popped the top off and drank from the bottle. He wiped his mouth. 'Yeah.' Suddenly he seemed exhausted.

Mum didn't say anything. I was glad. She put the kettle on.

My brother was sitting in the corner, his stockinged feet pulled up on the armchair, looking at a book or a catalogue or something.

'How are you, kids?'

My brother put his feet down.

'I'm all right,' I said. I was sitting at the kitchen table with the paper. A sickly air of sweat trailed behind Dad as he passed me to sit down in the other armchair.

I noticed the laces on his plimsolls were undone.

He put the tips of his fingers together, puffed out his cheeks and exhaled slowly. 'Nice to just relax, isn't it, Mart, eh? Just relax and take it easy, eh?'

I nodded. I saw Mum roll her eyes.

'They love music up the 'ospital, you know – they love it.'

Ian glanced across at me.

Dad pulled a cigarette out of his little pack of ten Embassy filtered, then a match. His eyes were glassy. He was, as my mum always put it, 'miles away', moving in a sort of stunned slow motion.

He worked his lips a little, then put the cigarette between them. As he took the first puff, he seemed to wake up. He cast a glance over his shoulder, and cocked his head at me. 'She don't fucking understand that, of course. Eh?'

I froze.

'*Dad*,' said Ian, wrinkling his nose.

But our dad was off on his theme now. 'I said you don't understand about how it relaxes people, do you, Peg?' His face was angry now.

Mum brought some tea in for me. 'Do you want a cup, Ron?'

He ignored the question. He seemed to be miles away again, thinking about something. His mouth hung open. His right lower leg and foot were vibrating, his heel going up and down, up and down.

'I might go up there again tomorrow,' he said, licking his dry lips. 'Help 'em out.'

'Why do you want to—?'

I knew, the moment Mum began to utter that sentence, that it was the breaking point. For weeks we could watch Dad move through every strange – and strangely predictable – step of his illness. But at a certain stage it would become less predictable: the illness would shift, somehow, into the atmosphere around him. When Mum began to speak there was a sickness in my stomach, a rushing in my ears, and it was as if the air was vibrating.

He was up out of the chair and on his feet in a second. Mum shrank back, her mouth opening and closing, and he was in front of her, his fists clenched, his face red and contorted, dribble and spit on his lips and across his mouth.

'*Why do I want to? Why do I want to?*' he mimicked, and he was working his right hand like a chattering mouth in front of Mum's face.

She flinched away, a look that was half-anger, half-fear, etched on her reddening face.

'Why do I wanna do fucking anything, eh?' He was yelling now, screaming. 'But *you* don't fucking do any-thing. You do fuck all!'

'Dad, stop!' Ian was up now.

Dad hardly seemed to notice. His head jutted forward, his eyes were wide and he was roaring at Mum:

'Why don't you fucking leave me alone! Why don't you fucking . . . leave me alone!'

I thought he was going to hit her – thought for a moment: this is it, the big breaking point, the point where Mum will say, 'Enough!' – but the blow didn't come. Instead he spun, reached up, closed his arms around the top of the kitchen door, locked his enormous hands across the top of it and wrenched it forward.

Mum screamed. My mouth had gone dry; my heart was hammering.

There was an awful sound of splitting, groaning, screaming wood and then he'd wrenched the entire door off its hinges, the plaster in the door jamb cracking and spattering across the carpet. I had never witnessed such terrible strength.

The tears welled up in my eyes. 'Stop, Dad, oh, please stop,' I shouted, rushing forward.

Ian had a half-grip on his arm, his mouth opened in horror, but now Dad was stomping, staggering, into the front room like a drunkard.

He raised his right arm and fist and, with the back of his hand, swept everything – the clock, our bits of china – straight off the mantelpiece. He kicked the television over and it lurched and crashed heavily against the bay-window curtains. Then he began picking up framed pictures, ornaments, knick-knacks, and flinging them against the wall.

My mum was weeping uncontrollably now. I had my

arms up to her shoulders, trying to get to her face to comfort her, to kiss her, to stop the terrible anguished sounds coming from her lips. 'Don't cry, don't cry,' I cried.

My brother was frozen in the doorway, hopping from foot to foot, not knowing whether to shout or to cry.

Suddenly, unexpectedly, Dad was crying too – a sustained and awful howl of absolute sadness and frustration. He sank back on the sofa, his arms stretched out either side across the back of it, his mouth opening and closing. There was spittle on his lips, his nose was running and the tears streamed down his sick and reddened face. He seemed to be having trouble breathing. His head lolled back and forth, back and forth, and then he lurched up, tall and momentarily frightening again in his bulk, but broken, hopelessly broken, in the middle like a great worn-out puppet. He staggered, half-blindly, towards the hall door, weeping and crying: 'Oh, Peg . . . *oh, Peg.*'

Mum came to him then. She put her arms up around his neck and her face against his while I clung onto her hips, her tears falling. He shook his head back and forth, slurring, '*Sorry, sorry,*' again and again, and Mum was stroking his hair and his face. Gently now, he pushed her away. His face was wet and red, crumpled up in pure misery, and as he finally got a hold on the door handle and stumbled out into the hall he began crying again: a low, awful moan.

My brother and I followed them up the stairs. Dad sat on the edge of his bed, his head in his hands, his fingers digging into his half-closed eyelids, snuffling and sobbing. 'I'm so sorry.'

'Please stop saying sorry, Ron,' Mum whispered: 'there's nothing to be sorry for' – and she hugged him and kissed him again.

I was in tears myself now, clinging to Mum's hands and to Dad's back. My brother was on the bed, holding and stroking our dad, trying to make everything all right when everything was far from all right.

Dad sank back onto the pillow, holding Mum in his arms, and Ian and I snuggled in on the other side. Dad half-turned to hug me, too. He kissed my forehead and I could feel his tears on my skin and on my hair.

After Dad fell asleep, I lay for a long time in the closed-in dark of my parents' room, listening to his snoring. I thought of the room downstairs, the destruction. I heard the sound again of tearing wood and I felt sick deep in my stomach. Is this what it had all come to?

I could just make out the shape of my mum lying on her side next to Dad, but I didn't know whether she was awake or asleep and I didn't want to speak. I didn't want to risk waking him.

My brother whispered: 'I'm going to my bed. See you in the morning. Wake me up if anything happens,' and I felt his small, light figure slip away. A thin shaft of light fell across the crumpled sheets as he let himself out.

Eventually I heard my mum stir, saw the shape of her shadow change, and then she whispered: '*Martin, are you awake?*'

The two of us crept back downstairs. It was about 10.30 p.m. Broken china, smashed picture frames and various shattered treasures lay strewn across the carpet and scattered on the hearth around our gas fire.

We had a little metal clock on three legs, which had been in the room for as long as I could remember. It had the smallest of ticks, like the peck of a bird. Now it was face down on the floor. I picked it up. I don't know why but the fact that it was in one piece and still working set me crying all over again. I sobbed to my mum: 'It's still ticking.'

Dad was up early as usual the following morning – and quickly out of the house. I crept to the top of the stairs to watch him go. He seemed preoccupied, his mouth working silently, and he had his Green Flashes on. Mum had straightened the front room the night before and I wondered what he made of it all, but his face gave nothing away. He plucked his old black duffel bag from the coat peg, slung it over his shoulder and walked through the house and out of the back door. I heard him wheel his bike down the alley and the gate at the top of the slope pushed back against the hedge.

At school, we had been promised treats for the last few days of the summer term. That week we were to be allowed to bring toys and games in, and, on the last day, to wear our own clothes instead of uniform. I should have felt excited, but I was tired and a bit deflated. A long summer of uncertainty stretched out in front of me.

My mum contacted Dr Hicks again and called Edgware Hospital, where she left a message for Dad's boss.

Auntie Ellen called round that afternoon to say that there was a doctor on the phone from Edgware. The record-player, he told my mum, was down in the hospital recreation room. The doctor himself had been given the painting. There was an affectionate chuckle in his voice, Mum said, but he was pragmatic: 'We're going to try and take Ron in,' he said.

'In there?' my mum asked.

'No. We're going to refer him to Shenley this time,' he said.

The hospital had spoken to Dr Hicks. I didn't know whether they'd spoken to Dad's doctor too. Something, somehow, had been arranged.

8

Shenley

Dad was taken into Shenley Mental Hospital near the village of Radlett in Hertfordshire. That full title is exactly how he always referred to it – 'Shenley Mental Hospital'– seemingly proud of what it did for him and, of course, what he had done for it in return. He talked about it for years after he was discharged, as others might refer to their old school or college, and this was entirely understandable to me, my brother and my mother, because his residence there seemed like a privilege, almost an honour, that had been conferred. Shenley was more like a country estate than a hospital. Acres of lawns and playing fields rolled down from a series of white single-storey villas with green roofs where the patients slept and were treated.

Books on medical history would later describe these villas as 'Italianate', but none of my family had been abroad. To us these uniform buildings split by greenery and broad gravel paths were more like the Butlin's holiday camps we'd visited, Bognor and Skegness, with their rows of chalets and neatly kept borders ablaze with seed-packet colours.

Visiting Shenley felt like going on holiday, too, because it seemed so far from where we lived. I cycled there from Harrow years later and it took me about an hour. In a car it might take half that. But there was no car in our family. Our world was proscribed by how far, as a family, we could pedal our bikes and the limits of the bus routes from Harrow.

To reach Shenley we took a bus to a little terminus at the railway arches in Bushey, then caught another bus out to Radlett. At 'Bushey arches', where we waited for that second bus, there was a shop specializing in dry-rot treatment that had an enormous model of a wood-worm over the door. This fascinated my brother and me and became one of the indelible elements of that Shenley summer.

Mum had travelled up as soon as Dad was admitted, 'to settle him in'. She came back so impressed with it that she could have been describing a country-house hotel rather than a mental institution. 'Oh, he's got a beautiful room, and there's lovely gardens – and there's a club where you can play snooker.'

My brother and I visited for the first time on a blazing-hot Saturday, the day after we'd broken up for school holidays.

Dad plodded up to meet us at the gates of the hospital grounds. He looked thinner, suddenly, and very tired. All the aggression from just a few weeks ago had gone.

''Ello, tiddlers.'

He took our hands and kissed my mum and led us across from the hospital gates to a pub called The Black Lion.

'They said I could stay out for half an hour.'

We all sat outside on a long bench and Dad bought us Cokes and salt-and-vinegar crisps.

'They been very good,' he said, 'very good indeed, but some of the blokes...' He rolled his eyes and glanced back across to the gates.

My mum sipped her shandy.

'Some of them are very ill,' said my dad. He crossed his arms and gazed up at the lowering sun and blew his cheeks out.

I thought he would ask how he'd ended up here: who had made the call; why we thought he was ill. I thought he'd run through the usual litany of angry enquiries, but that stage had passed. He was like a prisoner on the run, somehow, when he was high. Once he was caught, he was caught – and no questions asked.

We strolled around behind the pub. There were a few pretty little houses and a square, shallow pond with weed and sticklebacks in it. This was a plus. Shenley was starting to feel more like a holiday every minute.

My brother and I leant under the guard rail, our

hands on the narrow concrete kerb that marked the perimeter of the pond, and stared into the brackish water.

'This is great, Dad.'

Then Dad was down on his knees as well, his hand pressing on my shoulder. I felt very happy then.

'Look at the little 'uns.'

There were stickleback fry in the water – tiny, clear points of darting baby fish.

We walked back across to the hospital and up along the grey tarmac drive. To our right, little paths pushed up between lines of bushes and shrubs to the verandas of the various villas. To our left were dinner halls and administration buildings.

'Bloody mess in that dinner hall last night, Peg – food everywhere and the nurses having to come down and sort it all out.' He shook his head.

The 'nurses' were all men: the classic 'men in white coats' that people joked about. They were all very young and had the sort of quiet resolve I'd got used to among the male staff at Edgware. They were involved, nightly, it seemed, in 'sorting things out' – mainly patients who refused their medication or who picked fights with others. But all these revelations were still to come. Shenley, that evening, seemed the most peaceful spot on earth, a place in which to get truly well, away from the stresses of everyday life.

We walked up to the Alpha Club, a long, wooden hut

that sat on a raised area of ground between the villas and shielded from them by trees and hedges. Inside, there was a full-sized snooker table with a proper, oblong aluminium light over the top.

My brother and I had never played snooker, so my father taught us. He chalked one of the shorter cues, set me in front of him, between his arms, then, with his left hand, placed my right hand on the edge of the table and, with his right hand, ran the end of the cue over my knuckles and down, in the correct way, between my fingers. I liked the feel of the heavily polished wood on my skin.

'Now look down the cue,' he said, and I squinted down, closing my right eye, feeling like I was aiming a rifle.

'Evening, Ron.'

A young man with a bright-red face and ginger hair had entered the hall. I smelled the sweet gust of body odour. He must have been about twenty-five.

'These your kids, then?' He beamed down at us.

He seemed very spare and strong and there was something in the straight, square set of his teeth that suggested spitefulness. He had very bright blue eyes and strange, gingery-white eyelashes like the soft fuzz of a baby chick. I didn't like to look at those for very long.

'Yeah: Martin and Ian. And this is my wife, Peg . . .'

My mum smiled across from a little table. She still had

her green mac on, which seemed incongruous next to this sweating boy in his T-shirt.

'This is Alan,' my dad said.

Alan nodded, the smile never leaving his face. He scratched his chest and I noticed the gingery hair on the back of his hand. He glanced up at my dad. 'I'll see you later, then.'

'Yeah, yeah,' my dad said. He watched Alan go back out of the door.

'You 'ave a go,' he said to me, handing me the cue.

He walked back over to my mum, picked up a shandy, sipped it and then shook his head. 'He goes out in the bloody sun. I've told him. And of course with that skin . . .' He rolled his eyes. 'Then he gets *nasty*. Loses his temper. He loves football but you can't have him on the pitch like that. It puts the others off.'

My mum nodded. Her eyes looked a bit panicky. 'He hasn't had a go at you, has he, Ron?'

My dad screwed his eyes up. 'No. I'd fuckin' kill him if he did. Mind you, he's got the strength of a fuckin' ox. Big boy.'

Alan didn't seem like a big boy to me, but he did seem wiry and dangerous. I wondered what I should say or do if I saw him again, but Dad was ahead of me.

'I stay out of his way,' he said. 'He's already got himself in trouble with the doctors. And I don't think there's much wrong with him except he should stay in on days like this. Come on . . .' He scraped his chair back. 'I've got to get back for my medicine.'

We didn't go back to the villa with him that night. He kissed Mum goodbye back at the gates and we crossed the road to wait for the bus. It was getting chilly. My brother found some ants under the seat in the shelter and we played with them, making them march around twigs in the dust.

My mum was scratching her chin and thinking but she cheered up when, eventually, the little single-decker bus came shuddering around the corner. 'I'll be glad to get home,' she said.

We went up to Shenley twice a week during that summer. At home, my brother and I had 'dust fights' in the garden, scooping up earth in handfuls, piling it onto old pieces of hardboard and then tossing it high in the air to produce 'explosions'. Other children came over to play from neighbouring gardens: Peter Wyatt, who didn't have a dad; Paul and Mark MacManus, who lived at the top, 'right' end of the street and whose father, a genial and ancient white-haired Irishman, would always pull into the kerb on his bike when Mum was on the wall and ask about Dad.

There was nobody, not a single person, in our neighbourhood who looked upon Dad's illness and his stay at Shenley with anything other than sympathy. It was only years later – long after I'd left secondary school and was at college in London – that I realized fully how notorious Shenley was, both in the type of patients it took on and the 'experimental' manner of their treatment.

I did have an inkling, though. The third or fourth time we visited Dad, he met us at the gates with a plastic bag. Inside was a copy of 'Sugar, Sugar' by The Archies – the big hit of that summer and the best record I had ever heard. The voice of the American girl in the middle who said, '*I'm gonna make your life so sweet*,' made me feel hollow and peculiar in the stomach and I never grew bored with hearing it.

I later found out my mum had bought the record and slipped it to my dad on an earlier visit so he could present it to me near my birthday, 11 July. At the time, though, it seemed an indication that he wasn't entirely cut off from the world and I found that comforting. Shenley was beginning to feel rather unreal. That evening we went inside Dad's villa for the first time. It was single-storey and had no ceiling, which meant you were looking up to the inside of the roof and cross-beams, on which dangled heavy, old-fashioned-looking lights.

There was a central meeting or recreation area and, around the edges, individual rooms. There were no wards and no corridors. Dad took us into his room. It was larger than I'd expected, with a bed, a table to work on and a window. It reminded me, as had the Alpha

Club, of a building in a prisoner-of-war camp. I half expected someone to move a stove aside, to reveal a half-finished escape tunnel.

Dad seemed to be composing himself to tell us something. He sat uneasily on the bed, feet flat on the floor, and looked at his shoes. 'Bloke came in last night, Peg,' he said, 'and peed all over me.'

'Oh, no.' My mum looked pained. We both glanced up at the closed door as if the same man was about to enter and repeat his exploit. 'What did you do?' My mum took his hand.

My dad shook his head. There were tears welling up in his eyes and suddenly I wanted to cry too.

'Did you tell the doctors?'

'The doctors . . .' He shook his head. I thought that the doctors, even though they were young, had an air of real authority about them, but Dad was shaking his head. 'I don't think they really know what to do.'

'Well, can't they just lock you in?' said my mum. 'I mean, for God's sake!'

'They don't like locking our doors. It's not that sort of place.' My dad lifted his glasses on his wrist and wiped the back of his hand across his eyes. 'I tell you I've had it, Peg. I've really had it.'

There was a lot of commotion suddenly outside Dad's room and I wondered if one of the raised voices belonged to the man who peed.

'Not Alan, was it?' my mum said suddenly.

My dad gave a low laugh. Even Alan, it seemed, was not that mad. 'No, he's in another villa,' Dad said. 'But he reckons it's as bad in his one. People shouting. No, this was an old bloke. He was perfectly nice to me today – "Good morning, Ron" – doesn't remember a thing about it. Just came in and opened up the front of his trousers.'

'Perhaps he was asleep,' my mum said. 'Perhaps he was sleep-walking or he couldn't find the toilet.'

Dad shook his head. 'He was laughing. Then he stood there for ages just looking at me. They dragged him out ... Anyway,' Dad stood up suddenly as if to bring the matter to a close, 'forget about him, there's something I want to show you.'

We left the villa and Dad led us up behind the row of buildings to a fringe of trees on a slope about a hundred yards beyond.

'Where we going, Ron?' my mum said, laughing.

'You wait,' replied Dad.

The sun was getting lower and I knew that it would be dark within the hour. I too wondered where we were going.

We made our way gingerly over the fallen twigs and uneven soil under the trees, pushed down a small wire perimeter fence and stepped over onto the grassy edge of a huge ploughed field. I'd never seen one before. My brother crouched down to pick up a big lump of soil. It was light, slightly sandy: dried clay.

'We'll have to go across here,' my dad said, indicating the field.

'I'll take Ian back to the club,' my mum said. 'You go.'

My brother didn't say anything. Back then, he never liked to walk very far. My mum was sure he had something wrong with him.

'OK. Come on, Mart.'

It was difficult to pick my way across the field. It sloped up and over in a big dome, the surface of it, kissed by orange sun, lumpen and hard under my thin-soled Startrite sandals. I squinted across to the other side but could see nothing except another row of trees.

'Where are we going, Dad?' I said, but I didn't complain about the pain of walking on that surface.

'You wait,' he said.

As we approached the trees, Dad veered off to the right. I followed, and we came in behind the end of them. There, deep in shadow except where the sun glinted through the mesh of twigs across the rapidly darkening sky, was an enormous, still pond. There was complete, dead silence.

My dad carried on walking, his arms swinging in his light-green, short-sleeved shirt, his booted feet swishing and crackling through the undergrowth and onto the faintest of paths around the edge.

I had an enormous sense of arrival in that place, a feeling that somehow all the paths my dad and I had taken led here. I felt very strongly that this was where Dad was always meant to be: outside, free, moving, walking.

For years he had wanted to be a park-keeper in our local park. It was the job he felt he was most cut out to do because he got along with children and young people of all ages and because he always wanted to be out, out – out of his clothes on the sofa, out of the very neck of his shirt. His face, his skin, always yearned for the fresh air. He flung windows open all around him.

'What do you think?' He turned to me.

'It's fantastic.'

'I'm going to get Mum to bring my rods up,' he said, and he crouched down at the edge of the pond to touch the water.

'Good idea,' I said. A little breeze had come up now and I shivered slightly.

'We'll just walk round once and then we'll go back,' he said, and he disappeared off into the shadows along that little path.

9

The Match

Our visits to Shenley began to settle into a pattern: Coke and crisps at The Black Lion, a look at the little pond, back across to the hospital for a long walk around the grounds, then a stroll up to the Alpha Club for a cup of tea. It was hard not to drift into the notion that we were on holiday.

During his first few weeks at the hospital, Dad had gone through a period of supernatural calmness. His gentle smile had reappeared. His face, somehow, had lost its lines. At times he had seemed very close to the 'normal', balanced dad I knew, even moaning about one or two of the other patients and criticizing some of the doctors to my mum – something he'd never have done when he was high. He had been allowed to fish in his 'secret' pond, had begun making a raffia-seated stool in one of the craft classes. There had been no talk, it seemed, of discharging him, but I assumed it was only a matter of time: when our school holidays are over, I thought, Dad will come home with us.

Then, quite suddenly, his moods began to change. He seemed restless. The pacing started again during our visits and I noticed his fists clenching and unclenching at his sides. When we walked into the sweltering heat of his room at the villa, the air was sickeningly sweet with the odour of his sweat.

There had been long exchanges between my mum and dad about his medication, and my mum seemed aggrieved about something, but none of these conversations were shared with me and my brother. My dad kept touching my mum and saying, 'It's all right,' as if it was she who was the patient. It all seemed very odd.

About three weeks or so into his stay, we travelled up to Shenley for a Saturday afternoon visit. My brother and I lingered on the edge of one of the football fields, leaving our mum to walk up to Dad's villa on her own.

There was a game going on and Alan was in one of the teams. My brother and I, in one of our many bedtime conversations about Shenley, had decided that, compared with Dad, this bloke was genuinely 'mad'.

In many ways the hospital had brought Ian and me closer together. We were not estranged as children – we played and fought together all the time – but the twists and turns of Dad's illness had leant our conversations a more mature edge. We were growing up quickly. Even then, as a nine-year-old, I could feel that happening.

It was mid-afternoon on a hot day and the 'pitch', which was just a big, square lawn sloping away from the line of villas, offered no shade at all. Yet Alan – red-haired, fair-skinned and wearing long trousers, socks and ordinary lace-up shoes – was dashing around. Years later when I read the phrase 'blushed to the roots' in some Victorian novel or other I would think of Alan's face that day: striped red across the forehead under the baby roots of his ginger hair and beginning to peel on his nose and chin. Spotting us on the perimeter, he stopped running, raised his head and smiled. He jogged across, puffing and blowing. 'How's your dad?' he said.

It seemed a strange question from someone who was in hospital with him. Ian and I, unused – like all small children – to conversing with older people, and more than a little wary of this particular example, just shrugged.

I wondered what he meant. Alan squinted against the sun and glanced up at the villa. I noticed his socks were rolled down over his shoes and could not tear my gaze away from his blazing face.

'Do you like football?' he asked, after a while.

'It's all right,' I said.

He put his hands in his pockets. He seemed to be the one who was embarrassed now. He shrugged and then turned away. 'See you later.' He half-jogged, half-strolled, back to the game, although he seemed to have lost his enthusiasm for it.

Ian was squatting on the ground, pulling up handfuls of grass. He looked, suddenly, very small in his sandals and shorts and for some reason I felt rather sorry for him.

I heard our mum calling, and I saw that she was walking down from the steps of the villa. Her arms were folded and she appeared to be annoyed about something. Dad was just behind her. His arms were straight down by his sides, which seemed odd somehow, and he was moving stiffly as if learning to walk for the first time.

'There you are,' said my mum. She wasn't smiling.

Dad came up, his footsteps heavy on the grass. His mouth was trembling in a very strange way and there was dribble on his lips. He glanced over at the game of football and then at us. His eyes seemed to be glazed and tearful. 'All right, kids?'

As he came close I could see that his arms and hands were also trembling. His hands seemed elongated because the fingers were at full stretch and quivering at the tips. His legs were shaking too, which explained the awkwardness of his walk.

I thought at first he might be cold, but this was a different sort of shakiness: it was very slight, very rapid and it seemed to run the length of his limbs.

'Are you OK, Dad?' I said.

'Yeah, no, I'm all right, I'm all right,' he said. He half-raised his arm. His voice seemed slurry and clogged up inside his head as if he had a heavy cold. 'It's just the drugs.' He slurred the 'just the' so it came out as 'sus-de'. 'Let's go . . . let's go to the Alpha,' he said.

My mum hadn't said anything, but she took my dad's arm as we walked across.

My dad had been given some sort of electric shock treatment. I don't know how many sessions of it he had endured or what prompted the hospital to administer it, but it had obviously come as a surprise both to him and my mum.

'Don't worry,' he told her, in the Alpha Club, and he put his hand on her arm. 'Honestly, Peg.'

It struck me, yet again, as I'd be struck so many times over the years, how brave my dad was.

'But look at you, Ron!' my mum said. My dad was still shaking uncontrollably. She was close to tears.

'Come on,' he said, and he put his arm round her neck and pulled her face towards him. 'I'll be all right, but I don't want you worrying, OK? I don't want you worrying.'

For someone whose own moods see-sawed so wildly – and for whom peace of mind often seemed such a strange and distant place – my dad had always had a knack of calming others.

Mum nodded, and dabbed her nose with a hanky.

She had always described me as 'a natural worrier', but I am ashamed to say that after she drew me aside and explained, in obviously shocked tones, what they'd done to him I barely gave it a second thought. I suppose I just trusted the doctors. My mum's tears, though, turned to frustration and then real anger.

Over the years she had familiarized herself with the basic pattern of Dad's treatment, and had even, out of necessity, helped to administer his drugs, but this seemed to be a development out of her control, and it terrified her. Had she signed a form for them to do it? Her reaction suggested otherwise.

She had some private conversations with the doctors in various offices around the place and came out looking furious and flustered. I don't know what was said. She glared around at the villas as if they were an enemy crowding in.

'I don't like this place, Mart,' she said, and there was real venom in her voice.

Dad, though, seemed to bear it all with remarkable cheeriness. It very obviously cowed him, burned away, temporarily, his sense of humour and his quick wit, but all of those aspects of his personality, thank God, quickly returned. Recovering from ECT seemed to be just like recovering from flu, although I'm sure it wasn't so simple for my dad.

I didn't comprehend then, and I find it hard to consider even now, the amount of pain he must have gone through. I find it hard to consider that the shock treatment might have felt like a form of torture or torment. Perhaps my mum did tell me that he ranted and railed against it, but I can't remember him doing so. To me it seemed like a process of knocking a person down and then having to wait quite a long time for him to get up again. On a few occasions when we visited, he had been knocked down and was getting up. That's how I remember it.

Alan had begun to attach himself to my dad. They played cards and snooker together. On a couple of occasions when we visited, Alan would be strolling a few yards behind my dad as he came up to meet us. As Dad reached the gate, though, Alan would always give a half-wave to us and turn back.

'Coo, Peg, he drives me up the bloody wall,' Dad would say, shaking his head, as he watched Alan amble back to the villas. 'Always bloody hanging around.'

On other occasions, though, there'd be more sympathy: 'He 'asn't got any family, you see? No one visits him. He's not a bad bloke, really.'

But I wasn't keen on him and Mum didn't like him at all. He had a way of tipping his head back and looking at us as if trying to work something out. My mum thought that, of all the patients in Shenley, he seemed the most genuinely disturbed.

Dad had begun organizing one or two hospital football matches, as he did in Cullington Close. These, though, were slightly wilder affairs. One afternoon, in between spells of blowy rain, we all stood and watched. Two groups of about a dozen men were lined up against each other on the lawn in front of Dad's villa. They were a strange amalgamation of young and old. Some of them, like my dad, wore shorts and T-shirts in a rough approximation of 'football kit'; others sported big coats or dressing-gowns flapping open over pyjamas.

My dad had a whistle and some folded-up paper as a 'notebook'. These accessories were enough to assert his authority – and make him a figure of strange fascination to some of the more unwell men.

As the match progressed numerous patients who were watching from the sidelines joined the fray, wandering on and attaching themselves to one or other of the 'teams', so that, by the end, there were fifty or sixty involved. Many seemed to have no idea that any sort of game was going on: the players were just a crowd among whom they could wander and fool around.

My dad, who was pretty 'casual' and 'relaxed' – two of his favourite words – about life in general, liked sport to be properly organized, so he did his best to referee the match properly. Every few minutes as the game descended again into a crowded scuffle, the little orange ball bouncing around in the middle somewhere, Dad would blow his whistle, leap in, grab the ball and insist on a 'bounce up'.

The sound of the whistle confused some of the players, who would stop and glance anxiously over to the villas every time it sounded, but it kept the match in some sort of order.

After about an hour, an old fellow with very neat grey hair and beard but a ferociously hurt look in his eye grabbed hold of the ball up at the end of the pitch and refused to give it back. Dad blew his whistle sharply and pleaded with the old man to return the ball, at the same time arguing with Alan, who was all for taking it back by force and kept charging at the fellow, shouting, his thin, gingery arm raised as if to strike him.

A large group had gathered behind Alan and my dad, some of them also wanting to tackle the old man directly, others just watching, curiously, to see what would happen.

But the old fellow would not give it up. He would not even look up. His chin rested on the top of the ball as if it was the head of a baby. He twisted and turned his body away from the men, backing into the shrubbery at the edge of the pitch. It was raining and blowing quite hard now, and the old man's neat hair was flattened to his head.

Watching from the sidelines, my mum tut-tutted. She dug a little wad of clear plastic out of her handbag and unfolded it into a rain bonnet. Ian and I folded our arms and skipped around to keep warm.

'I think they've had it,' said my mum, clamping her hand on her head to hold the bonnet on. She looked disappointed for my dad.

People began to wander away, shrugging and laughing. Dad sounded the whistle loudly twice to signal that he'd given up and began plodding back over to us, face down in the rain, shaking his head and spreading his arms towards us as if to say, 'What can I do?' Half a dozen of the other patients followed him, thinking he was going to start the game elsewhere, but he waved them away. 'Tomorrow, tomorrow,' he said. He sounded very irritated. He put his arm around Mum, screwing his eyes up against the drizzle. 'Let's get in out of this and have a cup of tea.'

Dad was in Shenley for about six weeks. At home I missed him terribly. The summer holidays had always been about Dad, one way or another. If he was ill, the long days would be spent keeping out of his way or struggling to get him into hospital. If he was well we'd go on holiday – always in England, always to the coast – or have days out at different places: the zoo, the museums, up at Stanmore ponds, fishing.

That summer the days away from Shenley dragged interminably. The evenings, when it stayed light till 8.30 or 9.00 p.m., were the worst: all the neighbours out on the wall, the children on their bikes, dogs barking in the streets, but a huge void where Dad was supposed to be.

'How's Ron?' Auntie Ellen would ask, and all the rest of the neighbours would stop talking to hear what Mum had to say.

'I feel sorry for your poor dad,' old Mrs Herbert would say, but she never elaborated: just shook her old head.

* * *

Dad was discharged from hospital at the end of August. Granddad brought him home in his old Ford Popular. Auntie Ellen waddled up to her front door to see, and was joined by old Mrs Herbert and her daughter Ann. As he struggled to unfold himself from the front seat of the car Dad looked very brown, exactly as if he'd been on a foreign holiday, but had lost a lot of weight.

'You all right, Ron? Nice to have you back,' Auntie Ellen shouted across.

My dad raised a hand, but kept walking. His legs seemed very stiff.

'Ahhhh, look,' sighed Auntie Ellen, as if he was a kitten. Mrs Herbert gave a rare smile.

'Here he is, Peg,' my granddad said at our front door. He was carrying Dad's suitcase.

My dad was coming down the slope behind him, glancing across at our unkempt front lawn with the little stone donkey in the centre. I could see him calculating in his head all the work that needed to be done outside.

'All right, Dad,' my dad said, before he'd even got through the door – and he was fishing in his pocket to give Granddad petrol money. 'Oh, come on, take it, take it,' said Dad, when Granddad made a face and looked faintly annoyed. 'Oh, sod you, then,' said Dad in the end and thrust the notes back in his pocket. They both laughed.

'Bloody fool,' said my granddad, and he smiled the way he always smiled: with straight, white teeth, handsome like a gangster. He had his hat on but no jacket. 'How are you, Peg?'

'I think I'm bloody stupid,' said my mum: 'stupid to put up with him,' and she reached up and kissed my dad on the cheek.

My brother and I were so excited. We were leaping round him, holding his sides, his hands, pawing at his old green jumper.

He walked us both into the kitchen, his big hands resting on our heads either side. 'I'll 'ave a cup of tea,' he said to Mum and opened the back door to look out into the garden.

The garden calmed Dad like nothing else. It was not a prize-winning garden – he was not obsessive about it. But it was Dad's garden. It was unpretentious, a bit untidy. There were little stone figures that he'd picked up here and there: an owl and a sleeping cat by the pond, and a small grey statue of Laurel and Hardy sitting side by side on a bench, which he loved. Sometimes, when he was well and my mum told him off, he would imitate Stan Laurel being chastised, screwing up his face as if he was eating sherbet and twiddling the hair on the top of his head.

Dad strolled down the garden, his hands, as ever, behind his back. His baggy green jumper, which had long ago lost its elasticity at the bottom, flapped shapelessly over his backside. He had a look at the pond. 'You fed these fish, Mart?'

He fetched the large pot of fish food from the shed and came back down the path, smiling. He foraged around inside it, carefully locating the spare door-key my mum always concealed among the flakes – and which she was convinced he would one day throw into the pond by mistake.

He tossed some food onto the water. Then he stood, arms still behind him, nodding at his fish.

Happy. Happy now.

10

Breathing Out

For the first few days after he came home, Dad seemed like a man reborn. He stalked round the garden, tending his roses, cutting the grass: he seemed in no hurry to get back to work. Then there'd be periods of just standing with his hands on his hips, staring at the lawn. Our neighbour Reg would come down to the fence, as he always did, and try to start a conversation. I'd see him waving his thin arms at Dad's flower-beds, though his interest in his own garden extended no further than sudden darting runs into the weeds behind his shed with a very old, very rusty-looking scythe.

Dad would be nodding, nodding.

Slowly it became evident that Shenley had left its mark. The man who had almost swaggered into hospital, six or seven weeks before, determined that his mission was to 'help' the doctors, had been cowed. He would lie in bed until the dull mid-morning, then shuffle down silently, in his pyjamas, to watch TV. My mum wondered, ironically, whether the hospital had driven him back into a depression.

But it was less a depression than a gradual realization of what he had been through. One evening, he snapped the television off suddenly and came into the back room, where my brother and I were doing our homework.

My mum looked up from her paper. 'Ron?'

'I'm not going back in there,' he said, and he had never sounded so definite about anything in his life.

'Oh, Ron, no one wants you to.' My mum stood up and slipped her arm round his waist.

'We don't want you to,' I said.

'I do!' said Ian. I scowled at him.

My dad laughed, but he was wiping a tear out of the corner of his eye. He sat down at the table. 'The trouble is, Peg, everyone was so *ill*. So *ill*. I've never seen anything like it.' He rubbed his eyes hard, as if the images were imprinted behind his eyelids. His mouth was trembling and I thought he was going to cry, but somehow he sniffed it all back. 'I'm not going back anyway.'

The impetus was for change. He handed in his notice at Edgware Hospital – a scene of so many small incidents but a place where he had always been happy. It was never quite clear why he felt he had to go. He had worked there for eleven years and would talk about it, on and off, for the rest of his life, but suddenly, somehow, in that strange, still period at the end of that extraordinary summer, it didn't fit in with his plans.

He sat in the back room, with his one evening cigarette, and scanned the small ads in the *Harrow Observer* and the national evening papers for a week or so. I looked at them myself, out of curiosity, but could not understand the abbreviations. Most of the jobs, it seemed to me, involved the skills to 'operate' some 'tool' or other to a certain prescribed standard. I thought of Dad's toolbox: the blunt hack-saw I'd once used to saw a line across the arm of his chair, the hammer I used to kill woodlice, the fascinating spirit-level.

Dad applied to a company called 'Franco Signs'. They needed a sign writer. But he came home from his first day grim-faced. There were long, anguished conversations with my mum that I preferred not to hear. I was becoming adept at dodging unnecessary anxiety.

The obvious problem was that he had never, as far as I knew, painted words onto glass, or anything else, and his lack of skill had been ruthlessly exposed. He was desperate to get on, to earn a wage, to get back to normal, but Franco Signs was not going to be the place to make it happen. After a month or six weeks he handed in his notice.

Dad was keen to get a job that was in some way creative, that involved drawing or printing, but he also needed to be among people who would understand him, who would, in some way that I was still trying to work out, sympathize. He'd worked for tough bosses in the past, and he was not afraid of hard work, but some other element had to be there; some regard, I think, for what he might achieve if he was allowed to go beyond the boundaries of the job: if he was allowed to be 'himself'.

There was a printing works close to Moorhouse Road. A series of huge, oblong, 1930s-style buildings in rusticated brick, it sat back from the edge of the busy Honeypot Lane.

Dad heard of a position vacant there – some sort of general assistant or handyman. He applied, and was accepted.

I was delighted for him. He had found, I thought, a big company to look after him. There might be prospects for him to 'get on', to be part of the team.

Years later, when I was at sixth-form college, I was in a production of *Death of a Salesman*. As the main character of the title, Willy Loman, built up hope after hope – for himself and his two sons – I thought of Dad, first at Franco Signs, then at the printers, trying his hardest but waiting, always waiting, for the inevitable knock-back.

A few Saturdays after he got his job we cycled up to the three ponds at Stanmore Common to go fishing. Dad had packed up all his gear in the morning, tying the canvas bag with his rods along the crossbar of his bike and stuffing his bait-box and tackle into the old black duffel bag with white piping that he always carried.

To begin with he hadn't asked me along, but as he was wheeling his bicycle out of the shed he looked up and saw me watching from the kitchen window. 'Coming, tiddler?' he said, and he raised his eyebrows and smiled as he said it, so I couldn't refuse.

Mum and Ian had gone out shopping and I was facing the prospect of just rattling round the house on my own, so I nodded and ran out to the shed to get my own bits and pieces. I very rarely 'fished' properly when I was with Dad. I preferred to take a little net, some jars and plastic bags and see what I could dredge up from the mud and reeds. I liked to watch Dad fish. I liked to see him lost in it.

You could not get to the ponds without cycling up one steep hill or another, either Green Lane, which wound up gradually towards the common, or Dennis Lane, which was like a steep ramp up to it. I'd always loved Dennis Lane because it challenged you not to dismount, and because it was lined with the sort of houses Americans lived in on television: big, chalet-style dwellings with no fences or hedges, but immaculate lawns that spilled down to the pavement, and hose-sprinklers that were connected to outdoor taps rather than, as in our house, running up through the kitchen window.

I had puffed up Dennis Lane with Dad before,

watching his big, white calf muscles expand and contract as he sawed up and down on the pedals in front of me, but today we opted for the more gentle Green Lane. We were only a few yards up the first incline when Dad dismounted, blowing and breathing heavily.

'Can't do that, son. Can't do it.' He propped his bike against a wall and straightened up, wrenching at the big black buttons on his donkey-jacket. His face was red and he was labouring to breathe.

'You all right, Dad?'

He waved his big hands at me. He couldn't speak. Finally, he said: 'I'm fine.' He expelled air again. 'I just haven't done anything like this . . . for a long time.'

I nodded, but I wondered about this. He'd had plenty of exercise at Shenley – walking, playing football. He should have been fitter than ever.

We plodded up the hill, resting every ten yards or so for Dad to get his breath back. This was an odd feeling for me. I'd never known my father to be physically weak in this way. I added up in my head how old he was – forty-two – and wondered if this was what suddenly happened to people at that age.

We crossed the road by The Vine pub and saw the low, uneven concrete fence that bordered the first pond. This was always a thrill for me – like the drum we used to look at on the Boosey & Hawkes factory. That nondescript fence meant that, within a few more steps, the surface glint of the pond would come into view – a sight more thrilling to me than almost anything in childhood. Water, mysterious open water, and the fish waiting.

On every previous trip we paused for a little while at this first pond, which was the smallest of the three, before wheeling our bikes across the rough grass and rutted mud of the common to 'look in' on the second – the banks of which were too covered in thorn bushes and trees to offer many places to sit – and then on to the third.

The third was always the place we ended up fishing because it was the largest and deepest and had big, wide areas of open sandy bank interspersed with overhanging trees.

Today, though, my dad crouched down on the dry, light earth and pulled all his stuff out of his duffel bag straight away. He was making himself at home at the first pond. I watched him carefully to see if he was show-ing any other signs of tiredness, but he seemed bright enough. Every so often, though, he would straighten up and blow out his cheeks.

I started dipping my fishing net into the shallow, brackish water along the far end of the pond, where lines of bushes and small trees had crept down the bank and formed a dense, low canopy. The water was only an inch or so deep here, sitting over layers of rotting leaves, twigs and rich, dark, stinking mud. Heaven for newts. I loved newts.

Suddenly I was aware of Dad close by. He was

bending down and whispering to me under the spiky branches of one of the trees, gingerly holding them out of his face. 'Martin,' he whispered. 'Follow me.'

I picked up on his silence and stealth and crept across the mud to come out of the pond the long way, the sticky mud sucking and pulling at my wellington boots. I didn't want to make a noise swishing the water.

He was crouched on the bank near his fishing tackle, peering out across the pond. He beckoned to me. 'Look,' he said, and pointed to a spot six or seven yards out.

I leant in close to him and squinted along the line of his finger. It was difficult to separate the reflection on the water from what was going on beneath, but the more I looked the more I was aware of a long bar of greyish-brown colour just below the surface.

'Pike,' said my dad. 'Big one.'

I looked away, to try to clear my confused vision, and stared again, but now all I could think about was my dad's breathing: a low, whistling rasp in his chest. Where had that come from?

As if suddenly aware that I was listening, he dropped his arm and reached for his rod. 'I'll cast out,' he said.

I set the problem of his breathing aside; parked it back in my mind with all the other pointless worries.

He skewered a fresh maggot on his line, drawing pus-like liquid from its side, then let it dangle for a moment. He ushered me back a little, then gently flicked out the maggot, weights and a tiny feather float. The float

142

plopped softly into the water about nine inches from the snout of our 'pike'. I peered out to see if there was any movement, but the shape did not change or move. It had still not fully formed itself into a pike and I wondered if my dad and I were seeing things.

The little orange float bobbed gently, its reflection dancing in the water. Then suddenly, languidly, something large and terrifyingly alive in that warm afternoon silence turned and flipped up against the grey surface and for a split-second – in its movement and the merest hint, so I thought, of a feathery dorsal fin – defined itself as 'pike'.

Dad's mouth opened – 'ha' – and then we both watched as the surface of the pond re-formed itself in shimmering stillness.

'Gone,' he said. He smiled at me.

We cycled back around four o'clock, free-wheeling down Dennis Lane into the rushing wind and the teeth of the big old Volvos and Jaguars bringing the rich residents of the lane back from their afternoons out.

When we got to Cullington Close there was a police car outside our house. I felt a lump in my throat. Was Mum ill? Had Ian had an accident? Perhaps it wasn't anything to do with us: perhaps one of the Ludbrooks was in trouble. But the moment my mum emerged from the door of number 32, her neck flushed red, I knew what had happened.

'Where have you been!' she screamed at me, her neck

jutting out so that I could see the tightened tendons. 'Where have you been!'

'I went fishing, Mum . . .'

My dad raised his hand to his mouth. 'Oh, Peg.'

'For God's sake. You can't just bloody . . . disappear. I've been worried sick about you.'

The policeman was starting to put his helmet on, fussing with the strap, his eyes downcast as the row blazed. I'd never come across an embarrassed policeman before. He began to make his way up the path: an older man, with heavy legs.

'I'm so sorry, I really am,' Mum called after him. She had subsided a bit now. 'My stupid husband!' She indicated Dad, as if there might be some doubt about the relationship. He smiled.

'OK,' the policeman said as he brushed up along the hedge to the gate.

Mum shook her head and went inside. Dad looked across at me, made a funny face and winked.

Dad's breathing was getting worse. He couldn't climb stairs without the air rasping and whistling in his lungs. He'd sit down in his armchair, after some exertion or other in the garden, the palm of his hand clapped flat on the front of his pullover while a whole ragged symphony of low honks and murmurs sounded from his chest.

He'd been to see his doctors but I wasn't made aware of their verdict. When I asked Dad what was wrong, he'd just shake his head and say: 'I need to get fit.'

What I did begin to realize, though, was that there was some trouble over Dad's job at the print works. It was beginning, my mum told me, 'to get him down', and though he hadn't sunk into any sort of clinical depression he seemed preoccupied, anxious. He appeared too to be waiting for some sort of cue from my mum.

'I would like him to get away from that bloody job,' she said to me.

'Why?'

'It's not doing him any good.'

'Why doesn't he, then?' I said. 'There are lots of other jobs.' I thought of the rows of small ads.

She shook her head.

One low, grey, drizzly afternoon, my mum, brother and I set out for Honeypot Lane. Dad had called from the works to say he had the chance to do some overtime and could we bring him up something to eat.

Ian and I were both a bit reluctant. Like most children, once we were in from school we considered the hours to be our own and anything we were forced to do seemed like a theft. But we couldn't let Dad go hungry and we couldn't let Mum go on her own.

We sat on the bus, watching the big windscreen wipers alternately revealing and obscuring the grey houses sliding by, the yellow splodges of headlights. I don't remember any details of getting into the building, whether we had to give our names or wait to be taken through, but the room in which we ended up – the fumes, the noise, the mundane horror of it – will stay with me for ever.

We found ourselves in a noisy, cramped, industrial-looking space of guard rails and pipes, the air thick with the acrid stench of chemicals. I did not want to breathe in. My brother pulled a face. Some sort of heavy machinery was thumping and rattling away around us. We were behind a low barrier at the edge of a large vat set into the floor. On the opposite side was Dad, dressed in brown overalls with his shirt-sleeves rolled up. As we watched, he stirred gently at the thick, brownish-clear liquid it contained with a long broom handle, his hands high up on the pole.

Someone said something sharply from a half-closed-off cubby-hole behind him, drawing his attention to our presence, and he looked up. Glancing across, he mouthed a 'hello' at us and attempted a smile, but the smile did not quite reach his eyes. He was winking and blinking at us from behind the fog of condensation on his glasses.

We watched him for a few more moments until the smell – the terrible smell – in that hellish room became too much for us. We waved, he waved back, and then Mum led us, gasping and grateful, into the cool, clear and welcome freshness of the drizzle. I turned to say something to my mum, something about the fumes, about the terrible things that choking atmosphere must have done to Dad's lungs, day in, day out. But she was already nodding and agreeing and shaking her head, tying on her headscarf, her face set in a look of pure fury.

11

Alan

Dad had been at the print works for six months. He must have cycled up every day to that grim factory, and clocked in to that low, windowless, fume-filled room, driven only by the thought that, somehow, the situation must improve before his lungs were ruined for ever. Years later, stuck in a dead-end job on one of my first magazines – and so bored that I would retire to one of the toilet cubicles mid-afternoon and doze on the closed lavatory lid – it was only the thought of my dad stirring those vats of printing ink, day in and out, of his resilience in a much worse situation, that kept me there.

Now Mum's mind was made up. Dad had suffered years of mental illness, but he wasn't going to endanger his physical health too. His lungs would never properly recover. The one release that he had always had, the ability to walk miles without tiring, would never again be easy to achieve. Within days of our visit to that hellish print room she had persuaded him to leave. At long last then, a stroke of luck: a job in the kitchens at Kodak, the biggest factory in Harrow.

Dad celebrated by buying a new bicycle 'off the boards'. He immediately covered it in hideous green emulsion paint – 'so no one will bother to steal it' – and cycled to work every day: a twenty-minute pedal through the then busy and traffic-congested Wealdstone High Street.

His was dull, repetitive work – washing-up, cleaning the big, grease-clogged trays, mopping down the canteen floors – but he loved the company, or 'firm', as he'd always call it. It covered a vast campus, employed several thousand people, and there were all sorts of 'perks' to be had – from regular entertainments in the large, well-appointed 'Kodak Hall' to free use of the tennis courts.

Dad also paid in sixpence every week so that my brother and I could go to the big Christmas show, where there was a pantomime and singing acts – and, at the end, everyone received a 'free' gift. In the first year mine was a beautiful tin Mercedes car wrapped up, impressively, in a tissue-lined box.

Dad devised other perks, too. Much to my mum's consternation he began bringing home bottles of foul-smelling chemicals and sheets of photographic paper. These were too shiny to draw on but turned from white to blue instantly when you exposed them, disastrously, to light – a phenomenon that amused my brother and me until Dad flew into a sudden rage and bundled the boxes into the top of the box-room cupboard out of our reach.

'You two are a fucking nuisance.'

'Ron!' Our mum was coming up the stairs.

'Well, I want to use that paper. I want to do some developing.'

Dad's temper calmed Mum: while he was shouting at us, he was not high. But the prospect of Dad throwing himself into a new hobby did not please her at all. She still had raw memories of the painting, of where it had all led.

Dad bought, 'off the boards', an ancient-looking enlarger – a strange contraption of metal arms with a huge lamp-head. From Kodak he 'acquired' shallow chemical trays and more opaque bottles of various liquids. It was all ferried into the box-room, the door of which he kept resolutely shut behind him with strict instructions that he was not to be disturbed.

One evening, when Ian and I were in bed, I heard the door of his box-room open and Dad pad across the top landing. He called down the stairs: 'Let's take some pictures, Peg.'

He looked round our door. He was in his pyjamas too. 'Shall we do some pictures, kids? Eh?'

Mum had been heating some milk for herself downstairs, prior to coming up. 'Oh, not now, Ron.' But she'd already put her milk down on the little table in the hall.

'I got it all set up.' He rubbed his chin. 'I wanted to try it out.'

When I look back at these pictures now there is something inestimably sad about them: me, my brother and my mum, at carpet-level – because Dad had to set up his lights on the floor – peering out of the darkness.

Ian, with his raging eczema, looked, my mother later said, 'like a Belsen victim'. But I can't help thinking of the man behind the camera – trying, trying, with his lack of education, with his lack of money, to get ahead, to change his life in some way.

He spent most of the night developing them. In the morning they were scattered on every flat surface about the place as he, dark-eyed, exhausted, cycled off to work.

Kodak had enviable sports facilities and, during those spring days of 1970, Dad took up tennis again at the factory's courts. He hadn't played properly since he and my mum were courting, fifteen or twenty years before. But it had always been 'his' sport and he persuaded himself that regular games might help clear his lungs.

He had a good if elderly wooden racket propped up inside his wardrobe and bought several boxes of brand-new Slazenger tennis balls from 'Jacks', a secondhand and army-surplus shop in Harrow that seemed to be able to get hold of anything at a knock-down price.

Dad took my brother and me over to Kenton Park to play tennis, too. He couldn't move about the court very quickly, and his breath was still a cacophony of gruff wheezing, but he served and hit the ball well and had soon taught us some of the techniques. Before long we were both dashing about, trying to return the shots our dad casually scooped to us, at a careful half-speed, over the net. After a while he would lope off court and sit on a bench at the side. I'd see the front of his jumper rising and falling as he struggled to get his breath back. Then he'd lean back, stretch out his long legs and tuck his hands behind his head to watch us play, his eyes half-closed and dozing.

When the park-keeper came round and told us, 'Last fifteen minutes,' we loved to put the big bolt across on the tennis-court gate – we were always the last to leave – then stroll back across the park, chatting to Dad about school and television programmes we'd seen. I'd slash at the grass on the football fields with my racket as we walked, till Dad said, 'You'll ruin it, Mart,' or suddenly smashed a ball up the football pitch for us to chase.

One evening as we came back towards the house, Mrs Herbert, sitting on the wall, said: 'You've got a visitor.'

'Peg says you'll know him,' Auntie Ellen added.

My dad smiled. 'OK.' He didn't like surprise visitors.

As we let ourselves in the back door, we could hear an oddly familiar voice coming from the back room. It was Alan. He was sitting at the end of our dining table. The sleeves of his white shirt were rolled up and his pale forearms rested on the tablecloth. There was a chunky gold identity bracelet on his wrist that I hadn't noticed before. It worried me, this bracelet, although I wasn't quite sure why.

My mum was sitting at the opposite end of the table. Her neck was flushed. Her hands rested in her lap as if she was being interviewed. I knew she was furious.

Dad put his racket down on the armchair and stripped off his sweater. 'What you doing here?' he said.

'He only lives round the corner,' said my mum, before Alan could reply.

Alan glanced across at her. My mum was looking straight at my dad: her expression gave nothing away.

'How are you?' said Alan. He looked round Dad at me. 'You all right, Mart?'

I nodded.

My dad put his hand on his hips like he always did when he was uncomfortable. 'Have you had a cup of tea?' he said, for something to say: an empty cup and saucer sat in front of Alan.

Alan nodded a little too strenuously. 'Yeah,' he said, 'yeah,' but he didn't look at the cup.

It suddenly occurred to me that he might be high.

My dad was not going to sit down.

Alan started talking about leaving hospital and feeling lonely. He was living in a room in Christchurch Avenue, which was literally round the corner from us. It was being let by an old lady who was deaf. 'I can't make her understand,' he kept saying.

My dad was nodding, nodding, but he stayed on his feet. He kept shooting glances at my mum, who was watching Alan as if he was giving evidence in court.

'I tell you what we'll do,' said my dad finally – and he glanced, instinctively, at his watch – 'what we'll do, old mate, is we'll get together next week and go swimming.'

I'd never heard Dad use the expression 'old mate': he was making up lines for himself.

Alan nodded again. 'Yeah, yeah . . . swimming.'

'We'll go up there together,' said my dad, 'me and you, Alan. Have a swim.'

This was clever, I thought, because Dad had calculated that Alan's house was directly opposite Wealdstone Swimming Pool. They wouldn't have to come to our house at any stage.

Alan stood up, scratching his chin, a quizzical look on his face, as if he hadn't quite got what he wanted. He smoothed his shirt down at his sides and I caught a whiff of his body odour. He yawned. 'All right.'

My mum got up as well.

'Thanks for the tea, Peg,' he said, as if only noticing her again now that she'd moved.

'It's OK,' my mum said.

When the door had closed behind him my mum turned on Dad.

'What are you doing?' she hissed, very suddenly. 'Why is he here? You know I don't like him.'

My dad backed, theatrically, against the wall as if my mum were a leaping dog. He made a mock-terrified face at me, but I wanted no part of it. He was going to try to joke his way through, but I could see my mum was furious – and I thought she was right to be.

'I've got bloody kids in this house, you bloody fool!' Mum shouted, belting his shoulder. She stomped off to the kitchen.

Dad looked at me. He'd given up on the joke. 'I didn't know he lived so close,' he said quietly. He looked really upset. 'I thought he was up in the East End somewhere.' He seemed to turn this over in his mind for a moment. 'Peg!' he shouted. 'I didn't know he was living round here – he told me he was in the East End!'

In reply I heard my mum bang the washing-up bowl into the sink and begin filling it, ferociously, from both taps at once.

My dad scratched his head and examined his chin in the hall mirror.

The following Saturday there was a knock at the door just after 8 a.m. Dad was the only one up and about – he got up early most days – and he answered the door without thinking.

Alan stood there with a rolled-up towel under his arm.

Mum and I came to the top of the stairs. She glanced at me and tutted. I could hear my dad saying, 'They won't be open yet,' and laughing unnaturally.

Suddenly, Mum was charging down the stairs and talking at the same time, her right arm pulling her dressing-gown across. 'He doesn't want to come today, Alan,' she said before my dad could say anything else.

Alan was trying to peek round the door without stepping on the doormat: there were all sorts of random rules in his head. He looked as if he'd got up without washing or brushing his hair.

'No, not today,' said my mum. She was suddenly gentle, as if talking to a child. 'All right?'

Alan lifted his hands hopelessly, the lime-green towel slightly unravelling, not looking at my mum but appealing to my dad.

'It's very good of you, Alan, but Ron's got plans,' she said, and now she had her hand on the door. 'He'll be in touch.' She closed the door.

'Peg!' said my dad.

'Don't you "Peg" me, Ron.' My mum's expression was fierce. She wagged a finger in his face.

'I could go round there.'

'Round where?' said my mum. 'You leave him alone.'

My dad put his hand on his forehead. 'Blimey. What am I going to do now?'

'Don't do anything,' said Mum quickly. 'He'll get fed up.' She turned on her heel.

Dad shuffled his feet for a minute or two, then breezed into the kitchen. 'He's not a bad bloke.'

Mum said nothing. She was wiping surfaces ferociously, an angry look on her face.

'I said I'd go round there in the week anyway,' Dad said.

Mum paused and looked up. 'Do what you bloody like,' she said fiercely.

'Oh, come on, Peg.'

'Do what you bloody like,' she said, 'but if he comes here I'll call the police. I've got enough to handle with you. I don't want another one. I mean it.'

My dad wandered into the front room. On the sideboard he had a large china squirrel that he'd found in a charity shop. Its head unscrewed and inside he kept crisps and nuts. He took out a bag of peanuts, sat back in his armchair, ripped it open and then threw a handful into his mouth. He looked at me as he chewed and then lowered his voice: 'Do you want to come swimming with us, tiddler?'

Before I could answer I heard my mum's voice from the kitchen: 'Don't you bloody dare!'

My dad and Alan went swimming, they went out for

drinks at the Kodak social club, they played snooker and tennis. They liked Kodak, I decided, because it was a community, like Shenley. Sometimes they went back to Alan's lodgings, to chat, I supposed, and smoke the packets of cigarettes Alan always had clutched in his hand. Mum had maintained her ban on him coming to us.

Alan, I soon decided, wanted, more than anything, to be at our house, in our house, all the time. He wanted to be part of our family. That was the impression that I'd had of him at Shenley, and it hadn't changed. I could feel his yearning, almost see it in the quick glance of his eyes at my brother and me when we met him and my dad in the street.

There was always an amused half-smile and a ready bounce in his knees as if to say: let me come home, let me join in – I can be your big, playful brother. It unnerved me because I thought, oddly, that at some point my dad might persuade my mum it was a good idea. That was the fear that I always, eventually, located when I plodded home from school feeling mysteriously unhappy. *Alan*, I thought, it's *bloody Alan*.

There didn't seem to be any point to his friendship with my dad, I decided, other than for us to 'adopt' him eventually. I imagined my mum and dad filling out the forms at our kitchen table while he sat there, that big, sinister gold bracelet resting on the table. But he wouldn't be looking at the forms, he'd be looking at me, as if to say, 'I've won.'

The end of it all came very suddenly, as I suppose we always knew it would. Alan became ill and went very high. It was interesting, comforting, in an odd way, to see how my father handled it. Alan came to the door one night, quite late, and insisted on coming in. My dad waved my anxious mum back into her armchair. Suddenly, almost for the first time since we'd gone to that QPR match and he'd grabbed hold of the boy's legs, there was a light in Dad's eye that glinted and said: *enough*. I followed him out to the hall.

'What do you want?' Dad said.

Alan was on the doorstep, his legs spread wide apart as if he was ready to fight. His hands were in the side-pockets of his bomber jacket. I thought of running up to get one of the Browns.

Alan didn't say anything for a long time. His head was tilted up and he seemed to be thinking, thinking, but nothing would come.

'I think I've had enough of this,' said my dad.

'Eh?' Alan's mouth barely moved.

'I think,' said my dad, 'you can fuck off back to where you came from now.'

Alan's eyes narrowed. He was puzzled and, I thought, angry. My dad pushed him. Alan lost his balance, and he couldn't get his hands out of his pockets quickly enough to steady himself: he swayed, his mouth open. Dad had him by the shoulder now and spun him, not roughly but not gently either, towards the path. Alan's mouth was opening and shutting, but he didn't seem inclined to argue.

My dad pointed a finger. 'I don't want you coming round any more, eh? Enough. All right?'

Reg Ludbrook had his head out of his front door now. 'Everything all right, Ron?' He came round our bay window, his hands in his pockets as usual. He had a jacket on with pens in the top pocket – the jacket he wore for work – and a grubby nylon shirt with worn-out collar, open at the neck. He was painfully thin. I could see his glassy skin over the bones on his breastplate and a few coiling wisps of grey hair there. He was smiling.

'Hello, Alan.'

'Hello, Reg.'

'Everything all right, Ron?' he said again.

My dad didn't answer. He turned to Alan, his eyes wide, a determined look on his face, forming the words before he spoke them. 'Get out of it, all right? Get out of it.' It was a phrase my granddad used all the time, or shortened, if he was really angry, to 'gertcha'.

Reg laughed – a deep, machine-gun cackle. He was a great fan of slapstick, of Laurel & Hardy, and he looked on every scene in real life with the anticipation that he'd find something funny in it: that someone would do him the favour of giving him a laugh.

I was used to it, but it must have been unnerving for Alan. He glanced at Reg, whose mouth hung open over a mouthful of broken teeth chipped and stained brown

160

from the roll-ups he smoked. Reg's face had about it the forward-jutting leanness of the starving dog, the lurcher.

'See you, then, Reg.' Alan backed up the path a few feet, as if afraid my dad was going to chase him, then hurried up to the gate, keeping close to the hedge.

Reg was already onto the next thing. He glanced across at me. 'I got some great Abbott & Costello, Martin – I'll lend it to you.' He owned a cine-camera – his pride and joy – and had various cine-films in little square, dog-eared boxes. He'd bring them out into the garden like a pack of cards.

Before I could say anything he turned his skinny dog face back to the retreating Alan, as if still hopeful he'd crack a joke or slip on a banana skin.

My dad sighed. 'Thanks for that, Reg.'

Reg's expression didn't change. Throughout it all his hands had remained rammed in the pockets of his trousers, as they always did. 'Blimey,' he said at last, and gave that unearthly cackle again. He turned back to his front door, raising his hand to signal goodbye as he went.

Dad came inside and closed the door gently. He put his hand on my shoulder and steered me into the front room.

My mum had been standing and watching from the bay window.

'I'll tell you something,' my dad said, and he wagged a finger at Mum. 'I'll tell you something and I mean it,' and he turned his wagging finger towards me, too. 'I am not going back in Shenley. I am not. I'll 'elp 'em but I'm not going back.' He sat down heavily on the sofa. 'Fucking idiot,' he said, probably about Alan but perhaps about himself – and then he laughed.

12

Creosote and Carousels

That summer, using big oblong planks of dark, knotty wood obtained from somewhere or other, Dad and Granddad built us a Wendy house under the trees at the end of the garden. Over the course of a week or so, various neighbours were drawn into this construction, bringing with them extra materials, such as tarpaulin covering for the roof. Assorted Brown brothers turned up and were soon employed nailing things together. My dad loved nails and used them in the building of everything in our house, inside and out. He had so little truck with screws that if he was ever forced to use them – which was only when ('Sod it!') he ran out of nails – he banged those in with a hammer too. Nine years later, this minor peccadillo of my father's would help me get my first job.

Granddad was everywhere during those few days. He was short and strong, like a small barrel-shaped dog, and he scuttled around on his little legs like a circus performer, as the Browns made lewd and rude comments about his age or his clothes. 'You're cheeky buggers,' he'd half growl, glancing up from whatever he was doing. He laboured at a furious speed, always with a roll-up hanging damply in his mouth, one eye closed against the smoke. My dad would often stand back and watch him work, a look in his eyes that was half admiring and half suspicious that some corner had been inconspicuously cut.

This period of building work delighted Reg Ludbrook, who came dancing down his path, smile on his face, as soon as anyone appeared. He stood with both hands on his fence, as if about to give evidence. My dad would glance across and force a smile: 'All right, Reg?'

From the moment he reached the fence, Reg's mind would be working on a witty comment. His mouth would drop open in readiness to deliver it – or to laugh at something someone else said, at which point he would rock the wobbly fence with his hands until Dad frowned and said: 'Careful of that, Reg.' None of the comments were ever very funny – 'You'll do yourself a mischief there, Ron! Ha, ha, ha!' or 'Don't nail your finger to it, Elb! Ha, ha, ha, ha!' – but they were delivered with such gusto that it was hard not to laugh along.

Reg had a shed at the end of his own garden – a neat, twelve foot by six foot construction with a roof that sloped back. He recreosoted it every year with the same big paint-stiffened brush. The shed sat back against a hopeless, thorny tangle of low trees and bushes, threaded with nettles and creeper, into which, from time to time, Reg would plunge fearlessly in order to retrieve one of our footballs or a Frisbee. He would never refuse a favour.

In this shed Reg had, at various times, a miniature model railway and various items of electrical and telephonic equipment that he was repairing or tinkering with. He also had a cassette-player and speakers.

Reg had three real passions in life, based on the different careers he had led: the navy and its ships and anything to do with the War; railways and steam-locomotives; and telephones, particularly the old, black bakelite ones. He had four or five of these phones bundled up in a great tangle of brown wires. He'd often rush out of his shed with this bundle, swearing and cursing and bouncing it around like some strange puppet in a vain attempt to separate the different phones. He also loved old radio programmes like 'Round the Horne' and often would lapse into the voice of the Goons to deliver the same old lines: 'Turn the knob on your side!' *'I haven't got a knob on my side.'*

Early one evening, about halfway through the building of the Wendy house, Reg did not come down to the fence as usual; instead he swept along his path and down to his garden shed. He was carrying a small cardboard box. My dad, granddad and three of the Browns were in the garden. I was crouched on the crazy-paving with Peter Wyatt, playing with some toy cars.

Reg disappeared into his shed, but left the door wide open. A few moments later, at very high volume, the Band of the Scots Dragoon Guards struck up, filling the air with the sound of braying bagpipes. Roger Brown looked at my dad, a huge grin on his face. Dad shook his head in disbelief.

Then Reg emerged from his shed, waving his right hand like a conductor with a baton. He mouthed something at my dad.

'What?' said Dad.

'What do you think of it!?' yelled Reg.

'Yeah,' my dad was nodding, 'yeah, it's good,' but he didn't say it sarcastically: he was only ever sarcastic when he was high. 'What is it, Reg?'

'Eh?' Reg cupped a dirty hand over his right ear. 'Eh, Ron, what?'

Meanwhile, the Browns had started marching. Roger and Pete had picked up slats of wood, tipped them back over their shoulders, and were high-stepping up the lawn. My granddad, hands on hips, grinned from ear to ear, casting glances up to the kitchen window to see if my mum was enjoying it too.

I thought Reg – always waiting for the joke, the quip – would laugh, but he didn't. He was furious. He took one long look at the marchers, then stalked back into the shed, bumping his shoulder on the door, and snapped the machine off. The Browns were laughing and coughing. Reg re-emerged, the cassette in his hand, and shook his head at them, slowly and mournfully, as if about to announce a death.

Up on the crazy-paving, Peter Wyatt and I were open-mouthed. What would happen? Would Reg pick a fight with the Browns?

My dad was at the fence now. 'It's all right, Reg, they're only mucking about.'

'I don't understand you,' Reg said over my dad's head.

But the Browns were sitting on the grass, their backs turned to him. I saw Stephen, one of the older boys, spit onto the lawn. Roger grinned up at me. I didn't dare grin back. I was glad I hadn't marched too. I still shuddered at the thought of the Steptoe incident with poor old Mr Saville.

Shaking his head slowly and theatrically, 'I'll see you later,' Reg said at last. Still shaking it, he stalked back up the path.

Roger smiled. 'Sorry, Ron,' he said, standing and stretching, as we heard Reg's back door bang shut.

My dad tutted but said nothing.

'It was very good,' said my granddad. 'Very good.' He smiled his big white gangster's smile.

Unwittingly, of course, by showing a vague interest in Reg's cassette my dad had declared himself pro-bagpipes, pro-marching bands, pro-any sort of loud music in the garden. I felt a bit sorry for my dad. When he was well, Dad always prickled at the very presence of Reg at the fence. If he and Mum were sitting out there in their deck-chairs and Reg suddenly appeared behind them, Dad would fold his arms more tightly round himself and scowl, dreading the moment that Reg began to speak.

'Look at this, Ron,' he'd say, and he'd have brought something down to the fence: tatty pictures of ancient relatives, or yellowing press clippings. Once he produced a book of photographs from the war years including pages and pages of the victims of the Holocaust at Belsen and Auschwitz, the corpses piled up, pale, doughy and unreal. My brother and I stared at these, turning the pages round to try to make out heads and feet: we'd never seen dead bodies before.

Now there was a new tyranny: his tapes. I wondered what else lurked in Reg's cardboard box. I didn't have to wait long to find out.

By Friday of that week, the Wendy house was finally finished. Our garden seemed to be full of children: the MacManuses, Peter Wyatt, two of the Ludbrook girls – Kerry and Jackie – in grubby floral frocks. Even Fred and Ann Herbert were craning their necks over their fence to see our playhouse.

Granddad, who had nailed up most of the finishing tarpaulin on the roof single-handed, was in his vest, drenched with sweat, wiping his chest and armpits with his shirt. My dad was smoking a little cigar. He'd paid the Browns in cigarettes and they'd disappeared to help their father, Neville, exercise his racing pigeons. In their garden, two fences away, we could hear Neville – dark-skinned like a gypsy, and sullen – shaking a tin of peanuts to encourage the grubby birds out of their loft. *'Come on, come on!'*

My mum brought some tea out on a tray, and fizzy lemonade for us. She had on a blue-and-white-striped V-neck top, blue flared trousers and white shoes – Mum always had dozens of pairs of shoes – and looked oddly elegant bearing that tray down our plank-strewn garden.

My dad grinned. 'Here she comes: Lady Muck!'

We danced and skipped around with the excitement of it all, and I felt vaguely sick.

'Can we go up there, Ron?' said Peter Wyatt, who was always the most adventurous of us all.

'Yeah, yeah.' My dad was already sipping his tea.

The Wendy house had a window opening at one side, with no glass or frame, and Peter put his plimsolled foot on the sill and clambered up to the roof.

Suddenly, the air was filled with the clanging bells and trembling organ of a fairground carousel. It was deafeningly loud. Reg had ghosted up the garden to slip the tape into his machine and now stood at his shed door, in his threadbare old slippers, grinning at the ground, shaking his shoulders theatrically.

My dad, obviously irritated, was not going to let it spoil the mood. 'Ha, can you hear that, Elb? It's the bloody fairground now!' and he grinned across at Reg, with a wink.

'Yes, it's very good,' said my granddad vaguely. He scratched his stomach.

'I tell you what,' said my mum, only half-jokingly, quickly scooping up the tea tray so as to make her exit, 'he's as bloody mad as you are,' and nodded from Reg to Dad, wide-eyed.

Auntie Ellen, who had followed Reg out and now stood halfway down her path, exchanged exasperated glances across the fence with my mum as she rattled in with the teacups. 'I'll bloody kill him for you,' she shouted over the music. '*Reg!*'

'All right, all right...' Reg waved his arms in surrender and then slipped back into the shed to turn it off. 'I was only having a bit of bloody fun,' he said quietly across to my dad as he popped back out. 'They never understand, do they?'

'What's he saying, what's he saying?' snapped Ellen, who was picking her way down the garden. 'Is my old man having a go?'

'No,' said my dad, 'no, Ellen – you know what he's like: he'd never want to upset you.'

A few days later, my dad and granddad brought home a small heavy sapling, its trunk shrouded in a plastic sheet and sticky tape. After much huffing and puffing and stabbing the ground with shovels to find somewhere not already congested with tree roots, they planted it a few yards in front of the Wendy house. It was a Victoria plum tree, with torn and yellowish slivers of young bark around its trunk.

'Victorias are flatter than normal plums,' my granddad told me – he liked to be an expert on many things – 'and not quite as sweet.'

My brother and I were not particularly bothered about the fruit – Mrs Herbert gave us bagfuls of the stuff every year, from her apple and plum trees – we just wanted a tree. Or, more particularly, a tree-house. We dreamed of linking it to the Wendy house by a length of rope so we could swing across.

Sitting in the back room, after he'd washed the soil – which my dad always called 'mould' – off his hands, we cross-examined Granddad on how big it might grow.

Granddad shook his head over his tea. 'I don't think you'll get a tree-house up it. Anyway, you've got a bloody Wendy house.'

'Yeah, but you never know, Elb,' said my dad, who could see Granddad had made us feel awkward, and who never liked to let us down. 'You never know.'

When I returned to school that autumn of 1970, I was in the top class – Class 1 – for my final year, and had a new teacher: Miss Ashcroft.

She was from a generation of women teachers who

had served in the armed forces and remained resolutely unmarried. Always immaculately dressed, in cashmere sweaters and prim, A-line skirts, she had extraordinary clear brown eyes, a down-turned mouth, and was handsome, in a rather imposing and firm-jawed way. She also had an unlikely but endearing weakness for a certain amount of silly, schoolboy humour. Not too much, though: I can still remember my face burning with shame and embarrassment as I was sent out of class for messing around with one of those silly trolls on the end of a pencil.

We had been back only a few weeks when a letter was passed round the school inviting pupils to join a local church choir. Miss Ashcroft read it out to our class. 'And,' she said at the end, 'all choristers will be paid quarterly – and for weddings.' She folded up the letter and dismissed the class.

I was quite interested. I looked round at my friends to see if the promise of extra pocket-money had enthused anyone else, but there seemed to be no other takers. Chairs were already being noisily scraped back and lifted onto desks.

Back home that evening, Dad nodded but looked puzzled. 'Church choir?' I could almost see him mulling it over, turning it around in his mind. But then something seemed to register. 'Still, to get paid to sing. *That's* good.'

'It's only £1.20 every three months,' I said.

My mum was actually more worried. 'Will you have to go to church?'

'Every Sunday.'

'You didn't like going to church with the cubs.'

I wanted to say, '*Yes, but I didn't like the cubs.*' But that felt like a betrayal. For nearly six months I'd pretended to go happily. Instead I said: 'It was St Anselm's and the church was always really cold. Plus I had my bad knee then. All the kneeling . . .'

My mum was nodding but she still didn't seem very happy. 'Well, if you want to do it . . . But once you've started you can't just give up. It will be every week.'

My dad smiled. 'You go, son. Enjoy yourself: it'll do you good.'

That was enough for me.

13

Life of Brian

St Mary the Virgin, Kenton, stood at the top of a steep little hill about a mile and a half from our house. My mother and father had been married at St Mary's, and my brother and I christened there, but none of us were really familiar with the place. A cathedral-sized building, it would have been forbidding if not for the leafy memorial garden that broke up the imposing southern wall, and the square tower, which had no heaven-pointing steeple and anchored the whole building firmly to earth.

Services here were 'high', there were regular visits from church dignitaries and local Tories such as the mutton-chop-whiskered Dr Rhodes Boyson, but the atmosphere of the church itself, its congregation, was much more homely and parochial. Largely this was due to the vicar, Father Hedley Shearing, a small, balding man in his sixties or possibly even early seventies, with tiny, glittering brown eyes, pointed nose and chin and a general air of inquisitiveness and good humour. But it was also the influence of one or two of those he employed.

The audition for the choir was on a Wednesday evening. I cycled up on my own – my brother enrolled a year or so later – and joined a crowd of thirty or forty boys milling around on the flagstone square in front of the enormous main doors. One or two, I noted enviously, had a Chopper bike: an item which was way beyond my parents' budgets but which I'd been trying to win in competitions in *Disco 45* and *Popswop* magazines.

A pale-green and cream Triumph Herald drew up and a youngish man with thinning sandy hair in beige cord trousers and Hush Puppies stepped out. One or two of the parents who had turned up seemed to recognize him and moved over towards the car. He raised his head and took in the crowd of boys as if looking for someone in particular, then headed into the church. He had music books tucked under his arm.

We followed him inside and to the left, up a winding staircase of cream-coloured stone to the choir gallery. Our clumsy feet clattered on the steps, the sound combining with our excited whispers and echoing out into the near darkness of the church. He beckoned us to wait in some rows of chairs at the top of the stairs, then made his way across to the organ. I noticed he walked very fast – strutted, almost – with a purposeful, slightly pompous air.

The organ was positioned halfway along the front edge of the gallery, the console occupying a little balcony. The sandy-haired man settled himself down on the polished pew behind the console, nimbly flicked out combinations of stops, and flexed his Hush Puppies on the pedals.

We all watched in silence, suitably impressed by his briskness and the way he sat with his nose ever so slightly in the air. He spread and cracked all of his fingers (which provoked a half-giggle from one or two of us) and then lowered his hands to the keyboard.

One, two, three thunderous minor chords echoed off the stone walls and vast hammer-beam roof. I noticed that the choirmaster was almost 'vamping', swinging his shoulders slowly back and forth, his gaze directed beatifically upwards.

Then, to our astonishment, there boomed from the organ the theme from *Monty Python's Flying Circus* . . .

One or two of us giggled, looked at one another to make sure our recognition was correct, then – seeing the half-innocent smirk that had appeared on the organist's face – we all started laughing. The sound echoed back at us out of the gloom.

I had never come across anyone like Brian Apperson. He was in his early thirties, only a few years younger than my dad, but, as I got to know him better, seemed of a generation that I'd never encountered: one who knew about all the groups we listened to, the television programmes we watched, but who was definitely an 'adult': someone to look up to and confide in.

He was the funniest person I'd ever met, peppering every conversation with little quips and asides, suddenly gurning out a funny face or impersonating one of the screeching old ladies Terry Jones and Graham Chapman were then creating in *Monty Python*.

It's hard to overestimate the impact Brian had on me and my family. I was not an introverted child, but I was a shy one. If I was ever required to push myself forward, to show what I could do, I'd shrink back. I lacked confidence in my own abilities. I always took the view that everyone around me could kick a ball, tell a joke, sing a song, better than I could – even if I only half-believed it. If I recited or sang anything, my voice would tremble with fear.

Brian changed all that. By simply insisting that I sing solo in church he imbued me with a faith in my abilities that, quite simply, changed my life. Under his tutorship I went from a shy ten-year-old to a confident young teenager.

The choir met twice a week, on Wednesday and Friday evenings. For an hour we rehearsed the mass-setting, hymns and anthems we'd be required to sing the following Sunday, followed by the hymns for the weddings that required our services on the Saturday. Then we'd dash down the stone steps and into Father Shearing's vast vicarage garden to play football on his lawn. The vicar would watch us from his living-room window, or wander out, sometimes with Brian in tow, and chat on the path while we ran around. When it grew dark, we'd take the lamps off our bikes and put them in the damp grass round the perimeter of our 'pitch' as floodlights.

There was never any question that Father Shearing wouldn't let us into his garden. Brian, in his half-smirking, cod-solemn way, had announced the privilege at virtually our first rehearsal. Before long, we even discovered a small overgrown orchard beyond the lawn, where in late autumn we'd throw rotting, cider-smelling apples at one another.

A year or so later, when he'd encouraged about a dozen of us to take the 'catechism' – leading up to our Confirmation as Christians – Father Shearing said that he would conduct the instruction in the study of the vicarage itself. This room, which overlooked the vicarage's front garden, fascinated me: everything seemed to be covered – the backs of the chairs, the cushions, the side-tables – with little embroidered cloths and mats. There were various religious artefacts, such as garishly over-coloured prints of St Mary and the Saints; a little crucifix on a stand. The vicarage was very large and Father Shearing, I knew, had a 'housekeeper'. (I imagined myself living there, but couldn't quite place my parents in the rooms: Mum sawing at the carpet with the Hoover, knocking over the ornaments and scolding herself as she dislodged another embroidery.)

We all considered the catechism would be a serious process and had such respect for Father Shearing that we were quite prepared to see it that way. But prior to the very first lesson he gave us all cups of orange juice, turned on his colour TV – a real rarity then – and announced that we'd better watch *Best on Soccer* before we started. 'God is important, of course,' he said. 'But we mustn't forget about George.' He winked at us.

The other boys in the choir fascinated me. They were from various schools around Harrow and Wembley – most of which I'd only vaguely heard about – and seemed to be more fashionable, more bohemian, than those of us from Priestmead.

Two boys in particular caught my attention. The first, who was called Mark Elliot-Smith, wore corduroy suits, which made me almost sick with envy: he seemed to wear a different-coloured one every week. He also wore cravats, sometimes held in place with exotic-looking gold rings. He had longish hair of a sort of orangey-blond and walked with a strange bow-legged, bouncing gait.

The other boy, who emerged very quickly as our natural 'leader', was called Steve Carter. This was a name that made me jealous. Imagine being called 'Steve Carter'. He looked almost leonine in appearance, with shoulder-length hair he was always stroking down, and a long, pale, handsome face. He was older than the rest of us, wore silk psychedelic-patterned shirts and the sort of wide flares that were expensive and hard to find. He was friends, so we all heard, with various cast-members from *The Double-Deckers* – soon to be a massively successful children's TV show – and even went to stage school himself. He also knew Jack Wild and Mark Lester from *Oliver*. But he didn't seem to have a dad, only a dark-haired, rather glamorous mum, so I contented myself with the thought that his life couldn't be perfect.

Brian Apperson had known Steve and his mum before he'd put the choir together, and had invited Steve to join, it seemed, almost in the way that you would invite an exotic foreign football-player into a struggling team.

One evening, at the Wednesday rehearsal, Brian announced that Steve was just going to rehearse a solo that he would perform at Sunday's big 11 a.m. service. Steve stepped up out of his pew, already peering closely at his manuscript, then made his way down to the front wall of the gallery.

Brian played a single, slightly wavering chord. Steve, his manuscript book balanced on the palm of his right hand, seemed to hesitate for a moment, then began . . . '*Pie Jesu . . . requiem.*'

I had never heard a voice – or a piece of music – that was quite so beautiful. I know now that the soprano solo from Fauré's Requiem is probably the most famous piece of choral music for a woman or boy soloist that has ever been written, but it seemed, back then, so strange, so exotic, so other-worldly. I wanted to cry. I can still hear his voice in my head now. It was not a classic treble tone – it was much too rich and strong for that – and he delivered it, seemingly, from the top of his head and just one side of his mouth, his shaggy, curly-haired head tilted over. He sang out into the pitch darkness of the church and, behind him, in the brightly lit pews, nineteen boys, in shoes still muddy from football, were open-mouthed with wonder and envy.

Church, as far as my family were concerned, was for weddings, funerals and christenings; it was not somewhere you went out of choice.

Mum was especially wary. She did not set foot inside the church unless she was obliged to. The idea of going voluntarily, I knew, seemed very odd to her. One evening, though, for reasons I have now forgotten, she had to cycle up to meet me.

As I came skipping down the stone stairs I saw her peeking in at the back doors, her handbag clutched tightly in front of her.

'What's it all about then, Mart?' she said to me when we got home. 'All them candles . . .'

I understood her suspicion. There was something very odd about young people who went to church regularly just to pray. But as the weeks had gone by some sense of

181

our place in the scheme of things had begun to take shape in my mind. As choristers, I thought, we were the 'professionals', ranked alongside the clergy, the choirmaster and the old ladies who came in to do the flower arrangements. The congregation were the 'audience' and any young Christians among them, especially ones near to our age, were nothing to do with us.

Dad had been much more enthusiastic about it all from the start. 'It's good, Peg: he's getting out. Meeting people.' He leant down to me, and put his arm half round my neck, leaning in close. 'I'm proud of you, son.'

Brian Apperson lived in a large ground-floor flat on Harrow-on-the-Hill. Again, this seemed overwhelmingly exotic to me. I had no idea about the price of houses – our home was rented from the council – but it seemed impossible that anyone could actually *live* on the Hill: it was so famous, so historical, so rarefied. I thought of everything in terms of film and television. The way in which the entrance and entrance sign to the block of flats Julian Court was almost half-concealed in some bushes and that it was approached by a long, winding, virtually unlit drive, reminded me of so many of my secretive heroes' hide-outs: from Thunderbirds' Tracy Island to Batman's gadget-filled cave.

It seems odd now, filtering that world through my own experience as a parent, that none of our mums and dads minded a bit when Brian Apperson invited us, in groups of ten and twelve, to come up, have dinner and play snooker with him at Julian Court. Were we living in so much more of an innocent world or was it just that Brian was so solid, so trustworthy? He was unmarried – all of us knew that – but there was no suggestion of anything untoward in his nature or his behaviour. There were rumours of women friends in the background and, later, I'd come to meet one or two of them, but for the most part Brian was an enigma to us: in the five or six years we knew him we didn't really know him at all.

His flat was magnificent. A huge, expensively decorated lounge opened onto a smaller room, where he had set up a half-size snooker table. This was a huge luxury for all of us. I'd only ever seen a snooker table at Shenley – how lucky I felt now that my dad had taught me to play – but one or two of the other lads had only ever seen one on TV, in *Pot Black*.

We would sit at his table and pick at a few sandwiches and crisps, then Brian would put records on as we trooped off in twos and fours to play snooker. He played mainly classical music but had a taste, which I was soon to share, for John Betjeman's poetry records with the Jim Parker orchestra. Brian was a talented mimic and could reel off virtually any British accent. As Betjeman intoned, in some sort of obscure Northern dialect, the words to his poem about the swimmer Captain Webb, we'd all join in, trying to match Brian's impersonation.

The gas was on in the institute
The flare was up in the gym . . .
A man was running a min-eral line
A lass were singing a hymn . . .

Dad had been well for a while and in my mind I'd begun to view his illness – not for the first time when a long period of peace and quiet had lulled me into a false sense of security – as an experience in my past. The fact that my father was a manic-depressive set me apart from other boys: from time to time I felt that it gave me, a nervous boy who didn't play football and 'muck in', a sort of street-credibility. Until it happened again, of course. Then it was just miserable.

I'd told Brian about my dad, hoping, I suppose, to impress him. I knew that his job, never precisely explained to us, had something to do with the Health Service, and I thought he might be the sort of person who would then nod sagely and launch into a whole explanation of the illness and why it was such hell for a boy like me. But he didn't. He just looked pained and nodded. I didn't know what this meant. Was he silently chiding me for trying to use my dad's illness to gain kudos? Or did he simply not like to be confided in? Whatever the explanation, it left me wondering what would happen when he met my dad for the first time.

It happened one evening after Brian had driven me home from Julian Court. It was raining and, as my dad came to the door to let me in, he naturally invited Brian in out of the rain as well. My mum, who hated anyone being brought in late, was already in her night things in the back room.

'Oh, Brian.' (She'd met him once or twice at the church door.) She glanced at my dad.

'I'm not staying; I just brought Martin home.'

'I'll make you a cup of tea,' said my dad, ignoring my mum's glances and Brian's embarrassment. I loved this about Dad.

Brian looked very odd in our back room. We didn't have visitors like him – in Hush Puppies with light socks and cords. Nobody dressed like that in Cullington Close. No one was so carefully put together. They didn't cross one leg over the other like he did, or seem so perfectly relaxed at our kitchen table.

My dad handed Brian the cup.

'Thank you, Ron.' Brian glanced at me. House-point straight away for Brian: my dad liked his first name being used.

'How's it all going, then?' said Dad. 'Martin loves it. I've never known him get involved in anything like this.'

'He's doing very well.' Brian smiled at me again. 'But they're all good boys. I'm pleased.'

'Good, good. It's nice to have a choir. I like choirs,' my dad said. 'I like music. It's so relaxing. I'd love to be able to do what you do – play the piano.'

I knew all of this was true – and so did Brian.

My mum had brightened. 'Well, he says you make it funny,' she said. 'You have jokes with them.'

Brian was straight into one of his Monty Python women. 'Jokes with them! I don't make jokes with them, Mrs Townsend – perish the thought!'

My dad's mouth opened in a big grin. 'Oh, that's that wotsisname, isn't it, Peg? *Monty Python*. We've seen that.'

'Oh, it's daft,' said my mum, wrinkling her nose, but she looked up slightly coquettishly at Brian as she sipped her tea.

'Anyway, I think you're doing great for him, Brian, I really do.' My dad was effusive now, and I knew I could add Brian to my allies: someone my dad liked and my mum was impressed by.

'Well, it keeps him out of trouble,' said Brian, standing up and stretching, 'and you're doing a solo next week, aren't you?'

'Ooh, a solo!' This was my mum.

I felt my stomach drop and my head was suddenly slightly dizzy.

Brian saw my expression. 'You can do it,' he said.

''Course you can, Martin. Can we come and listen?' Dad asked Brian.

I felt worlds whirring around my head. A solo. A solo in church. It seemed like a mountain to be climbed. I knew I could do it but if I could have got out of it in any way I would have grabbed the chance. I stood back from myself and imagined the others watching me step up. *Look at his hair, his trousers. He's trembling, he's actually trembling. And he will certainly sing flat. He must sing flat. His voice will tremble and he will sing flat and how we will all laugh!*

Brian said nothing about the solo until we were nearly at the end of the Wednesday rehearsal. We hadn't practised anything in which I could take a verse or a chorus, so it had to be something special. *Pie Jesu* perhaps? Not *Pie Jesu*. Only Steve Carter could sing *Pie Jesu* and I didn't want to be compared with him. Steve had, by then, been appointed Head Chorister. He was an obvious choice. We all loved him – actually loved him in the way eleven-year-olds love one another for their skill and their coolness and their perfect clothes. Perhaps he himself had suggested I could sing *Pie Jesu*? I got on very well with him.

'We have a wedding on Saturday,' Brian announced from the organ console, though we had already seen it posted up on our little choir notice-board, 'and Martin Townsend will sing a solo.'

A solo at a wedding? There were a few murmurs from the other boys – and my best friend Lee Waldron nodded his encouragement.

'He'll take the first verse of "Love Divine" . . .' said Brian, half to himself – he was already packing up the rest of the books. I didn't move, but Brian, once he'd scooped all the books into a heap, looked up towards me, shielding his eyes from the glare of the overhanging lights that always flooded our little choir area. 'Has he escaped? Has he tunnelled out?'

There was laughter and while it was still subsiding I got up, wobbly-legged, and made my way to the front, banging and knocking into the other boys in my excitement and fear.

The concrete ledge at the front of the gallery felt rough under my skin, almost powdery, as I rested the back of my wrists against it, the hymn-book flat open in my palms. Why was I thinking about concrete? I shook my head so violently to lose that distracting train of thought I felt sure someone would comment, but there was only silence from the choir gallery and the soft click-click of Brian readjusting the organ stops. My mouth had immediately gone dry.

'Head up, Martin,' said Brian softly.

I looked up and out into the darkness where, at the far end near the altar, a little blue lamp flickered and one or two long hanging lights pierced the darkness. This, I thought, is what Steve Carter sees.

'Are you ready?' Brian whispered.

I nodded.

He played a single note. It seemed to hang in the cold air for minutes until, out of the corner of my right eye, I saw him glance across at me and then, very theatrically, lean into the first chord.

'Love divine, all loves excelling . . .'

There was, surely, no shorter line in any of the hymns I knew, yet my voice wavered and broke halfway through 'excelling' as I ran out of breath. Then I had to swallow to get my voice back in place and I felt my fingers dampen under the hymn-book. Redness prickled my skin. Don't go red, *don't go red*.

I was aware of Brian pausing slightly at the end of the line as he detected my distress, then he gave another theatrical sweep of his shoulders into the next line as I struggled to regain my confidence. By the third line, which seemed like hours later, I was in my stride. Three more lines and it was finished.

Brian stood on his pedals and clapped lightly, glancing across to the rest of the choir, who joined in. Then he was turning, scooping up his music books once more. He put his hand on my shoulder as he passed by. 'Good,' he said.

I walked back to the gallery on wobbling knees but inside I felt a great surge of pride and confidence. Nothing would ever be quite the same again.

14

Butlins

It had been three years since we'd had a holiday. That first summer after Dad's breakdown, 1970, my mum had declared herself 'in no mood' to go on holiday anywhere. Instead, we'd built the Wendy house, watched the World Cup, pottered around the garden, over the dump and in Kenton Park.

I knew what she feared: that a change of scene might trigger something in my dad, might alter his mood strongly, for better or worse, and set him back on the slow and miserable road to hospital. But Dad was desperate, as he put it, 'to get away'. He'd always loved holidays – the chance to be out, constantly, in the open air, to fritter away money on silly things.

Early in 1971 he'd bought my brother and me money-boxes especially designed for holiday savings. They were oblong and made of tin. Each one had slots and compartments for 'Sweets', 'Funfair Rides', 'Days Out' and

'Beach Treats'. Ian and I pored over the childlike little drawings that decorated each section – the yachts, the beach-balls, the starfish – and chattered about where we'd most like to go. We had the Butlins brochure and often sat up on our beds, flicking through the print-perfumed colour pages, comparing the pictures of the various fairgrounds and of the sleek and futuristic monorail that threaded through every camp.

As the moneyboxes began to rattle – with our choir money, the two-bobs Granddad gave us every Sunday and the few pence we 'earned' doing errands around the house – Dad worked on Mum: 'Oh, let's take the tiddlers away, shall we? After all, it is his last year at school,' he added, nodding at me.

It was indeed my last year at Priestmead and I'd begun to feel the weight of the weeks leading up to my departure. I had high hopes of getting to grammar school – Harrow County, one of the very best in the country – but this was an ambition that trailed with it all sorts of unwanted baggage. My father, not to mention one or two of my friends in Cullington Close, had a rather ambivalent attitude towards Harrow County: they thought it was a great school that would somehow 'change' me; turn me into a toff, someone who wouldn't want to mix with them or live in the road any more.

'It's a posh place, you know, Mart,' my dad would say, his eyebrows slightly raised, his voice heavy with significance. 'The uniforms, the *cane*. You might not like it.'

I was already beginning to wonder how much this attitude would harden when he was high. To some extent he'd rowed back on making a 'man' out of me; it was an idea I thought had somehow evaporated during that summer at Shenley. But he hadn't been high since then, so it was impossible to say for sure.

'You won't want to know us lot when you get to 'Arrow County,' Mark MacManus had declared to me one night, when we were sitting up on the roof of the Wendy house. He was Irish, with a spectacularly snotty nose. 'My mum says no one from up 'ere 'as ever gone there,' and he nodded, significantly, back along the gardens.

I thought I'd probably need a holiday just to escape from such speculation.

'Oh, Ron, I don't know about Butlins,' my mum had said. 'Are you sure you're well enough?'

'Yeah,' my dad was all confidence, 'I feel great. In fact, I feel bloody marvellous.'

'We'll see,' said my mum at last.

'Well, we'll have to get it sorted out pretty soon, Peg,' said Dad: 'you know how it gets booked up.'

There were dramas, of course, in the weeks leading up to our holiday. In June, Dad found himself at the centre of a furious row at Kodak because the chef, a fat and lazy man who all the kitchen workers detested, had heard they'd been spitting in his tea. Everyone had tried to laugh it off – taking the chef out for a drink, telling him how much they all liked him – but he'd registered an official complaint. For a few nights Dad thought he, and some of his mates, might get the sack.

Then, on the night before we were due to leave, I was playing out on my bike when I was chased down the road by a dog. I took it into my mind, for some reason, to 'bale out' like a stricken fighter-pilot, caught my foot under the pedal and skidded along the pavement on my knee. Ann and Fred Herbert, who'd been working in their front garden, helped me back down the path. Mum poured Dettol into a bowl of warm water and helped me up on to the draining-board: the usual place for emergency medical aid. She was relieved it was not my 'bad' knee – the left one, which had been infected with an abscess two years previously. Carefully, she lifted the big flap of partly detached skin on my newly wounded knee and bathed away all the dirt and grit underneath.

'Typical,' my mum tutted: 'the night before we're supposed to go on holiday.'

But Dad was in like a shot before she could continue in this pessimistic frame of mind. Hours before, he had carried the suitcases down into the hall and, in his own mind, was already on the coach and halfway there.

He was a great believer in the power of anti-tetanus injections; any serious cut or bruise in our house and this magic solution would soon be advocated. 'I'll call me dad,' he said, 'and we'll run him up the hospital for a tetanus.'

At the tiny old Harrow hospital, on the slopes of Harrow-on-the-Hill, the injection was administered by a couple of nurses who took a shine immediately to my dad. He liked nurses and was all winks and nudges and sly jokes when he was around them. My knee was layered with a complicated dressing of lint and plaster. I particularly enjoyed the way the damp lint was laid on with tweezers, and tried to enthuse about it in the car.

'Yeah, it's interesting,' said my granddad kindly. 'They can do wonders these days.'

But my mum's face was dark. 'You're a bloody nuisance,' she said.

The next morning we took the interminably long coach journey to Butlins in Skegness, arriving, hot, headachey, our backs wet and itching from the scratchy seats, sometime during the mid-afternoon. My dad, as ever, swaggered ahead, carrying both our big suitcases into the enormous and crowded reception hall.

He sat the three of us on one of the little vinyl-covered benches at the perimeter while he 'sorted everything out'. We watched him sign us all in, then dart about, booking excursions, snatching up colour leaflets. He made friends, instantly, with a little knot of Redcoats, acting out some mime or other that reduced them to gales of laughter. When he was on holiday, nothing could spoil his mood.

I had to attend the camp surgery every day to have my

knee re-dressed. It was a bland little room with green walls and strange, painted lino on the floor. I seemed to be the only patient. My knee felt very stiff and I had waves of nausea from time to time, but it didn't hold me back too much.

Every morning, early, we were one of the first groups into the big Butlins dining-hall as the uniformed waitresses came round with huge baskets of toast and containers of tea. Tables were shared with a couple of other families, but Dad, usually so sociable, could not be chatty at breakfast: he was already thinking about the beach.

Dad attacked the beach every morning. He prowled along the Skegness promenade when the tide was still fully in and crashing up over the rails, watching, watching, for the tiniest patch of sand to be uncovered for more than a few seconds at a time. As soon as it was, he was down the stone steps, his two deck-chairs dangling from his big fingers, claiming the tiny area by digging the runners of the chairs in deep and then tossing the big shopping bag full of towels and sun cream and sandwiches from the café down onto the candy-striped cloth.

'There,' he'd say, and we'd follow him down gingerly, well aware that the sea was still pounding inches from our feet. He sat there, the tide swirling around his deck-chair, squinting out to sea through his clip-on sunglasses. 'This is lovely, Peg, isn't it?' he'd yell, as the wind gusted along under the promenade wall, and the salt spray splashed and cascaded over us.

He'd breathe in deeply, theatrically, the sea air, great gusts of it – 'Mmmm' – then dig into the bag for his first sandwich. He was proud of the fact that this, his first pioneering foray onto the sand, would effectively 'open' the beach to everyone else. 'See, they're all coming now,' he'd say, tossing his head back towards the stone steps as another laden family made their way down.

In mid-afternoon, when the sun was at its height and the beach chock-a-block with screaming, yelling families, he'd gaze around and say, 'Look at 'em all, Mart, look at 'em all. This morning we had it all to ourselves. Amazing, isn't it?'

Every night there were entertainments in one of the big 'ballrooms'. These vast halls were works of art in themselves, the walls and ceilings 'themed' with fishing and pirate paraphernalia – complicated arrangements of nets, corking, plastic fish – or Hawaiian knick-knacks: canoes, bongos, plastic flowers. A tropical fantasy such as this might have seemed a long way from this salt-sprayed, windy coast but Butlins sold it to us relentlessly, the female Redcoats decked out in hula-girl outfits for various song and dance numbers, the men in Hawaiian shirts with cream slacks and white soft-soled shoes.

One evening, after we'd watched a strange man in a leotard with jet-black hair fold himself, slowly, into a fish tank, there was a look-alike competition. One of the campers, a man of about fifty, his round red face bulging from the collar of a shirt checked in an even brighter red, claimed to be a character called Hoss Cartwright from the TV Western series *Bonanza*. The crowd cheered and whistled. He really did look like Hoss. Another woman, whose only claim to any sort of likeness was that she had wavy blonde hair, wiggled on as Marilyn Monroe.

Then my dad walked out onto the stage! We were sitting in some tiers of seats at the side of the ballroom, high above and to the right, staring down onto my dad's head, and it was odd and rather frightening, suddenly, to see such a familiar figure under those lights and to observe the other contestants turn and watch him walk on.

I told myself at first that I must be mistaken. Perhaps, I thought wildly, it was a look-alike for Dad. How had he suddenly got down there? How had he managed to slip away? I leant across my brother to where my mum was sitting. She was shaking her head, her face ashen. Next to her was a vacant seat with Dad's jacket draped on it.

I felt in that moment as if the whole hall must now know about my father; that he wasn't 'right', that he had, in that dread phrase, 'a history of mental illness'. I pinched and squeezed my arms and legs, and yelled at myself under my breath to try to make those treacherous thoughts go away. I had done this so many times over the years, and would carry on doing it right through my adolescence. Time and again, feeling light-headed, guilty, I found myself battling my own conviction that he – and we, his family – had been 'exposed' by his behaviour, whether it was during one of my dad's loose and rambling conversations with strangers at a bus stop, or at times like this. Always the same argument played out in my head – an argument staying just the right side of calm discussion between myself and someone who sounded, suspiciously, like Dr Hicks: '*You say you love your dad, so why are you ashamed of him?*'

There was applause in our ears now. My dad was the new victim on the stage, someone else who wanted to humiliate himself, but the audience knew, didn't they? They *must* know. I glanced along the row past my brother, whose eyes were transfixed on the stage, to my mum, but her expression gave me no comfort: she still looked terrified. Neither she nor I had thought he was going anywhere other than to the Gents or to get crisps or peanuts: Dad would always leave his seat once or twice for something. What the hell was he doing on that stage?

'And you are . . . ?' the Redcoat was saying. I put my hands over my mouth as if that would stop my dad speaking, but he leant across and whispered his name in the man's ear. 'Ron Townsend!' announced the MC, in that tone of surprise that suggested he knew Ron Townsend would turn up eventually. 'Ron Townsend from Harrow . . . Go ahead, Ron.'

My dad pushed his black-rimmed glasses out of line across his nose and mugged some sort of strange face that I couldn't quite make out in the glare of the lights.

The MC leant down conspiratorially to the crowd, before announcing: 'That's right, ladies and gentlemen, boys and girls: Ron Townsend as *Eric Morecambe*.'

I felt a strange rush of relief, as if, somehow, Eric Morecambe had got my dad out of something, saved him at the last moment.

There was wild applause – and laughter. My mum was clapping too. The man next to me patted me on the shoulder and smiled.

'So now,' the MC was saying, 'it's time to vote.'

I noticed, with horror, that some of the crowd were already losing interest and I found myself thinking, Stay, don't wander off. My panic had evaporated: my dad was a palpable success in his new disguise and I didn't want the moment to be spoiled.

The audience was asked to clap each 'act' in turn. The winner would be the look-alike who received the loudest applause. I was relieved that Hoss Cartwright won, with my dad in second place. Not humiliated, but not forced to do anything more than smile when people came up to him and said, 'You should have won, you really should.' As he turned to walk down the wooden staircase and off the stage, I couldn't wait, suddenly, to hug him.

We were in our little chalet later and it was quite dark, the only illumination coming from a bedside lamp and the moonlight at the little window. My dad was lying on the bed, fully clothed, reading a library book. The pillow was folded double under his black hair. He had his right hand behind his head, his left hand clutching the book and turning the pages. I could hear my mum washing her make-up off in the bathroom. My brother and I were on the floor, talking over what we were going to do the next day, where we were going to go.

I loved the smell of the chalet. It was unique, a mix of sand, soft sand, and polish. Once, years later, on a rainy day at Earl's Court station I had stood on the very edge of the platform, waiting for a City train, and that smell – that same unique, half-polish, half-beach smell that was in every chalet at every Butlins – wafted up along the tunnel. It was so sudden and so distinctive that I had not wanted it to end, but a train announcement distracted me and when I turned back it was gone.

My mum clicked the bathroom light off. When she came out, she was ashen-faced. She sat down on the edge of the bed and my dad looked up, like a boy. He said nothing. She leant down and spoke to him.

'What is it, Mum?'

She turned and gave me her brave smile: the very straightforward one that always said, 'Everything's wrong but nothing's wrong.' 'Time you were in bed,' she said simply.

My dad had put his book down and was just looking

at my mum's back, a little frown on his face that I couldn't interpret.

'Time for bed, you two. Come on,' said my mum, and then we were pulling off socks and pants into a bundle over our knees, trying not to touch the stone floor with our bare feet and carry sand back up into our bunk beds.

My mum turned off the light and I heard the springs sigh as she sat down, in the dark, on the bed.

It was, perhaps, two decades later that Mum told me why she looked so upset that night. She had remembered, with chilling clarity, that it had been on an earlier holiday and in a very similar chalet that she suddenly realized she had miscarried. This was before my brother was born.

'It might have been a little girl,' my dad had added. He had always wanted a little girl.

It rained, on and off, for the rest of the week, leaving big damp shadows on the new-made concrete paths around our chalets and a glistening across the deep rows of pink rhododendrons that we passed every morning on the way to the dining-hall. My dad had brand-new tennis gear and, almost for the first time, his tennis shirt was his tennis shirt and his white plimsolls not some terrible flashing sign of his illness. I don't think that any of us thought Shenley had 'cured' my dad – even at ten, I was not that naïve – but it had calmed him, eased him onto a level that was not just the final ledge before a depression. This was the dad, I thought, I had always wanted.

One evening – and it may have been the last evening before we came home, such a mixture of excitement and sadness seemed to be coursing through our little family – we were walking back to the camp from a stroll along the sea front. My mum, who was not often mischievous back then, but seemed oddly so that day, darted up behind my dad and yanked his shorts down.

'What the fuck . . .' squawked my dad, but he was laughing before he could finish the sentence, laughing and turning and trying to pull the leg back up even though she'd pulled it so far down it was caught round the top of his knee. He had no underpants on.

It was a ridiculous thing. Silly. But I can rarely remember feeling happier, in my childhood, than I did at that moment: something vital had been restored between my mum and dad, some connection. All through Shenley, and in the following year, they had been circling each other – and my brother and I circling them. The ill-ness had moved among us and divided us, as it would, I knew, again, but on that warm evening as Dad struggled with his shorts, roaring with laughter and mock right-eous indignation, the unit moved back together again.

Families can do anything, I thought. Anything at all.

15

Grammar School

My dad would sometimes call me over to his armchair in our back room, or into his bedroom when he was sitting on the edge of the bed, hands folded, and he would talk to me, very quietly and frankly, about what he wanted for me and what I might want for myself.

He had a way then – when he was well, and when I was old enough, I suppose, to notice – of looking me straight in the eyes and of talking very seriously, so that I would half want to get away and half want to be there for ever, just talking, talking. His words, at root, always carried the same message: '*I don't mind what you do. I just want you to be happy.*' It was the same message, I suppose, that flows between parent and child the world over, except that each parent and each child is different and so the message means very different things.

My father spoke to me, I always thought, from a battlefield, his battlefield. I could never hear that message without thinking: he wants this for me because he has never really had it for himself. This was at the heart of the argument that always raged in my mind – and, I suspect, in my mum's – when he was ill and indulging in all sorts of strange behaviour. For my part, at least, I'd think: why shouldn't he? In this illness, in this state of mind, why shouldn't he take this particular chance of happiness – to paint a picture, to play his music loudly – because what other chance will he have? But life cannot be lived like that, or it certainly couldn't in our family. We were close to one another and to the rest of our family but to almost nobody else: it was only, years later, when others outside my family began to be important to me, that I could view his behaviour, when ill, with that sort of detachment. I had, then, my chance to be 'clever' about it, to rationalize it, even to ignore it; but my mother, who was always close to him, who was never that close to anyone else, did not have that luxury.

So my dad would talk to me and I would weigh every word and believe every word, and everything, *everything*, he said to me seemed to be true and wise. Is that the way, always, of sons? And in not pushing me, in never wanting anything for me except my 'happiness' – in that most liberal of messages that I now, years later, might sneer at and dismiss as too easy a regime, too light a burden, for a child – he planted the seeds of a ferocious ambition. For what greater ambition can there be than to strive for one's own happiness?

* * *

It was the morning after our return from Skegness that the letter arrived informing me in which secondary school I had been placed.

I had my own bedroom by then: the little box-room overlooking the street at the front of the house, where my dad had painted and later developed his pictures a few years before. The old enlarger, and some of the chemicals, were still in the wardrobe, now sharing space with my *Victor* and *Beano* annuals.

Dad, who had been up for a while, but was still in his pyjamas, handed me the letter unopened. Mum came in, smiling and excited, wrapping her housecoat around her nightie. They sat on my old green candlewick bedspread as I tore open the envelope. The letter was very straightforward and simple: 'We are delighted to offer you', etc., etc.

'It's Harrow County,' I said. 'I've got into Harrow County.'

My mum clapped her hands and my dad leant across and kissed me on the cheek. I felt his bristles on my face, and a gust of bad, sleepy breath. 'Well done, son.'

My mum read through the letter herself, shaking her head, then picked up the accompanying sheet of paper, which listed all the sportswear and other equipment new pupils were required to buy. It added up to hundreds of pounds.

'You won't need all this stuff, Mart, will you?' she said. 'Green rugby shirt and white rugby shirt?'

Rugby! I hadn't considered that horror at all.

My dad took it from her gently, as if handling some sort of precious legal document, and read through it. He sniffed. 'We can get some of this second-hand, Peg – and you won't need a cricket-box, son, will you?' He was staring at the paper now, doing that thing with his lips, the pursing and un-pursing, that always worried me.

'What do you reckon, then, Dad?' I said, though he had already told me. I wanted to hear it again. I wanted to make sure he wasn't drifting off, drifting away, when there were just a few weeks to go until my first day at the new school. The thought of Dad being high at the same time as I was starting at Harrow County made me feel suddenly tired.

He rubbed his eyes, nodding ahead of the words. 'Yep, yep . . . I'm very proud of you, son. Very proud of you.'

I didn't like that strange 'yep, yep'. I didn't like any of this silence, this staring. I glanced at Mum, but she didn't seem to have picked up any sort of odd mood from him. She was chewing the end of her forefinger and, I knew, mentally adding up the cost of all the equipment.

Dad reached up suddenly and stretched, yawning, his pyjama jacket gaping open over his big, wide hill of stomach. He let the paper slip from his fingers onto the bedspread but he still kept staring at it. I couldn't read his thoughts.

'Let's get a cup of tea, shall we?' he said, partly to himself but mainly to Mum.

* * *

The first few days at Harrow County were oppressive and confusing. We 'new boys', with our conspicuously clean blazers, our newly cut hair – and carrying around virtually every piece of equipment we'd been bought just in case it was suddenly required for use or inspection – were herded from room to room. My head throbbed from the constant anxiety that the group would shuffle round and I, somehow, would fail to shuffle with it. We were given teachers, timetables, form and house groupings. Our names were constantly called. All the teachers seemed very stern and serious.

The buildings, sixty years old, were very run-down. A rumour spread round on the first day that the whole school had been declared 'derelict' in an inspector's report published in the newspapers. Not one of us doubted it. Most of the desks, stained with ancient ink, scribbled over and engraved with compass points, had broken lids. No chair sat steadily on its legs. Gas-light still illuminated many of the subterranean corridors. The high, narrow windows were fogged with dirt and dust.

The older boys, terrifyingly bristled and side-burned, pock-marked with acne and enormous, angry pustules, seemed to have adopted the school's shabbiness. Their lapels were encrusted with food, top pockets hung off their stitches: ties, never properly undone but just slipped in a loop over the head, had hardened into frayed bottle-green and blue tatters.

We newcomers seemed to be adrift in a dusty ruin peopled by young savages.

The teachers were a grand collection of donnish and elderly men, some of whom still bowled along the battered old corridors in gowns and mortar-boards. They were interspersed with eager-faced young liberals like Mr Burt, our moustached English teacher – who reminded me of the then-popular TV star Peter Wyngarde of 'Jason King' fame – and Mr Tufnell, my form teacher.

The headmaster, Joseph Avery, was a red-faced man with a great heap of curly red hair piled up higher on one side of his head. This made him easy to caricature and drawings of 'Joe', his hair spiralling away like an ice-cream cone from his forehead, were to be found all over the school. He was a popular head: clever, kind and almost indestructibly positive about the school and its boys. I remember being impressed that his name was in the copy of *Who's Who* kept in our school library and would read his brief biography again and again. For me, a council-house boy, to be delivered into the charge of such a man seemed to be an honour I barely deserved: what did I know about anything? Someone soon, I felt, would 'find me out' and deliver me back to my shame-faced family.

Joe and his Scots deputy, 'George' Cowan, were among the teachers in the school on whom the boys conferred the secret privilege of being referred to, privately of course, by their first names: 'Dave' Burt, 'Hughie' Skillen, 'Bernie' Marchant, 'Harry' Mees.

Mees, in particular, was an enigma: gammy-legged and with an awkward gait like old Mr Rawlins, he spoke in a broad and easily imitable West Country accent. He was a brilliant history teacher who would simply announce a title at the beginning of the lesson – 'Craarmwell', 'Gaarge the Thurrd' – then orate, his gaze directed almost permanently at a point high on the back wall. His knowledge commanded respect. Like high-court judges we simply sat, listened and wrote. I never saw Harry Mees so much as glance at a textbook. I never heard of pupils misbehaving in his class. There was no time: the course of history was off and running; it was impossible for us to interrupt or divert it.

Harry would, though, interrupt himself from time to time. One day, in the middle of an oratory, he stopped, sucked at his big yellow teeth and fixed us all with a stern gaze. He had very small, very pale blue eyes.

'Some of you,' he said, 'may be tempted at some point in the future by a loife of croime.' No one said anything but he raised his palm to stop our imagined protests any-way. 'No,' he said. 'You may.' He sniffed, leant both hands on his desk and swivelled his head to scan the room. 'I'll say this: if you do an armed robbery, do not take a shooter. Understand?'

We all nodded. He sniffed again and carried on with the lesson.

This interlude soon passed into school legend, with third- and fourth-formers advising younger children sagely, 'Harry Mees says: never take a shooter on a blag' – though the 'blag' bit was added later, with due reference and respect to *The Sweeney*. Why Harry Mees gave the advice, and at that point, was never known, but the only other time I heard him despatch a pearl of wisdom not directly related to a history lesson was when discussing Deep Purple. Members of that group – Roger Glover and Richie Blackmore, if memory serves – had attended Harrow County, holding one of their first band rehearsals in the 'Old Hall', and Harry Mees was hugely proud of the fact. 'Deep Purrple,' he'd say, 'what a group! And remember this . . .' He leant both arms on his desk and fixed us with a stare. 'There are only two toipes of music: good and bad. There are no other categories.' Brief pause. 'Now . . . the Corrn Laws.'

The rest of the masters, feared, despised or merely pitied by the boys, were allowed only surnames or, worse, nicknames, which were hilarious in their bluntly direct cruelty: Bender, Porker, Gimpy, Pinhead.

So now I was a grammar-school boy, my green blazer, bottle-green and blue tie and smart new lace-up shoes a badge, so it seemed, of rare privilege. I felt awkward the first time I walked back into Cullington Close. I couldn't bring myself to take off my tie or to pull my uniform around – I was much too aware of what it had all cost –

but I knew that if I met any of the other boys in the street, Peter Wyatt or Mark MacManus, for example, I would have to exaggerate a cockney accent – 'Aw'right, Mark?' – just to give myself some protection.

At the wall, faced with the early spring evening of Herberts and Ludbrooks, I felt gauche, effeminate, though none of them – apart from the Ludbrook girls, who couldn't resist, and Reg, who had to find a joke – would ever say anything less than positive.

'Ooooh,' Auntie Ellen cooed, as my dad swung open our front door. I felt myself cringe as old Mrs Herbert, from somewhere behind me, added a wolf-whistle.

My dad was in his light working trousers and open-necked cream shirt. 'Ow'd it go, Mart? What was it like? You make a lot of new friends?'

I couldn't wait to get my blazer and shoes off, but I didn't want to let my dad down: he wanted to talk to me, I knew, in my uniform. The worries I'd had a few weeks previously when he was reading my letter of acceptance had subsided a little. He seemed to be OK.

'You look bloody great, Mart. Bloody great. Doesn't he look bloody great, Peg?'

My mum came into the hall, pulling off her rubber gloves, and gave me a kiss. 'I've made you some soup.'

My brother came bouncing down the stairs. 'You look great, my brother.' Ian has, for years now, referred to me as 'my brother'. He touched my lapels. 'Lovely cloth.'

He'd obviously been watching *Never Mind the Quality, Feel the Width*.

I wanted to tell them everything but I couldn't think of where to begin. My overall impression had been of the grubbiness of the place – how poor and run-down and forgotten it all felt – but they didn't want to hear that.

My dad lit an Embassy. 'Some bloody clever blokes there, Mart, eh – the teachers?'

'Very strict,' I said. At that stage I had had no other impression.

'There'll be very clever blokes,' my dad decided. He blew a smoke ring in the air.

'Leave him alone, Ron; don't nag him,' my mum said, putting soup on the table.

'I'm in'erested. It's in'eresting,' my dad complained. 'We're having a nice chat, aren't we, Mart?'

There was a knock at the door. Mrs Herbert from number 28 had brought her daughter-in-law, Sylvie, 'to see Martin's uniform'.

I didn't mind this. Sylvie was about twenty, kohl-eyed, and she wore cream gloves to go out. I was beginning to notice girls and she seemed very elegant to me.

She looked me up and down. 'You look very smart.'

'He says they're very strict, Sylv,' my dad said.

'Oh, they will be, Ron,' said Mrs Herbert. She crossed her arms.

Sylvie nodded. 'Our Les'd like to see you like that.'

Sylvie's brother Les was a car mechanic, always covered in grease, who raced stock-cars at the weekend. These battered and windowless vehicles would sit, incongruously, nose up to the road, on Mr and Mrs Herbert's drive: Ford Anglias with flames clumsily emulsioned up the side. I liked Les.

'Still, mustn't keep you,' said Mrs Herbert. 'Come on, Sylv.'

Sylvia leant across and gave me a peck on the cheek. I caught a whiff of suffocating perfume. 'You look lovely, Martin, really lovely.' She turned to my mum. 'Peg must be very proud.'

'Well, the uniform cost a few bob,' said my mum.

My dad tutted. 'Peg. It's only money!' He flinched, knowing what was coming, and my mum swiped at him with her tea-towel while Mrs Herbert cackled.

'You!' scolded my mum. 'You! Who went out and bought it all?'

'It's miserable here, Sylv – can't I come and live with you lot?' pleaded my dad.

'You're bloody welcome to him,' said my mum, trying not to laugh.

By the spring of 1972 the plum tree in the back garden had grown to an impressive height, or at least it had as far as my brother and I were concerned. We would take turns climbing to the first and only strong fork, then kick down at whichever of us stood below. It produced no plums of any note, although our mum said it was because Dad pulled them off too early. 'Give them a bloody chance, Ron.'

Dad would spit the shreds of skin into the grass. He suspected Elb had got the tree cheap. 'These are supposed to be bloody Victorias. My old man!'

It was about three months after I'd started at Harrow County and my dad, I noticed, was moving into a stage of getting irritated by things. The tree angered him and the outside flue attached to our kitchen boiler angered him even more. Smoke was drifting back into the kitchen as if there were some sort of blockage, but Dad couldn't trace it. The smoke from the top of the chimney seemed to be flowing uninterruptedly. The flue stack, which was concrete, had a round lid about three or four feet off the ground. My dad had this off almost permanently and would cast around for sticks, rods, coat hangers – anything – to poke about inside.

One Saturday afternoon, when Dad had this lid off and was cursing into the blackened hole, Reg appeared at the fence. 'Ron! Ron!'

My dad turned, rather angrily, red-faced: he always found it hard to conceal his irritation at Reg's interruptions.

'D'you want to borrow some chimney-sweep brushes?' he said. 'I got some down my garden.'

My dad licked his lips and peered back, uncertainly, into the flue hole. 'Well, something's doing it,' he said, as

214

if making up his mind. 'It might be a blockage.' He squinted higher up the stack, wrinkling his glasses back up his nose.

'I'll get 'em for you.' Reg stalked back down his garden.

'Reg's getting me some brushes, Peg,' my dad yelled back through the kitchen window.

'Oh,' said Mum. She came out and crossed her arms.

My brother and I were in the Wendy house but we came back down to the crazy-paving to watch.

Reg had tucked the rods down behind his shed. There was a whole bundle of them, and a couple of wiry-looking brushes. They all sat across a strange black sacking bag. God knows where Reg had found them.

I thought of the chimney-sweeps in *Mary Poppins*. 'Step in time!' I announced to Reg.

He gave his machine-gun laugh.

My dad looked serious, though. He glanced at us. 'You two stay out of the bloody way.'

'They can watch,' said my mum.

'Yeah, they can watch,' muttered my dad reluctantly.

I wondered, not for the first time that spring, what sort of mood Dad was now in. It transpired that he'd worked himself up, somehow, into a fury. He rolled his sleeves up, cursing that his hands, which had already touched the rods, left soot on his shirt.

'It'll wash,' said my mum. She glanced across at me.

'Right, Peg.' He turned to my mum. He was sweating and working his lips. 'Hand me them up.'

My mum came forward and went to pick up one of the rods, but she did it so gingerly – the rods being caked in soot – that my dad was dismissing her before she started. 'Oh, leave it! I'll do it me bloody self.'

'I can pop over,' said Reg.

This confused my dad. He was grateful for the rods but never wanted Reg in the garden. He forced a half-smile, wiping his nose. 'No, no, you're all right, Reg.'

Dad began feeding the first rod into the flue hole, quickly screwing on another, then another. He blew air out of his nose. 'It's going up, it's going up.' He pushed at the rods and found a blockage. Furiously he screwed on another rod and jammed it in, then another, and another.

What happened next still shames me but I don't believe any of us standing by could have borne to bring the charade to an earlier end. Perhaps it was because Reg waited so long and so patiently for slapstick; perhaps it was because my dad was being rude and ungracious and angry – had sworn at my mum, had sworn at us children – and seemed to have no reason for this early springtime irritation. Whatever the reason, none of us said anything when the brush popped out of the top of the chimney, bent up and over and – as my dad continued adding rods like a man possessed – began making its way down the outside back wall of the house.

A half-smile played on Reg's face and he lifted a

finger to shush my mum. She rolled her eyes. She knew there'd be a row. Dad was in a sort of trance. My brother and I, feeling we'd literally been sworn to silence, shed all loyalty in the sheer anticipated joy of the moment.

There were more rods in the bag so my dad, oblivious to anything except that cursed hole in front of him and the job in hand, carried on adding them, vigorously screwing each on with a sooty wrist.

Then, with a precision that would make you believe in God or at least some higher force – and as Reg clamped a hand over his mouth, his face creased in delight – the brush dropped, *plop!* on Dad's head.

'What the f . . . !' He jumped back as if he'd been electrocuted.

Reg howled with laughter, swaying back from the fence and clutching his knees. I think I must have believed, even though I knew the sort of mood my dad was working himself into, that he would see the humour in it. How could he not?

But he didn't. He straightened, he clenched his fists and, staring straight into the black hole in the wall, he exclaimed: 'Bugger the lot of you!'

Then he turned on his heel and stalked off out of the back gate.

16

Do You Want Me To?

Of course it wasn't fair, I knew it wasn't fair. Who did we think we were? After my dad stomped out of the garden, slamming the back gate behind him, I wanted to chase after him, go wherever he was going. Tug at his sleeve: *Come on, Dad*. He was only trying to do his best for us and we had thrown it back in his face.

'Here y'are, Reg.' My mum handed the rods back across the fence. She didn't look sad or angry, she just looked fed up.

'Sorry about that, Peg.'

'Don't worry.'

I didn't feel like doing anything then. I wondered, as I always wondered, where my dad would go, who he would talk to. Over to Granddad's perhaps? My nana's? His sister Jean?

Jean's house in Canon's Park was a popular destination because it was a good, long walk. By the time he got there he'd have worked out all the frustration in his urgent, marching pace. I imagined him in her little back kitchen, his legs stretched out. His socks, his plimsolls. A cup of tea.

'*But you've got to admit it's quite funny, Ron.*' Auntie Jean's voice; her thin but kind mouth that smiled, even in repose. My uncle Ron, her husband, standing in the doorway with his teddy-boy haircut. Thick set, hands in pockets. Grateful that Dad was there because it might mean a fishing trip was in the offing. My dad, lost in thought, eyes cast down on his outstretched leg, shaking his head. '*She knows I've been trying to sort that chimney out for weeks.*' But, deep down, thinking he may have overreacted. Or did he think that? Was he beginning to get high, to not care?

I wanted to be in Auntie Jean's kitchen with him (if that's where he was). I wanted to touch his arm and say sorry so that he'd put his cup and saucer down gently on Jean's floor and bring his left arm up across his chest to touch my hand.

From the moment the gate slammed behind him I wanted to say sorry.

The television was on again in the front room, but only Mum was watching it. Dad was perched on the edge of the settee, loudly rustling through the paper as if there was nothing in it worth his time. My brother and I stayed out of the way. Dad's long walk over to his sister's after the chimney-sweeping incident had not really improved his mood. There had been no rows, just this mood of sullen irritation.

The house seemed numb. A thick band of anxiety tightened round my stomach. This was the sort of period my mum, with a chilling lack of drama in her voice, always described as 'the calm before the storm'.

School seemed to be difficult, but I couldn't work out whether it was the thought of all the uncertainty at home that was making it seem harder. From being in the top class at primary school I had descended to stumbling among the strugglers: I couldn't keep up in French and I couldn't understand the maths I was being taught: something called The School Mathematics Project had swept away the conventional language of multiplication and division; now we were dealing with 'matrices' and other abstractions. I felt as if I'd been cast adrift.

The shabbiness of Harrow County school was depressing – the dim lights, the dirt on every surface you touched – but the shabbiness of the boys was even more so: the constant spitting, the close, stale smell of cigarette smoke on war-torn blazers. These boys were from decent homes and were not poor – they had records to lend, cassettes, new bikes and football boots – but there was a dull savagery about them that was not the savagery of violence but that of disinterest, of boredom.

I began to dread school.

* * *

It was the Sunday after the chimney incident. Dad's mood of irritation had given way, quite suddenly it seemed, to lethargy. He had not taken his old winceyette brown and orange pyjamas off all day. This was unusual; he'd sometimes keep them on throughout Sunday morning but he usually only kept them on all day when he was depressed. My mum bustled around and stayed busy, not avoiding him exactly, but making no real effort to talk.

During the late afternoon he'd wandered from room to room, scratching his backside through the pyjama trousers. He wondered out loud, sleepily and with not much conviction, whether he should get dressed. 'What d'ya think, Peg?'

My mum didn't look up. She was reading the paper at the kitchen table, her arms folded on it. She seemed to be delivering rehearsed lines. 'I don't know, Ron – it's up to you.'

'It's just that . . .' He yawned expansively. 'It's just that Mum and Dad are coming over tonight.' He shuffled off into the front room.

Mum looked at me with something like panic in her eyes. 'Is it this week?' she said. She closed her paper. I couldn't remember.

Dad lay back down on the settee after his Sunday dinner – we never used the word 'lunch' in our house – and stayed there throughout *The Big Match*, the afternoon film and *Songs of Praise*. Mum took his cup of tea in on a tray and laid it next to him on the carpet. He raised it to his lips, half sitting up, his left hand cradling his head, one watery eye on the TV. Tea dribbled down onto his pyjamas.

I noticed Mum's neck was flushed red with anxiety. There was a bit more attentiveness about her now. She kept saying, 'Come on, Ron, up you get: they'll be over in a minute,' in the hope that Dad would snap to in his usual way: start organizing the drinks; digging the playing cards out of the drawer. But he did not look at her and he barely opened his mouth to reply, 'Yeah, I know.'

I sat in the armchair opposite him, half watching the telly, turning the pages of the Sunday paper. My brother was on the floor, his back against my chair.

I hated Sundays, had always hated them: they just seemed like weightless, wasted time, dead hours shuffling on to Monday and the new-week horrors of school.

When the door knocker rapped, Dad suddenly sat up. We hadn't heard the car. There was sleepy drool on his lips and red lines from the cushion scored into his pale cheek. His mouth dropped open limply. He seemed disorientated, unable to speak, though he hadn't been asleep.

I realized, in that moment, that Mum must have been crushing up his pills in his food.

He flipped his wrist over – he always wore his watch on the inside – and glanced at the time. 'Oh, bloody 'ell,

Peg.' His voice seemed to be coming from a long way away.

'I did tell you . . .'

'Hold on . . . hold on a sec, then,' said Dad. He was slurring his words now. 'Let me get up the stairs.'

It was like watching a ghost try to stand. Dad looked at his feet on the swirling green of our carpet as if he'd just acquired them. I heard him plod-plodding up to his room.

I touched Mum's arm. 'Have you given him his tablets, Mum?' I didn't know whether to be pleased or ashamed.

She looked at me. 'Don't worry about it,' she said: 'it'll be fine. Let's just get through.'

Mum opened the door on Gran and Granddad, and Granddad, as he always did, stepped forward instantly and said: 'Hello, Peg, where's Ron?'

It had been raining and my gran, who was always well dressed, wore an expensive-looking cream raincoat. My grandparents had become friendly in recent months with a lady called Dora and her husband, whose name I have forgotten. They lived a few streets away from Moorhouse Road. This couple, retired, had a house in Portugal, and enjoyed a lifestyle to which my gran and granddad certainly aspired. Something about the situation had irritated Dad: he thought that his parents were taking on airs and graces and that my gran, in particular, had even changed her voice a bit to sound more like 'posh' Dora. He said nothing about it to them, of course: it was never in my dad's nature to be rude.

'Where's Ron, then?' Granddad repeated. He'd kept his coat on. He shouted up the stairs, but I didn't like the way he looked across at my gran as he did it. He knew something was up. How did he know? 'Ron! You up there?'

I heard my dad's slippers flip-flop across the landing and then he appeared at the top of the stairs, scratching his head. 'All right, Dad?' *Awrida?* The slurring seemed to have got worse.

Granddad frowned. 'You been in bed?'

Dad was flexing his lips over his teeth as if he'd just brushed them and was checking the whiteness in a mirror. 'I was just 'aving a little lie-down.' *Shusavinali-lie-down.*

Granddad said nothing, just turned into the front room. He still had his car keys in his hand.

'Take your coat, Elb?' My mum was straight across.

'Yeah ... yeah. Thanks, Peg.'

Dad had entered the room behind him, his hands clasped in front. He was making some sort of supreme effort.

'Everything all right with him, then?' my granddad said, but he didn't look round to face my dad.

My stomach felt tight.

Dad was shaking his head, wordlessly.

'Yeah,' said my mum, trying to sound casual, but there

Dad with Ian (*left*) and me on holiday in Bournemouth in 1963. Dad was thirty and living in lodgings, having been thrown out of my nana's house. 'It was a miserable time,' my mum told me, 'but in the end, I suppose, it helped us get our first council house.'

Above: My mother's parents, George and Win Pattrick, in the 1950s. A lifelong railwayman, Grandad Pattrick also served as a Grenadier Guard in the First World War – and was gassed twice.

Above: My father's parents, Elb and Liz, celebrate fifty years together, 4 May 1980. My mum and dad bought them a telly. They were good, generous people who could not understand my dad's illness.

Right: Grandad Elb in the back garden of Cullington Close, 1984. He'd lost Gran the year before. My mum and dad brought him the cap back from holiday in Exmouth and it only added to his roguish charm.

Right: Dad was called up to his National Service in 1950, aged eighteen, at Bielefeld in Germany. It proved so traumatic that he was invalided out early – and never really recovered.

Below left: Mum and Dad are married at St Mary's, Kenton, 15 September 1956. Dad always joked that they wed on the anniversary of the Battle of Britain. Dad wore one of only two suits he ever bought. He had the other one made for my wedding, thirty-three years later.

Below right: My newly wed mum and dad at a party at Headstone Lane in Harrow in 1957. Dad looked like Buddy Holly back then – Eric Morecambe much later.

Far left: Ian and me (*on the right*), Butlins at Skegness, 1966.

Left: Mum, me – and a plastered knee – on holiday in the late sixties.

Below: My Priestmead school photo from about 1968–9.

Hullo Clouds, Hullo sky.

Left: The author at about fourteen. My brother wrote 'Hullo clouds, hullo sky' on this picture in honour of the 'utterly wet and a sissy' Fotherington-Thomas from the Molesworth books.

Below: My second-year picture from Harrow County School for Boys. I am on the extreme right of the back row with extreme hair.

Left: My father's sister Jean and her husband Ron in the back garden of my nan's house in Moorhouse Road. She met him at a dance at the Queen of Hearts pub and they were married in 1957. Like my father, he was to become manic-depressive.

Below left: The irrepressible 'Uncle' Reg Ludbrook, our next-door neighbour in Cullington Close, getting ready to fall over at our Jubilee street party, 1977.

Below right: 'Auntie Ellen' Ludbrook, Reg's wife, also at the Jubilee party. A strong, kind woman, she provided invaluable support for my mum. And a phone she could use.

Below: My brother Ian (*left*) and me at my wedding, 9 September 1989. Ian seemed to take Dad's illness in his stride, and – endlessly patient and unflappable – was still there for him years after I'd grown weary of his antics.

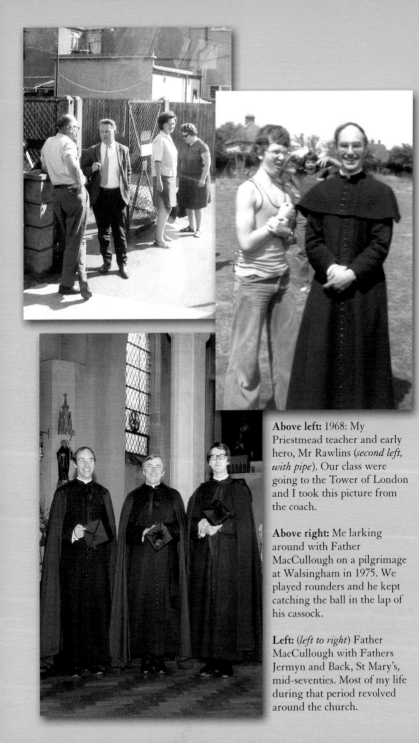

Above left: 1968: My Priestmead teacher and early hero, Mr Rawlins (*second left, with pipe*). Our class were going to the Tower of London and I took this picture from the coach.

Above right: Me larking around with Father MacCullough on a pilgrimage at Walsingham in 1975. We played rounders and he kept catching the ball in the lap of his cassock.

Left: (*left to right*) Father MacCullough with Fathers Jermyn and Back, St Mary's, mid-seventies. Most of my life during that period revolved around the church.

Top: My dad at a picnic table sent in free to *DIY* magazine in the early eighties. I was offered a free swimming pool too. Had Dad been 'high', we would have accepted it.

Above: My favourite picture of Mum and Dad, *c*.1993. They'd just joined the Kodak pensioners' club and this was taken on one of their outings.

Above: The last picture taken of my father, in September 1995, two months before he died. He'd had the suit made for my wedding. I miss him, but he still turns up walking and talking in my dreams. Speak up, Dad!

Above: Dad with my wife, Jane, at a little park at the end of Cullington Close, August 1994. Diagnosed as diabetic, he was desperately trying to lose weight and blamed his lithium doses for the pounds he continued to gain.

Left: Mum and me at a performance in Hammersmith of, er, *Summer Holiday* with Darren Day, a year or two after Dad's death. I was working for *OK!* magazine; Mum was brilliant at chatting up celebrities.

was a tiredness in her voice: it may even have been deliberate.

Granddad nodded.

'I'm fine, Dad, I'm fine. Do you want a shandy?' He was forcing his voice to sound more clearly.

My granddad had sat down and pulled his cigarette papers and Old Holborn out of his pocket. He still hadn't addressed my dad. Then he sniffed and looked up. He seemed angry about something. 'I think you should pull yourself together, Ron, eh? Pull yourself together.'

My dad had been heading out to the kitchen to get his dad a drink, but now he paused and, despite his drowsiness, looked quite angry. 'I don't know what he's going on about, do you, Peg?'

My mum sat down. 'I don't know, Ron.' Her eyes had widened ironically.

'Have you been to see the doctors?' my gran suddenly said. But Dad was in the kitchen and didn't hear it.

Mum baulked at doctors being mentioned. She didn't want the old lady repeating that when Dad came back in. She flapped her hand at Gran and said, in a lower but urgent voice: 'He's fine, Liz, honestly.'

But Gran carried on staring up at the closed door to the kitchen.

My dad came back in with the shandy. 'All right?'

'Have you been to see the doctors?' said Gran immediately.

'What doctors?' said Dad. 'What do I want with doctors?' He was irritated.

Granddad was licking his cigarette paper. He was frowning now, sitting very upright, his little legs crossed at the ankles. He was staring at something flickering silently on the TV screen. My mum had turned the volume down as she always did when there was a knock at the door.

'You've got to look after yourself, Ron, eh?' he said.

'I don't need any bloody doctors!' Dad was almost shouting now. He sat down heavily on the sofa, his face set.

Gran in her armchair folded her arms. 'All right, all right,' she said.

'Don't shout at your mother,' said Granddad. 'Pull yourself together.'

My dad was shaking his head. 'I'm not really ... I'm not really in the mood,' he said. He closed and opened his eyes.

Granddad had lit his little cigarette, but took it out of his mouth. 'Eh?' he said. 'What did you say, Ron?'

'We'll go, Elb.' Gran was standing up. 'He says he's not in the mood.' She'd made up her mind.

'No, don't go,' said my dad. 'Please.'

'Well, what's going on, eh?' said Granddad. 'Are you going to pull yourself together or what? Are you going to sort yourself out?'

'We mustn't row in front of the kids,' said Gran. She

touched Mum's arm. 'I'll give you a ring in the week,' she said gently.

Dad was standing up, half-pleading. 'Come on, Dad, stay and have a drink.'

'I don't want a drink.'

'We can play a bit of crib, eh?'

But Granddad had picked up his car keys.

'Come on, Mum,' he said.

Gran was turning and kissing my mum goodbye. She leant down and kissed me on the forehead too. 'We'll see you next week, Ron,' she said.

Dad, who was standing awkwardly by the settee, nodded. The effect of the tablets seemed to have worn off a bit and I thought there might be more shouting – was ready, in fact, to slip out of the room with my brother if there was – but this collapse in events was somehow worse. There was always such a good atmosphere when my grandparents visited, but nothing about this evening had been good.

'All right, tiddlers?' Dad said to us, after he'd seen them off at the door.

'We didn't get our 10p,' said my brother.

'No. Sorry about that.' He drifted back to the settee and lay down. He seemed utterly exhausted.

For about a week Mum had been crushing tablets up in my dad's tea; she had been breaking them up and inserting them between the slices of ham or cheese in his sandwiches. She knew it would be only a matter of time before he realized what was happening. But for the time being, at least, she was keeping him quiet.

We heard Elb's car pull away. Mum chewed her bottom lip and stared, for a long time, at the curtains in the bay window. 'I don't know,' she said, 'what we're supposed to have done wrong.'

Dad chose not to answer.

One day the following week I came home a little earlier than usual. In our weekly physics lesson – a ninety-minute 'double period' that sprawled across the afternoon – some of the boys had got into the habit of turning the Bunsen burners on and off without lighting them, filling the room with the metallic, heady fumes of gas. The windows wouldn't open, of course: the whole school was sealed tight by grimy, immovable sashes from which the cords had long been cut or stolen. The whole class had to sit and breathe this slow poison while our teacher, an infinitely patient Indian man called Mr Gupta, flapped the door back and forth, trying to disperse the fumes, moaning constantly at the 'rank stupidity' of some of his charges.

I had sat feeling ever more queasy, particular lines from Wilfred Owen's 'Dulce et Decorum Est', which we were learning in English, tolling on in my head: '*Gas, gas, quick, boys . . . an ecstasy of fumbling*'.

Mr Gupta allowed me to leave a little early. I trudged back into Cullington Close in the late-afternoon sunlight. I had a headache and felt sleepy.

Mum was tutting anxiously even before I got through the door.

'What's up, Mum?' I knew it was something to do with Dad. The television was off. There was an uneasy silence about the house. I could feel the usual churning panic in my stomach.

'He's in the garden,' she said. 'Go and look.'

I peeped through the net curtains in the back room, not, at this stage, wanting to be seen.

Dad had climbed the tree and wedged himself precariously in the same crook where my brother and I sometimes sat. He was holding one branch and sawing away at another with his old and very blunt hack-saw. Some smaller branches were already lying on the ground.

'He said he wants to cut it down.' Mum appeared at my elbow.

'Oh, *why*?' I said.

Mum sighed. 'I can't get him to take his tablets. He's stopped drinking tea because it tastes funny, and I don't know what's happening about his sandwiches. He doesn't know but . . .' She shook her head.

I was angry, but my stomach churned with disappointment and unease. He had given things away before when he was high but this destructiveness felt new to me. I had never known him ruin or destroy something he had made, and it seemed peculiarly odd that he'd wreck something in his garden.

'Why can't he ever bloody leave things alone?' said my mum. 'That's a lovely tree.' But I knew she was less upset about it than I was. 'Perhaps,' she said, 'he'll fall and break his bloody neck. *Go on*,' she shook her weak little fist through the window, '*break your bloody neck!*'

'I'll go out and have a word with him,' I said, though I didn't really want to. I could try to reason with him, I thought. Perhaps he just needed some reassurance, some sort of restoration of confidence.

I took off my blazer and tie and strolled out and up the path, trying to appear nonchalant. There were a lot of flies in the garden, clouds of them chasing about over the pond.

'You giving it a bit of a trim, Dad?' I shouted up.

He was sawing furiously at a branch. 'What?' He stopped sawing and, quite unnecessarily, cupped his hand to his ear.

'I thought you might be giving it a trim,' I said.

'No,' he said sharply. 'I'm fucking cutting it down and her sending you out here is not going to make any fucking difference.'

Dad was horribly alert and focused. He was never more dangerous than when he was like this. The question 'why?' at this point, I thought, could easily bring him down and into a much nastier confrontation with my mum.

But I felt the tears beginning to well up. I hated myself for it but I couldn't help it. I loved that tree. I wished Ian had been there by my side so that we could plead together, but he was still at school – and what would be the use of pleading anyway?

I decided to try a different tack; I had formulated the words in my head: *'Why don't you just trim it right back and the plums might improve?'* But only the sound 'wh . . .' came out of my mouth before he was scrambling, kicking among the branches, to get his big body down to the ground. The ruined tree rocked and swayed. I didn't dare move.

'All right . . . all right . . .' he was grunting, as he struggled. At last he was on the ground and brushing bits of leaf and bark off his sleeve. His face was soaked with sweat. His black hair stood up in clumps on his head. He thrust the hack-saw at me. 'Go on,' he said. 'You fucking do it. Go on.'

I wouldn't take it. He grabbed my arm. 'Dad!' I shrank in his grip.

'Ron! Ron!' Mum screamed from the house. 'Leave him alone!'

I saw Reg and Ellen's faces in the shadows at their kitchen window. Perhaps, I thought wildly, Reg'll come out and save me.

Mum was coming down the path now. 'Leave him alone! Leave him alone!' Her face was red.

He was in front of my mum now. There was dribble on his mouth. 'What do you fucking want? Eh? What do you fucking want . . .' His arms were raised, his hands gesticulating either side of his head, but the fingers were stiff and held strangely, in an odd position, the thumbs sticking out like the proverbial sore one.

This whole confrontation, I realized, was somehow alien to him. The words, the gestures, they were being performed by a person he was watching, a body that was at a distance from him. I imagined a little pilot in his head, sitting at controls behind his eyes.

'Just leave him alone,' my mum repeated.

Dad rolled his head sarcastically. 'Well, don't fucking send him out here, then! Keep him in' – he looked at me with sudden distaste – 'if he doesn't want to get his fucking hands dirty. Eh?'

I shrivelled. So this was what it was all about. I wanted to just laugh at him. If I hadn't been so scared, if I hadn't felt so humiliated, if I'd been a few years older ... But would he talk to me like this when I was a few years older? I wished then, in that moment, that the years would just roll on quickly and he'd be confronting a different me: one that didn't shrivel, didn't feel ashamed. Would that version of me ever exist?

He stalked back up the path and, putting his hands on one of the big lower branches, began hauling himself up again. I knew Mum couldn't say anything. In my head I'd already moved us both, stiff-legged, into the house.

Even inside she seemed terrified to speak – or terrified, at least, to speak about my dad. 'What do you want for your tea?' Her neck was flushed bright red. I could see the dark rings etched deeply under her eyes.

'Eggs,' I said. I don't know why.

She glanced out of the kitchen window and up to the tree. 'Don't worry,' she whispered. She cupped my face in her hands.

Neither of us saw Dad climb down from the tree. We didn't see him walk back up the path or hear him come down the side of the house. The first we knew was that the back door had swung open and he was there. He seemed huge, suddenly: huge and terrifying in that little kitchen with its miscellany of old chipped cups, the wooden egg-timer on the side and the radio splattered with paint from the time Dad had emulsioned the ceiling.

In that instant, in the face of his bulk, none of these things seemed properly real. It was as if Mum and I were living in some sort of fairy-tale place where everything was about three quarters of its real size. Anger had swollen him.

It all happened in seconds. He came from behind me and he grabbed my left wrist tightly with his right hand. Mum pummelled on his shoulder and I saw him wince, but he pushed her away. He took the saucepan of boiling water from the stove with his left hand.

'No, Ron, no!' My mum's cry changed into a sob.

Dad stopped and he froze to the spot. He held the saucepan, his wrist trembling slightly under the weight. I could see the wisps of white steam spiralling over the surface of the water. His eyes were wide, his mouth rigidly set: there seemed, suddenly, no trace of illness about him. I would never, in the whole of our lives together, see my father either so 'normal' or so utterly, utterly mad as in the terrible moment when he raised that pan from the flame.

He breathed once, twice. A strange, loud rasp. My mum had both hands on her mouth and had shrunk back. She was set in stone. I could hear her breaths too, and they were small and clogged. And in the ticking silence, when only the sound of all that breathing was evident, what he said was: 'Do you want me to?'

'Do you want me to?'

The words echo down the years. I have relived that scene again and again. I have studied it, I have analysed it, I have repeated it endlessly to myself.

'Do you want me to?' and the saucepan of water steaming in his hand: steaming and bubbling.

And what did I feel in that moment? What went through my head in that split-second? I felt no fear at all. None. I knew that, if my father took that saucepan off the gas, over and over, every year till the spades of cold black earth tumbled over both our heads, he would never be able to throw the water.

I don't know how long it was, after the question had been posed, before my dad simply put the saucepan back on the stove. He replaced it gently, almost tenderly.

There was no expression on his face as he did it. He gave nothing away.

'I'll finish that tree,' he said, as if the task now was just a task: something we'd all discussed and that he'd agreed, reluctantly, to do.

I don't remember what my mum did after Dad left the kitchen. I don't recall what she said. Did she grab me, hug me, smother me with kisses? Did she burst out crying? I simply can't remember. I can just see Dad's back disappearing down to the shed. I can see him picking up the hack-saw and pausing for a moment to peer up into the branches and assess what needed to be done. I can see him hauling himself back up again.

'*Do you want me to?*' It was the worst moment of our lives together and it was the defining one. It was, in the midst of all the sweat and the tears and the anger and frustration – all the loathing and the spite and the utter, utter frustration of his illness – my father's greatest act of love.

17

Men in White Coats

Where had manic depression taken my father this time? Not 'up', that's for sure, not into a 'high'. Dad was irritated, or verging on irritation, all the time. His behaviour was not erratic, it was aggressive – and that was more erratic, in the normal scheme of things, than anything we'd encountered before. Had my mother disturbed the normal rhythm of his illness by secretly feeding Dad his tablets? Or was the illness itself changing? Mum hadn't dared try since to slip him any tablets, fearing she'd be discovered and provoke another act of destruction or spitefulness.

He would come home from Kodak, fling off his donkey-jacket, eat his tea rapidly – almost choking himself in the process – then march out into the garden to do battle. There was no pacing or hand-flexing – none of the symptoms of his 'high' stage – or any indication of an oncoming depression, but he was very far from his 'normal' warm, funny self.

I began to wonder if Dad's present state was actually 'normal'. Perhaps this angry, frustrated man throwing himself into digging – a stage in complicated plans to replace our garden fence or build a new pond – was my 'real' dad. He'd always craved a job in the open air, one with responsibility and some degree of creativity. He would have given a limb, literally, to be a postman or a park-keeper and had even considered working 'on the dust', as others in Cullington Close did, because at least emptying bins would have got him outside and meeting people.

Such jobs were hard to get, though. The posts that had come my father's way in the past were listed in tiny, badly printed ads in the back of the *Harrow Observer* or *Hendon Times*. Time and again, he'd railed against the restrictions of his education – a poor secondary school, no opportunity for college or university – that had left him, stranded, in this series of dull and claustrophobic places: hospitals, factories, kitchens. Kodak, in some sense, was a step up from this: at least it offered its workers some sports and social facilities.

I looked up the schools policies for the Thirties and Forties and tried to work out which particular gap my dad – and Mum, come to that – had fallen through.

My mum had been much more affected by the

boiling-water incident than I had: 'What if he'd thrown it? We'd be in the bloody burns unit! Oh, Martin.'

I thought of a little girl – the sister of one of my friends from Priestmead school – who had been in the bed next to mine in Edgware when I had my abscess. She had curly hair and a doll's face like Shirley Temple. She had knocked a saucepan of boiling water over herself. Every day I would watch as a nurse, using fascinating tweezers, gently covered the lower third of her body with layers of moist lint.

I simply refused to believe my dad would ever have done something like that to me. *My dad? Naa.* Certainly his behaviour depressed me; it could send me off to bed with my stomach knotted in anxiety; but I couldn't ever believe he'd hurt me.

I stayed out of his way that week nevertheless: I had no desire whatever to watch the extremes of his illness unfurl.

Peter Wyatt and Mark MacManus came knocking on the door and I went with them to play on the large expanse of wasteland at the end of our road.

Something had once been built on this land – some sort of sewage farm, it was rumoured. The remains of low, powdery-grey walls were half-concealed here and there among the stinging nettles, bushes and tangled mesh of dead twigs. We called this place 'the dump', even though the real dump, the central refuse tip for the area, lay up behind and to the north of Cullington Close.

Our dump was adjacent to Kenton Park. We built 'dens' in it, screened by old candlewick bedspreads or curtains, and retreated to these hiding places with lumps of cheese and sugar cubes to have 'feasts'.

I played in the dump with Pete and Mark and a few other children from our street until it began to get dark. Sometimes my mum would go to our front gate, which was a couple of hundred yards away, and yell, just once: 'Maaaaartiiiiiin!' It would set a dog off barking somewhere and as I dawdled back, thinking of school, together with a little crocodile of other pals, I'd hear the animal hurling itself at a back gate somewhere.

That night, though, she didn't call. I felt the cold on my skin, glimpsed the yellow street lights beginning to glow in Cullington Close, and began walking back anyway. As I glanced up towards our house, I could see more light from the windows than usual, as if the curtains had not been drawn.

Nobody was on the wall. I could hear Frank Sinatra swinging along, and I shivered. *'Love and marriage, love and marriage, go together like a horse and carriage.'*

Then I saw my dad. Our front door was wide open, and he was sitting down on the doormat, his long legs stretched out, his sockless ankles showing above the unlaced Green Flashes. His eyes were half-closed.

'Hiya, Mark, hiya, Pete,' he called, and raised his cigarette to them in greeting. The two boys came along our wall, trailing their fingers on the brickwork, their eyes fixed on Dad.

He didn't say hello to me. He was letting me know that, though I was in the street and playing, these were the real, grown-up lads.

'Where's Mum?' I said.

He shook his head. 'Dunno.'

I brushed past my dad, and he made a big play of moving out of my way, as if I was infected. Mum was in bed but not asleep. I saw her red nose and fingers over the counterpane as she lay stiffly.

I listened in the half-light of my parents' room. 'When did the record-player come back?' I asked.

'He brought it back with him today. It's been at the hospital. I've got to ring them tomorrow.'

'Oh, good,' I said. I knew she'd already been on the phone to Dr Hicks.

'What's he doing down there?' she half-whispered, though there was really no need to lower her voice with Frank singing his heart out.

I sat down heavily on her bed. 'Just sitting there.'

She tutted and sat up. 'He's a bloody nuisance.'

'The front door's wide open,' I reported, feeling slightly disloyal. 'The whole street can see in.'

My mum tutted again.

My brother came up the stairs. He'd been in the back room, drawing: as much as possible he just got on with it when Dad was like this. 'He's an idiot, isn't he,

Mum?' Ian said. 'What's he want to play it that loud for?'

'Oh, listen to that. Bloody thing!' said my mum.

It was 'Nice 'n' Easy'. I had grown to hate it as much as my mum always had. It was the opposite of how any of us felt.

I wanted to go downstairs and make a cup of tea but I was nervous of being around Dad when he was high. I was afraid he might pick a fight. I went down anyway and put the kettle on. He wasn't on the doorstep now. I glanced out into the back garden and saw the shed door open. Long ago, he'd attached a length of yellow washing-line twine to the inside handle to stop it swinging back sharply and straining its rusty hinges, so that you had to duck under it to open and shut the door.

Dad came out now, a large tin of paint in each hand. He brushed past me in the kitchen and out into the hall.

When I walked past, and up the stairs, with a tea for me and one for Mum, he was back sitting on the step, his arms clutched across his knee, watching the night. He said nothing to me. The paint was in the hall behind him, on top of some old sheets of newspaper.

It was almost 9 p.m. I thought I might as well go to bed. I couldn't watch TV: Sinatra was in there.

I took Mum's tea in to her. She was sitting up now, with her knitting, her back against the headboard.

'He's still just sitting there ... He's got some paint,' I added.

Mum got out of bed and went to the top of the stairs. 'You coming to bed, Ron?' She knew better than to ask him about the paint, but she wanted to see it for herself.

I was behind Mum, peeping through the top banisters.

Dad looked up vaguely, as if not quite sure where the voice was coming from. I realized he didn't have his glasses on. He often took them off when he was high. He looked oddly bald-eyed and old.

'No. I'm going to do some bits and pieces.'

My mum said: 'OK.' She shrugged at me. After the events of the last few days, she was pursuing a policy of just trying to keep him happy.

I kissed her and went off to bed, Frank still singing his heart out below. It was a wonder that the neighbours never complained, but they didn't: either through sympathy for my mother or because they had problems of their own to contend with at nine o'clock at night. There wasn't much money in our street, and a tangle of different generations in many of the houses: I had no difficulty in imagining other people to be too pre-occupied to worry about us.

I was half asleep and half awake, not sure whether I had slept at all, when the music was suddenly turned up. I glanced across at my sleeping brother.

There was an oily taste to the air that I couldn't quite place. I swung my feet out of bed and crept across to the top of the stairs. I looked at the glowing hands of my little Ingersoll watch: it was past 11 p.m.

Downstairs, whistling to himself, half-bent to his task and caressing each stroke with the movement of his tilted head, Dad was painting the front door.

I could see a pair of feet behind him, and a beige nightgown tightly wrapped round. It was Auntie Ellen. She bent down behind my dad and looked up the stairs at me. She came into the hall gingerly, as if trespassing, and she said loudly: 'I told your dad he shouldn't be doing this in the middle of the night.'

My dad looked up and glared at me, then he turned towards Auntie Ellen, his mood changing in an instant. 'We're relaxing, aren't we, Mart? We're taking it nice . . . and . . . easy. Eh?' And he looked back up at me sourly.

Auntie Ellen, still in the hall, lowered her chin and fixed me with a gaze that held the message *'He's really gone mad this time.'* 'Anyway,' she said, turning to Dad, as if turning to go. He was engrossed in his work. She turned back to me quickly and mouthed: *'I'll see your mum in the morning,'* and wagged her finger.

Dad left the door propped open all night, sheets of newspaper tucked under it, and slept, in his clothes, on the settee, his arms folded, his plimsolls up on a cushion at the end. He was still there when I came down early in the morning to answer a knock at the door.

The milkman was half-leaning through the doorway. 'Everything all right?' he whispered.

'Yeah.' I tried to laugh.

'He's done a good job anyway,' he said, flicking a

glance towards the door. He gave a little wave and disappeared back up the path, whistling.

He hadn't done a good job as it happened: the bright-
green gloss had crazed in the damp overnight. I knew
my mum would be furious.

The house was freezing. We had no central heating. I
half-closed the door, hoping the rustle and bunching of
the newspapers wouldn't wake Dad. I could hear him
snoring like a drunk, and, somewhere behind that sound
the rub and thump of the needle on his Frank Sinatra
record, sliding back and forth on the run-out groove.

Mum had been making clandestine calls to Dr Hicks to
try to get my father sectioned into hospital.

Previously this had involved slipping round the bay
window to Ellen's house when my dad was out of sight.
Mum would take a cup for sugar or some knitting that
needed sorting out in case Dad spotted her and
she needed a covering excuse. But Nana had been ill in
recent months and, to keep in touch with her, we'd had
our own telephone installed for the first time. It hung on
the wall at the bottom of our stairs. Dad, rather
comically, gave it a wide berth as he came down past it,
as if it was about to shout at him. He'd resented its
presence from the afternoon it was installed. 'I suppose
you'll be ringing those bloody doctors day and night,'
he'd snapped.

Mum was having none of this. 'It's ... for ... my

mother,' she said, in the slow, deliberate way that so irritated him. 'All right?'

But the calls to Dr Hicks's surgery were frustrating. Mum was told that the doctors would like to visit Dad and see him for themselves. They were from the psychiatric wing of Northwick Park, a relatively new hospital just outside Harrow town centre.

'But after all the things he's done . . .' my mum argued.

I could hear Dr Hicks's calm, patient voice in the receiver and my mum nodded and rubbed the side of her face slowly, as she did when she was trying to think something through.

'Why can't they take him back into Shenley?' my brother had asked, in all innocence. Shenley, for us, was like an enchanted land we'd visited and then dreamt about ever since.

'I wish they bloody would,' said my mum. 'It's like living with an unexploded bomb.'

In the end, inevitably, the whole process took too many calls. Even then, at eleven years old, I could see the ludicrousness of it: my dad had a record of mental illness, an absolute pattern. Why, each time, were we forced to start again?

Mum was upstairs one evening when the phone rang. My brother and I were in our pyjamas. It was just after nine o'clock and none of our family would call this late.

Dad, who had been in the kitchen making himself a sandwich, was through the room in seconds. I glanced at my brother.

'Hello? Who?'

I heard my mum's urgent footsteps on the stairs. 'Ron?' There was a whimpering panic in her voice.

'Well, fuck that!' yelled my dad and I heard a terrible, wrenching snap and then the sound of the telephone receiver clattering off the wall.

'Oh, Ron!'

'Don't do it to me, all right? Don't do it!'

My mum made a sound, either a whimper or the beginning of some sort of protest, but it was drowned by the deliberate thump of my father's feet pounding up the stairs.

The door from the hall clicked open and Mum came in softly, seemingly trying not to give away where she was. She sat down heavily on the sofa, clasping her hands in front of her as if ready to watch something really important on the television. She was shaking.

She looked at me. 'Northwick Park on the bloody phone. He's torn it off the wall.' She wiped her eye once and gave us the thinnest of smiles. 'Well,' she said, 'there'll be no argument about it now. If they don't take him in, they can take me in.'

I didn't like that sort of talk – and neither did my brother. 'There's nothing wrong with you, Mum,' said Ian, and he crawled across and clasped her hands.

'No,' said Mum. 'I'm sure there isn't.'

About a week after all this a smart Volvo Estate drew up outside our house. Ian and I saw it from the bay window, and called our mum in from the kitchen.

'Where's your dad?' she said simply.

'I think he's gone up the road to Mr Chapman,' my brother said.

Mrs Chapman, a small, colourless sort of woman, highly nervous, had become very friendly with Mum, and Dad had somehow latched onto her husband. They had a son, David – a prodigiously talented young foot-baller – who Dad had tried to involve in a few Cullington Close kick-abouts.

'What's he doing up there?' Mum said, still keeping her eye on the Volvo.

'I dunno,' Ian replied. 'He said he was going to have a chat with him.'

It was a chilly, darkening afternoon, and a couple of the lamp-posts outside our house already glowed im-patiently. But like a pair of old soldiers who never leave their post, Ellen and Mrs Herbert had been sitting out stoically on the wall with their knitting, occasionally turning to each other and pointing at one or other house across the road. The neighbours over there, somehow, were always worth gossiping about.

When the Volvo arrived they both stood up, Ellen

smoothing her skirt and primly tucking her knitting back into a plastic carrier-bag.

Two men in white coats got out, looking up and down the street before turning to my mum.

White coats! The old Napoleon Bonaparte song 'They're Coming to Take Me Away, Ha Ha' chimed away in my head. I couldn't help it. Reg had bought the record and at one time, four or five years before, couldn't stop playing it. He even dragged his little record-player out onto the stained and cracked area of paving by the back window of his house, trailed the electric lead back through the window, and played it to us in the garden. I don't think he did it to insult Dad – such things were not in Reg's nature – but it was certainly a song that lodged in the mind.

They're coming to take me away, ha, ha
They're coming to take me away, hee hee, ho ho, ha ha
To the funny farm
Where life is beautiful all the time . . .

The men stood at our porch, looking around and up and down the street as if aware of their own importance and eager to see how many people had noticed. One of them, a young Indian, was handsome, healthy and affluent-looking. The other, a slightly older man, was balding, with a long, mournful sort of face, like Pete Townshend from The Who. He had a way of looking down and then suddenly up, as if he was constantly hearing things that surprised him.

The Indian grinned and stuck his arm straight out to shake hands with my mum, as if she was a pools winner, and they came into the house, instinctively wiping their feet on the doormat that we never had.

'You keep this nice, Peg,' said the older man.

It was odd hearing my mum's first name used by a male stranger. It reminded me of Alan.

'Oh,' said my mum, slightly embarrassed. She never knew how to handle compliments.

The Indian looked round the top of the walls. Everyone noticed, somehow, our polystyrene coving. 'Where is Ron?' he said.

Mum scratched her chin and glanced out of the window. 'He's up the road with a family we know,' she said. 'Can you pop up and fetch him, Mart?'

'I'll go,' said Ian, and I was relieved, because my brother could always stay matter-of-fact with Dad, and Dad always detected a drama whenever I was involved. He started pulling on his plimsolls.

'What are you going to say?' asked my mum.

'I'll just tell him to come back,' said my brother.

Mum looked impatient and opened her mouth to say more, but he was gone, slamming the front door after him.

The Indian man laughed low. 'Lively kid.'

My mum chewed on her nail. I could see her turning

over in her mind how this meeting was going to go, and I knew what she was thinking. 'Erm, do you want a cup of tea?' she said quickly, and, while they were still saying 'yes' and talking about milk and sugars, she added: 'Are you taking him with you?'

'Oh,' said the Indian, as if that had not occurred to him.

But the older man was nodding. 'Yeah, yeah, we can do that.' He seemed to understand, as he should have, that they couldn't 'interview' Dad, obviously at my mum's bidding, then leave her to take the consequences.

'*Can* we take him?' mused the Indian. He balanced his weight on one leg, his head tilted to one side. He had the air of a man considering whether a piano could be fitted into his van.

'Yeah, yeah. We can.' The older man seemed in no doubt.

'Hu-llo, fellas.' My dad was suddenly there, filling the room, using the super-polite two-syllable 'hullo' I'd heard him employ with doctors at Shenley a couple of years before. It was his reasonable 'hullo'. It said: *I'll go along with this, but I'm not going along with you.*

I looked at my brother. 'Can we go in the garden?' I said to Mum. But she didn't hear me, or didn't want to. We were all in this together, I supposed.

The doctors gave my dad their names.

He leant in, as if eager to hear them, all smiles. 'And

you're from Northwick Park?' He didn't look at my mum.

'Ron . . .' The Indian wanted to get straight down to business.

'Yeah,' my dad interrupted, and he put his hand up, the palm flat, at just about the level of the Indian man's chest. 'Yeah. I'm not going in.'

'Ron . . .' This was the older man.

'I'm not going—'

'Let's talk about this. Let's sit down at the table and talk about it, shall we?' said the Indian, ushering Dad through his own front room.

And suddenly Dad was prepared to *be* ushered. He was putting one leg in front of the other.

The older man's face was more serious now, and he'd straightened up. No more nervous, upward glances. They were dealing with the patient.

'Yeah, yeah, we can talk about it.' Dad's attitude had changed, or was changing. Suddenly he was among his own, among the doctors. It was miraculous to behold. How had the pair of them changed the atmosphere; how had they suddenly taken the sting out of it?

'Shall we have that cup of tea?' said the Indian – and this was part of it too. He had his hand in the small of my dad's back and was steering him into the back room, towards the kitchen table.

'I haven't been feeling great, I really haven't.' My dad was at the table now. He had his elbows on it. He was staring at the table-top and he was talking at it. 'I've actually – Peg, tell 'em – I've actually been feeling really lousy.'

My mum didn't say anything. She looked across towards Dad as if she were seeing him for the first time.

'Just very, very . . . down,' he was saying.

I thought of the last few weeks: the rows, the irritability. Could it be possible that all of that was a sort of depression? I had grown used to there being two parts to my dad's illness, the high and the low, but it appeared there was also a third part: how my dad translated what he was feeling to the doctors.

'OK, Ron, well, you know what you have to do, and what we have to do . . .' This was the older man. It was as if he were discussing tactics for the second half of a football match.

My dad pushed his chair back. He was standing up. 'Where do you want me to go, then? Peg, are you going to get some clothes together?'

I couldn't believe it. I didn't want to speak. I didn't even want to look at him. What was this all about, this illness?

'Yeah, yeah,' said my mum, who seemed equally confused.

I thought that she might be about to start trying to itemize what he was going to need, and I prayed quietly to myself that she wouldn't: we seemed to be in the middle of a spell – a spell of complete logicality – and I didn't want her to break it by compiling lists. A few days ago he'd ripped the phone from the wall at the mere mention of Northwick Park. Now he was ready to go meekly. *Meekly*. It needed meekness around him: we all needed to bend our mood, change our stance, stay with him on this. Our reaction could not be relief or sympathy: it had to be as matter-of-fact as my dad's. It was like a game of diplomacy.

So my mother did not go into any detail about the clothes he'd need. She could do all that later, once he'd gone.

I saw his big old brown case appear from somewhere. The older man was staring out at our garden, perhaps considering a different tack now the job was done. I hoped he knew what he was doing. He lifted his cup to his lips, tasted the tea, and replaced the cup in the saucer, but he said nothing. A phrase like '*Lovely garden, Ron,*' I thought, might scupper us: might remind Dad what he was leaving behind and make him change his mind.

But what did I know now anyway? These doctors were in control: years of training had taught them the fine gradations of diplomacy needed to bend a mental patient to their will. *A mental patient*. Poor Dad.

Or perhaps the doctor just didn't think of saying, 'Lovely garden.' Maybe I was giving the pair of them too much credit, and my dad, by suddenly adjusting his behaviour, his viewpoint towards acquiescence, was playing a longer game. If so I couldn't, for the life of me, see what it might be.

Dad was kissing my mum now. 'See you, Peg.' Then he was kissing me: 'See you, son.' He kissed and said something to Ian, patting him on the back and laughing.

I was upset now to see him go – and I was confused too, because suddenly I didn't know why he was going.

'Hey, there's nothing wrong with my dad!' I could have said, and, despite everything, I came really close to saying it. Love wipes the memory, perhaps – or has no memory.

18

The Crow

The Browns had an old crow, with an injured foot and a broken wing, that couldn't fly. Roger Brown had found it one day, revolving helplessly in the dust by the kerb, dragging its useless, outstretched wing. He had put it in an old budgerigar cage for a while, fed it worms and nursed it back to health.

The crow now lived, I thought, under our hedge, but I couldn't really be sure. This is where it disappeared to, but perhaps it made its way from there back to the Browns' garden, two houses away, and into a nest I'd never seen.

The miracle, anyway, was that for nearly a year this huge, black flightless creature had not only survived with its disabilities – and in a street full of stray cats (the local paper had once published a picture of eleven of them sitting side by side on one Cullington Close wall) – but had actually thrived.

It was very tame. Roger Brown was, like many tough young men – one of those clichés that prove themselves by being unerringly true – 'very good with animals'. My mum said he took after his father, Neville, who kept the racing pigeons. Neville's relationship with his pigeons was more businesslike, though. I couldn't imagine him 'loving' any of them, even if they won money for him.

Anyway, this old crow, the morning after Dad had been taken into Northwick Park hospital, came out of its hiding place under our hedge and hopped down the slope, tick, tick, tick, on its one good leg. Its injured foot, which, Roger had once told me, had been flattened under the tyre of a car, was blackened and spread out, like old chewing-gum. It always made me vaguely queasy to look at it.

The crow came down to our door and began to tap on it. Inside the house, this sounded quite loud – like someone laboriously driving a nail in.

We were all still in bed but I heard my mum say, from her room: 'It's that bloody crow,' and then I was out of bed and downstairs, rummaging in the bin with the Sunblest and the cream crackers and assembling a little pile of mixed crumbs in my hand.

I didn't like opening the door on the crow because I was always afraid that it would hop in or flutter up at me, but of course it never did. Though tamed, it was still a wild bird, so that when I opened the door it hopped back as if this was the last thing it expected a door to do.

I put the crumbs on the ground. The crow, which looked very greasy and alarming close up, cocked its head and fixed me with its little eye like a bead of black gravel. I noticed that one wing stood proud from its body and that underneath it was wedged a confusion of fluff from its own threadbare body, and little twigs and bits of privet. This looked painful and I wanted to reach in with my fingers and dislodge it all, but of course I never would. I was too frightened of the crow to touch it. Dad had said matter-of-factly one day, 'Don't bend too close: it'll have your eye out in a second if you give it a chance,' and I never really doubted that.

The crow pecked critically rather than hungrily at the crumbs, occasionally pausing to cock its head, and when it had finished it simply fluttered backwards, like a swimmer turning round between lengths, and began hopping back up the path. I watched it until it disappeared under the hedge, kicking out twigs and leaves behind it with its sliding, skidding foot.

I was a dreamy, superstitious child. My dad had no truck with superstition, but my mum was so conscious of omens and signs, so keen to follow every little myth and rule that might bring good luck or chase away bad, that it seeped into my brother and me. We never walked under ladders, of course; Mum made us throw salt over our shoulder if we spilled any; we had to sit on the stairs before we went out anywhere, and we were never allowed to pass anyone else on the stairs, because it would bring that person bad luck. She'd fly into a fury if we ever blew up and popped a paper or plastic bag. 'You're banging someone out of a job!' she'd shout, and snatch the damp remains away from us. My dad, who laughed like a horse at most of Mum's superstitions – largely because he knew they'd been passed down directly from her mother – actually concurred with this one. He'd been unemployed too often.

How birds came into all this, I don't know, but Mum was not at all happy that the crow had visited us that morning, for the first time in weeks.

'I just don't think it's a good thing,' she said. 'I don't like it when it just turns up.'

We were all sitting at the table in the back room, eating toast. I felt a tremendous sense of relief that Dad had been taken away at last. I'd been quite upset about it the night before but now it seemed like the start of a holiday. There was so much going on at school, most of it awkward and frustrating, that the idea of coming home, at last, to a quiet house: of watching TV, playing records, having my friends round without the constant threat of something odd or eccentric happening was irresistible.

'It's just an old crow,' said my brother.

'It's a bloody nuisance.' Mum stared out of the window, chewing. 'It's not good news.'

'A cat'll get it in the end anyway,' I said, without enthusiasm.

'The cats are a bit frightened of it,' my brother said.

'*I'm* frightened of it,' Mum said. 'I don't know why it hangs around.'

Northwick Park hospital, where Dad had been admitted during those first grey, lowering days of winter 1971, was close to Harrow town centre and about two miles from where we lived. It had been built only in the last couple of years. In contrast to Shenley's Italianate villas or the elegant 1930s-style of some of Edgware's buildings, it was an exercise in concrete brutalism, with big, damp-stained ramps for ambulances and a series of forbidding-looking entrances.

The hospital complex covered several acres and backed onto Northwick Park itself, a rather bleak and formless area of fields broken by low hedges and pathways but with very few trees. Like many parks left unplanted and with no centre or reference points of any kind, it was oddly depressing. The psychiatric wing, which was at the back of the hospital, overlooked it.

My mum had been up to the hospital that first Saturday afternoon to see Dad and 'settle him in', but she was very non-committal about him when she came back. 'Yeah, he's all right,' she said. 'He's sent you home some comics from the shop.' She put her bag on the draining-board and pulled out some *War Picture Library* and *Commando* magazines.

'He's happy, then?' I asked.

259

'Mmm.' She didn't seem at all sure.

'Mum!' I complained. 'Come on.'

'I don't think much of the hospital,' she said. 'I'll be honest: I don't think it's up to much.'

We all went there the following Saturday. Dad did not want us to go up to the ward but insisted on meeting us downstairs in the reception: a huge, overlit area with big, dirty windows and low tables covered in torn copies of magazines.

He seemed preoccupied as he came out of the lift but he kissed Ian and me, his eyes darting across to the reception desk. He was wearing his green pullover, white shirt, light trousers and Dr Martens. This was exactly how he dressed at home, which was odd. In hospital the Green Flashes almost always went on – during the first few weeks at least – combined, if it was warm enough, with shorts. This was how we knew he was ill but in the process of getting better. Now, seeing him in these 'normal' clothes, I didn't know how to judge him; I didn't know what to think. Had he somehow got better before he went in?

'Let's go for a walk,' he said. 'I'll show you something.'

We swung out of the big glass doors onto a grim and grimy little road. Beyond it, scraps of patchy grass stretched away. My brother and I wanted to run onto it but it was pocked with holes and littered with bits of timber and concrete with rusting wires sticking out. It was as if the finished building, having reached this grassy fringe, had simply stopped and shrugged off these bits and pieces of building material.

'Lovely, isn't it?' said my dad, unsmiling.

My mum shivered. 'Don't like it down here.'

We walked past a high, blank concrete wall interrupted by a tall, wide chimney-stack. Sickly-looking grey smoke came from the top. 'Experiments,' my dad said. 'That's where they burn the dead animals.'

I stood back, taking care on the lunar-landscaped grass, and peered up at the chimney. I wasn't sure: did people do things like that in Harrow, in a hospital?

The service road changed into a narrow, gravelly trail rutted with old tracks of bicycle- and wheelbarrow-wheels. Beyond it was Northwick Park itself, sitting low and washed-out: a desert of sickly pale greens.

I'd never liked this park and didn't particularly fancy wandering over it. Years later, a little clutch of patients, over a period of a few weeks, had made this same dismal walk from the psychiatric wing to the platform of Northwick Park station, clearly visible over in the north-eastern corner of the park. There each had waited for one of Betjeman's silver Metroland trains to come rumbling in from the affluent worlds of Amersham and Great Missenden, before leaping in front of it.

'Let's go back,' said my mum. 'This is miserable.'

My dad turned on his heel. Mum slid in alongside him and he put his arm round her back.

The doctors had decided to try to reduce Dad's doses of lithium. 'It's not a good drug,' one of the doctors told my mum one afternoon, taking us into a strange little office off the main wards: a small niche of temporary wall-panels. Everything about Northwick Park seemed temporary, transitory. I wondered idly whether their advice had any permanence about it either.

'It's a drug that causes terrible side-effects – the knee jerks, the twitching, the lips: all that,' he said. 'But it is bad for his organs too.' He swivelled on his seat and stared at the ballpoint he was holding in his right hand. He wasn't writing with it, he was just inscribing circles in the air over his blotter as the seat turned back and forth. He seemed a strange man to me, with his thick black glasses, and his very thick black hair low on his forehead. I couldn't take my eyes off the pen.

'Will you be reducing it for ever, doctor, or is it just for the time being?'

He looked up from his pen, then gazed up at the ceiling, and he stopped swinging his chair. For a moment he looked like a proper hospital doctor, I thought. I wished he had proper walls for his office.

'We just have to find a way, long-term, of bringing the dose right down. Physically it is not doing him any good at all.'

My mum clutched her shopping bag on her knee, as if there were extra doses of lithium in there that she was never going to let him get his hands on. 'OK,' she said. 'Let's see what happens.'

Dad was sitting on his bed in the ward. A newspaper was next to him. The bed was made. He was in his 'home' clothes still. He looked, almost for the first time, more like a prisoner than a patient.

He gave Mum a list of things to bring in — mainly books and a bit of fruit.

'I'm fucking bored in here, Peg.' He breathed heavily through his nose. There were windows on both sides of the ward: one side looked over the rear of the big ambulance ramps; the other over that wretched park. It was one of those rare rooms where looking out of the window would make you feel worse than staring at the walls.

I thought Dad was going to cry and I think he nearly did, but instead he said, 'You get off,' and touched my mum on the elbow. 'I'll see you in the week.'

Harrow County School and Northwick Park hospital were only a few hundred yards from each other. They stood either side of a large and very busy roundabout and though this was certainly hazardous to cross I convinced myself it was impossible. It made my stomach churn with guilt but I didn't want to think I could visit Dad at lunch-time, or after school. I didn't want to think I could visit him at all, on my own. I couldn't think of anything I wanted to say to him, and I was slightly afraid of what he might say to me.

I try to convince myself, now, that part of this was in the nature of being eleven years old – that parents suddenly start to seem boring and out of touch – but that is nonsense. I was so intimately involved with my dad's problems, and pulled so close to my mother in the need to deal with them, that it was impossible to think about a 'generation gap': we were all in it together. But perhaps that was the problem: perhaps I didn't want to be 'in it' any more.

I'd like to say that I wrestled with my conscience over this, day and night, but I didn't. When Dad went into Northwick Park that first time I was almost happy to forget about him. Almost.

At the end of the Christmas term the first-year boys of Harrow County were summoned, one by one, to see various senior teachers about 'career prospects'.

I wanted to write. I had never wanted to do anything else. But I couldn't comprehend how any money could ever be made from writing and so, expecting the conversation to concentrate on the practical matter of wage-earning rather than Literature, I prepared a passionate speech in my head about how writing was a need, a hunger, etc.

The interviews took place in Mr Mees's history room, a brightly lit cubicle that on one side overlooked the 'inner quad', a small playground hemmed in by the school's main buildings.

I was called in at lunch-time. I felt over-confident,

almost cocky, having cleared my head of all notion of taking an 'ordinary' job in favour of the uncertain life of an author or poet.

Mr Marchant – 'Bernie' as he was known to some of the boys – stood behind a desk. The sternest of our teachers, in aspect at least, Mr Marchant always wore a gown; he never smiled and his hair, coal black, with faint flecks of grey at his temples, was shaved square on his head. He had tiny eyes and a small, pointed nose, which, in conjunction with the haircut, gave him the look of an angry hedgehog.

When he spoke, which he did very slowly and precisely, he sounded his 's's harshly behind his top teeth. His habit of suddenly pushing back the tails of his gown seemed to be his only flamboyance. He was in all other respects, it seemed, a teacher designed to provoke fear.

Mr Marchant was not one of my teachers. I had never spoken to him. Everything I thought I knew about him had been gleaned from his appearance and from what other boys in my form – who, crucially, had not been taught by him either – had heard second-hand. So, in the presence of what I perceived to be Mr Marchant's hard pragmatism, the speech I had rehearsed evaporated in my mind; and in the face of what I expected to be an aggressive interview I decided to adopt a similar approach.

He sniffed and looked down at a single sheet of paper on his desk. He looked up. 'Martin?'

I nodded.

'Martin Townsend?'

'Yes,' I said, and I could hear the nervousness in my own voice. Come, come, I thought to myself, this is Bernie Marchant: show some backbone.

'What does your father do?'

In all my years as a journalist, I have never again encountered – still less been able or inclined to deliver – such a perfectly lethal first question.

Looking back on it now I wonder to what extent it was planned. I have to assume not at all; it was surely not possible for a Classics master, who had never met me – who could know very little from my school records, even if he had been inclined to look at them – *deliberately* to formulate such an unsettling enquiry. But that is exactly what it was.

We are all, these days, not supposed to regret anything: life moves on at such a pace and we, though only human in scale and form, are supposed to hitch ourselves to time's relentless advance: all things must pass; no sense in looking back. But I do regret my answer to that question: it stands above all other possible regrets. It represented such a wretched, hopeless misreading of the enquirer that the moment I said it I wanted to take it back.

'He doesn't really do anything,' I said.

Mr Marchant, who had been glancing back at his sheet of paper, looked up sharply and inclined his head just a fraction. That faint movement should have been enough of a warning sign, but I was eleven, I was frightened, I was, in an instant, way out of my depth.

'Doesn't do anything,' he repeated slowly. 'You mean he's unemployed?' – and he managed to express that word without the faintest hint of disapproval.

'No,' I said. 'I mean he doesn't really do anything *much* – just *manual* work.'

Mr Marchant sat back, drew his hands together on the paper and fixed me with a look of pure fury. 'So you are ashamed of your father?'

I felt my face burning. 'No, it's just that—'

'Don't you ever, *ever*, be ashamed of your father,' he said.

'No.' I felt crushed. I just wanted to go now, leave the room, do the whole thing again tomorrow starting on a different note, but Marchant was standing up. He flicked the gown behind him.

'Your father, how old is he?'

I had to think about this ... 1932 from 1971. 'He's thirty-nine.'

Mr Marchant nodded. 'Well, then he has had nothing like the advantages you've had.'

'No.'

'But he has done his best.' Marchant hissed the final word. 'He has done his best for you and given you a better chance so you had better make sure you don't waste it by making idiotic statements like the one you just came out with.'

I didn't know what to say, but Marchant had subsided

now. He sat back down, flicking the gown over the back of his seat. 'So ... Martin?' He glanced at his paper again. 'Martin – what do you plan to do with your life?'

I saw my dad again the following Saturday. Mum ushered my brother and me straight up to the ward: she didn't want to go anywhere near the waiting-room at the back of the hospital. There was one other patient on Dad's ward, an elderly man lying still, on his side. He had big brown eyes and they were open, staring. The covers of his bed were miraculously unrumpled as if someone had made the bed around him and he hadn't dared to move since. The whole place had the sweet, depressing odour of stale bread.

I was oddly comforted to see Dad in his Green Flashes. The laces were undone, as if he'd put them on and then lost interest. Mum unpacked things in front of him – grapes, lemonade, papers – but he just stared at Ian and me, a half-smile on his lips.

'You two all right, you tiddlers? How's school?' and he was nodding before either of us answered, so I know he wasn't really listening. He was on a very reduced lithium dose now, Mum told me later.

'Me mum and dad are coming up tomorrow,' said Dad. He plucked at the grapes.

My mum gave me a look as if to say: God knows what they'll think.

We chatted for a bit, but Dad stayed sitting on the bed.

There was no thought, now, of a walk. When Mum indicated that we'd better go he seemed almost relieved and stood up straight away. He had the air, I thought, of someone waiting for something to happen to him.

'I'll see you, Peg, then. All right, kids?' He kissed me on the lips. He almost always kissed me on the lips.

19

The Balloon

As well as the battles my mother fought with various doctors – to get my dad into hospital; to ensure he was given what sounded, at least, like the 'right' treatment (though none of us were ever sure what that was) – there was the constant struggle she had with his employers too. He had run through a series of jobs before becoming an electrician at Edgware Hospital, all the time day-dreaming of the little café or jewellery-repairing business he and his dad might one day start. But most of these posts had evaporated when a long spell of illness dragged him back into hospital. My mum must have been relieved, finally, when he was appointed as an electrician at the hospital: at least they had a responsi-bility, and were in a position, to understand his problems.

Kodak had been understanding too, but their patience had begun to wear a little thin. At some point, either when he was still in Northwick Park or just after he was discharged, the job slipped away from him.

I can't remember my mum ever announcing to us that Dad had lost this or that job, and I don't think she ever did: bearing in mind her fear of the popping plastic-bags, undoubtedly the whole subject of unemployment was one of her greatest terrors. But the message would eventually get through to us.

I never worried that Dad wouldn't get a job, or that we'd be thrown out of our house or starve or not get any toys for Christmas. But I wanted Dad to be happy in his work; I wanted him to come home whistling again with a 'Lucky Bag' in his pocket like he used to when he was at Edgware.

I'd add my concern about his job to the general stock of nameless dreads that always seemed to be turning round in the back of my mind – school, choir, girls – and then take off on my bike. I would ride for miles, always north, always on my own, to Elstree, Aldenham reservoir, Letchworth village green. I would never let my own twelve-year-old son travel so far now, but back then, in the early Seventies, there was no concern about paedophiles or child-murderers. I felt protected by the rigidity and seriousness of most of my life. I had it in my mind that if I had never committed a crime, or even considered it, then it wouldn't happen to me: I was armoured, I thought, by my own common sense.

So I pedalled along, peering into the unfamiliar front

gardens of Hertfordshire – always on the look-out, as my dad was, for the tell-tale reeds or rushes that would indicate a garden pond; the gnomes or stone animals that might be lurking near – and I wondered what would happen with our lives. Would Dad always be ill like this? And would I, one day, be ill too?

I had found an article in one of the dull news magazines – *Newsweek, Time*, or some such – that they insisted on keeping in our school library. It posed the question 'Is mental health hereditary?' There were diagrams of brain-wave forms, small black-and-white photographs of obscure institutes in somewhere-or-other, 'Mass.', whatever that meant. But the only answer that could be gleaned from those grey, apologetic pages was 'possibly'. I photocopied it and took it home to show my mum.

She scanned the serried lines of closely printed text for a few seconds and nodded. 'Yes,' she said, 'I've heard that.' But she didn't read the article.

I had made up my own mind, anyway, that mental illness must be caused by a shock, a trauma: something seizing your head and giving it a shake, so that everything flew around like one of those little snow-scene globes. It was a comforting thought, in many ways: I wasn't expecting any shocks.

Dad's condition was deteriorating rapidly at Northwick Park. He was being allowed, I thought, to fall apart. Each time we visited him, his bed and his bedside cupboard, and the general atmosphere around him, seemed to have fallen into disorder and disrepair. It was as if he'd moved in permanently and then been neglected. That's how it felt. He smelled of sweat; his hair was greasy and sticking up in tufts.

He was back, obviously, on lithium, or, if not that, then on something else that made him hollow-eyed and restless. The pacing and the constant shaking of his hands, as if trying to dry them, had returned, worse than ever; there were flecks of dribble at the corner of his mouth when he talked and in between the talking he'd flex his lips over his teeth constantly. It was the worst state, physically, I'd ever seen him in.

My mum seemed unsure what the hospital medics were trying to do. Initially, the doctor in the strange temporary office had said that they were going to try to liberate him from lithium and its terrible side-effects. Why had they changed their minds?

He sat on the edge of his bed, his hands clutched between his knees, his lips working, his knee bouncing on the floor, and I tried to engage him in a conversation about school. We'd built a hot-air balloon in our technical subjects class. It had a balsa-wood frame covered in tiny, tiny, squares of tissue paper. My dad's sad blue eyes – red-tinged – watched my fingers as I described how small.

We'd taken it out to the playground at the back of the school and lit a burner under it. Then we'd let it go. It floated up beautifully, ascending in perfect, measured increments like a real balloon. But as it began to rise towards the top of the 'Jubilee' elm trees planted when the school was founded, it suddenly swung to the left, and then lurched back to the right. A flame flared up, engulfing the delicate tissue paper, and the balloon was destroyed.

My dad looked at me for a moment, almost as if he was about to make a joke – make light of the moment as he so often did on sad or desperate occasions – then buried his face in his right hand and started sobbing.

'Don't cry, Dad,' I begged, 'please don't cry,' and I could feel the swelling pressure and tickle under my nose, the tears welling up in my own eyes. I took in the room in seconds – the chaos: all he had. The chaos that could be solved only by the intervention of someone else. I felt terribly sorry for him at that moment, not for the first time, not for the last: terribly sorry to be watching my father suffer and to have no idea at all how to put things right.

This was a terrible time. Even if I try to look back on 1971 and 1972 with the sort of nostalgia for the Seventies that I see on TV every other week, I tend to think of the bands that I loved – Slade, T-Rex, Gary Glitter and the Glitter Band – bickering and rowing through their early, less-successful singles. Sullenly smoking fags backstage at *Top of the Pops*. They hadn't had their big successes yet. How could they have been happy then when my family and I were not? There was nothing very happy about 1971 and 1972. It was a grey, confusing, headachy sort of time.

Dad came out of hospital just before Christmas. His mood had balanced out into a sort of neutral half-depression.

He stayed in bed most of the time. But on Christmas morning he was up, as ever, hours before the rest of us. He crept into our room – I saw him come across the half-light, like a man trying not to tread on glass – and I smelt his stale breath as he whispered first to me, then my brother: 'Come on, tiddler. Father Christmas has been.'

We always believed in Father Christmas. We knew exactly who he was and we appreciated his consistency.

Ian would always pretend that it was too early and he didn't really want to get up, but on this morning – 25 December 1971 – his play-acting grated: I was just relieved to see that one part of Dad's behaviour would never change. He always got more excited about the festive season than all the rest of us put together.

When we came down to the front room – yawning, dry-mouthed, sleepy-eyed, but actually desperate to open our presents – Dad was already there, sitting in his pyjamas in his armchair, a half-smile playing on his lips.

Our presents were always left in large plastic sacks with big, gaudy drawings of snowmen or reindeers on them – one each, either side of the hearthrug.

Seeing us shiver a bit, Dad leant down with a sigh and punched at the ignition on the side of the gas fire once, twice, four times. Usually he'd swear impatiently when it failed to take; his robust curses were often the first thing we'd hear in the morning on school days. But today he just kept punching silently. He wasn't well, that much was clear: his knee jerked – the ball of his left, then his right foot going up and down on the carpet – and he kept making a move as if to stand up, then changing his mind. Christmas kept him in his chair.

We crouched down, my brother and I, one knee up, one leg lying flat on the prickly rug, and peered into the top of the bags. We always took the smaller presents first, keeping the big surprises till last – partly to please ourselves but mostly to tease Dad, who couldn't wait for us to get to the 'main' present.

Mum came down, her dressing-gown wrapped round, just after we'd opened the first two or three, but then retreated to put the kettle on. She glanced at my dad and rolled her eyes at me. That was the year, I think, when I got a 'Johnny Seven', the oversized plastic machine-gun that fired seven different types of plastic rockets, grenades and missiles. It had been advertised constantly on TV.

Dad admired it for my benefit. Once our presents were open, the best of Christmas was over for him and he visibly subsided, usually disappearing off into the kitchen to get some more tea, then announcing that he was 'going back to bed for an hour or two'. This year, however, he just sat in his armchair as we made neat piles of our new acquisitions. Mum handed him his tea and he sipped at it in silence, staring into space or at our artificial silver Christmas tree, which he'd acquired through some sort of special deal at Kodak.

Perhaps he was thinking about Kodak if he was thinking about anything at all. Had he lost his job at this point? Did he know that he had? He remained off work, anyway, when my brother and I went back to school at the beginning of January.

He stayed in bed or lay on the sofa and watched TV. There was nothing for him to do in the garden. In the late afternoon, when I came home from school, and in the forty minutes or so we had before the daylight disappeared completely, we'd walk up the path together and feed the fish. He didn't say very much – just touched my head, then laid his hand on my shoulder.

On one occasion, touched by his touch – emboldened, suddenly, into talking like an adult – I did something that I never did and asked him how he felt. I remember he said, 'Up and down,' which was surprising, because he never commented on how he felt. He usually talked about the illness as if it was an entity separate from him that needed treatment and removal – like an infestation of wasps or mice.

* * *

A few days later he took an overdose of sleeping tablets. My mum and brother were at home. Mum had taken a cup of tea up to him at about three o'clock and been unable to wake him. She slapped his face, gently at first, then quite hard, and he moaned and turned his head. Then she spotted the half-empty pill bottle on the bed-side table.

My brother was nine years old, slightly built and asthmatic, but with our mum he hauled Dad off the bed, yanking at his arms, his legs, struggling to bear his thirteen or fourteen stones of floppy, mumbling, semi-comatose bulk. They forced him to stand up. They slapped him, pinched him, punched at his back and trunk, to keep him vaguely awake, as his head lolled and strings of drool spilled from his sore lips.

Then my mum had to leave Ian to do all this: to push and heave and half-prop Dad against the chest of drawers while she dashed down and rang, first, 999 and then Granddad. Whoever got there quickest could get Dad to hospital.

'Try to keep his eyes open, Ian. Don't let him sleep!'

I arrived home from school in the middle of all this, letting myself in the back door as usual. 'Mum?'

'Up here, Mart.' Mum was looking over the banisters on the top landing. 'Your dad's taken an overdose.'

'Oh, God.' I dropped my bag in the hall and quickly pulled off my blazer.

He was awake now and mumbling. He was sitting upright on the bed.

'Please get up, Dad. You need to get up.' Ian was holding his pale hands.

Dad was opening and closing his eyes: he desperately wanted to sleep.

'Give us a hand, Martin.' My mum brushed past me into the bedroom.

Between us, we got him up again. He wanted to stand. Some sort of message had got through, past the fug of drugs. Had he not wanted to, we could never have hauled him upright.

We walked him out and back into the box-room, and then round and round on the big mat in there.

'Sorry, Peg, sorry,' he kept saying.

'OK, Ron, OK.' But she didn't tell him an ambulance was on its way; didn't tell him that Granddad was, even as we spoke, cursing his way through the traffic.

We heard both arrive at the same time, Granddad's voice mingling with two others down at the front door seconds before the knocker rapped.

I knew my granddad would go about it all the wrong way; I knew his presence would, somehow, have a negative effect – and I knew my mum knew that.

The two ambulance-men seemed very young. My brother and I backed into our room and watched from the door as they took control.

'Come on, Ron, let's get you up.'

We could hear our dad mumbling, 'Sorry, sorry,' again and again.

Granddad stood at the door of my mum's bedroom as they walked Dad across the landing, but Dad seemed barely to notice his presence.

I watched Granddad's expression but there was nothing to be gleaned: he simply looked concerned. He was holding his car keys. 'Shall I run you, Peg?'

'Yeah. I'll get some stuff together.'

The two men were strong but they sweated and heaved and swore under their breaths at each other as they steered my dad – floppy-legged, heavy – down the stairs. They pushed him against the wall and then gradually slid him along and down it, one of them stooping to manhandle his legs onto the steps one at a time.

'Shall I open the door for them?' I asked my mum.

She shook her head. 'Let 'em get on with it,' she said.

So Dad was back in Northwick Park. I thought back to the days in Shenley. Was he worse than that now? Had something changed?

In the middle of it all I sought refuge, I suppose, in the choir. Once I had walked through the big back doors of the church and then run up the winding stone steps to the cool, light gallery, it was possible, for an hour or so, to slough off the world outside.

I told Brian about my dad after practice.

'He's just going to have to take time to get well,' he

said. 'The important thing is: is your mum all right? And are you?'

'Oh, yeah.' I tried to sound confident. 'You know my mum.'

He smiled. 'Have you seen these, then?' He took me across to the organ console. A pair of rear-view mirrors had been mounted either end of the keyboard. 'So I can see what's going on at the altar,' he said.

I sat down in the kitchen with my mum a couple of nights after Dad had been taken back into hospital.

'I don't think he did it deliberately,' she said.

'No.'

'I mean, for all he has some rotten times with his illness, I don't think he'd want to leave you two. I don't think he could do that.'

I gazed out into the garden. We were sitting in the back room, she up at the table, me in the armchair. She'd been reading her paper.

'He told me he couldn't sleep, that was all,' she said after a while. 'He said he'd gone back and lain there for hours but he couldn't get any rest. That must be awful.' She looked at her paper again.

'Mum,' I said, 'why don't you leave him? Why do you put up with all this year after year? I don't know how you can stand it.'

'I love him.'

'Well, I love him too,' I said, 'but it just goes on and on.'

'Oh, Mart, I've thought about it so many bloody times; I've turned it over in me head. I've spoken to Nan about it, but she just says: "Peg, I lost your dad all those years ago and there's not a day I don't think about that, how unfair it is."'

I thought about this for a moment.

'And Nan . . . well, you know how Nan is. She's had her ups and downs with Ron.'

My mum and dad had been living at number 72 when the incident between Dad and my nan had taken place. It was the very early Sixties and my parents were on the waiting list for a council house. My dad, in particular, was desperate to get a place of his own.

Granddad had not been dead very long. The atmosphere in the house must have been one of suspended animation: I still had a sense of that when I went over there.

I don't know what caused the row. My nan, who could be so pleasant most of the time, was absolutely immovable when she felt she was in the right, and if she did not get her way there could be long, silent sulks. Growing up with her, I always considered that she had two expressions: both to do with the position of her glasses. When they were down her nose, she was in a benign mood: friendly and patient. When they were fixed in position at the top of her nose – and sometimes I would actually see her push them into place and know, instantly, that she was irritated – then she was a match for anyone.

A quarrel began, anyway – possibly between my mum and dad alone, or possibly between my mum and Nana, then somehow involving my dad too. Mum never spoke about it. I only knew for certain about the end result – and that was that my dad pushed my nan down the stairs.

I don't know if Nana was badly hurt. I don't believe she went to hospital. Her hips were always bad; had the fall made them any worse?

All I see in my mind's eye is the hallway – dark, even during the day – and my nan tumbling down and against the wall at the bottom.

The part I needed to know was what was said afterwards. Did my dad run down the stairs to help her? I felt sure he did. Did she refuse his help? Did she push him away, curse at him? I was equally sure of that too. But what was the immediate aftermath: what sanction did Nana deliver? Did she issue an ultimatum: 'Get out of my house now. I don't care if you've got nowhere to go'? I felt sure she did.

For many months during those years, my mum and dad 'had' to live apart, according to Mum, and she always told me it was so that they could get a council house. In my mind I registered it as a sort of penance that had to be paid so that the council would relent. But I think the incident on the stairs forced them to live apart; certainly my nan had never forgotten it. She would hug my dad, kiss him, ask him how he was – and when he was ill she was as concerned as anyone – but when we sat down together on a Sunday evening at Cullington Close, or my dad took me over to number 72 for a 'bowl' and we were in her kitchen, drinking tea, I saw the tiniest glimmer of something in my nan's eye. It was unmistakable. It would go with her to the grave. It was suspicion.

20

The Belltower

I had never believed that Dad had tried to take his own life. Perhaps, out of natural compassion, Mum had sold me an account of events she didn't entirely believe – and God bless her for that – but I *did* believe her version. Dad had been desperate to sleep and had simply taken more and more tablets. I had no trouble accepting that. For years I'd watched him twitch, tremble and pace restlessly when he was ill. Many times I had got up in the middle of the night with a bursting bladder and opened the toilet door on my dad, sitting, hollow-eyed, on the lavatory with one of his library books. Once, I remember it was *The Carpetbaggers* by Harold Robbins. I went back to bed and had nightmares about that baffling title.

I found it much easier to understand the agony of no sleep than that of no hope. Dad was still wrapped up, it seemed to me, with the detail of life – music, humour, fishing, conversations at bus stops: surely people who committed suicide had swept all this away long ago? Or perhaps the saying was true that suicide remained, always, the ultimate unanswered question. Either way, I was about to come up against the horror of it for the first time.

It was early in 1973 and my brother and I had been singing in the choir for a couple of years by then. What had begun as an hour of practice twice a week, a wedding every other Saturday and a Sunday morning service had become a series of activities that occupied most of our free time.

There were football matches most Sunday afternoons and we had begun serving mass as altar boys, every few weeks or so, at a half-hour service on Sunday evenings. There were also, from time to time, recitals such as Benjamin Britten's 'Songs From Friday Afternoons', which I loved because they sounded like a series of short pop songs.

St Mary's itself became such a familiar place to me that, a few years later, when I took my O-level art exams and was faced with producing a piece that illustrated perspective I painted the interior of the church. I passed with an 'A'.

If my sex education mainly consisted of what I picked up from friends at school, I was not naïve. I did not expect any of the priests at my church to be married: surely that was against the rules? I did not assume they were homosexual either; neither that word nor any of the crude variations of it were ever mentioned by me or, to my knowledge, the other choirboys in the entire seven years of regular attendance. There was, though, a kind of gentle, artistic femininity around the choir gallery and vestry that, twenty years on, I'm sure, might have been translated in later parents' minds as something more disturbing. It was mixed up in a number of elements: it was a sort of perfume, an atmosphere.

The church was very beautiful, with its vast cream pillars; a delicate, turquoise-blue hammer-beam roof; an altar draped in delicately embroidered cottons with gold crucifixes of a very particular richness and delicacy. In keeping with this visual grandeur, services at St Mary's were 'high'. The congregation – over a hundred people at the 11 a.m. mass – was plucked from the middle classes of Kingshill Avenue and its environs: comfortable, long-serving professional men and their neat, upstanding families. For their delectation we would sing masses by Mozart, Dvořák, Palestrina, in later years accompanied by an orchestra.

Into this environment of beauty and gentility came the priests themselves, Father Shearing, an assistant and a young trainee, all of whom were very gentle, intellectual and holy. I never heard any of them raise his voice. When members of the congregation spoke to them they did so almost as supplicants – lowering their voices, choosing their words with infinite care – while the clergy took their lead from Father Shearing: standing with their hands clasped in front of them, nodding, saying a few words, touching a shoulder or a wrist. The conversations were rituals. Everything at St Mary's was, in one way or another, a ritual.

We had arrived for a choir practice, a year or more previously, to find something new on the altar. A large object had been set down in front of it – a long shadow: heavy, solid and blacker than the usual darkness of the church. A few of us had noticed it on our arrival and had peered down the nave, trying to make it out. The only illumination in the church came from a couple of very bright lights hung directly at our eye-level. They were hung much too high to pierce the darkness and, instead, served only to dazzle us.

Brian, in his breezy, matter-of-fact way, followed our gaze, shielding his eyes, but he already knew what it was. 'It's a coffin, boys. It's just a coffin.'

Just a coffin. There was a chorus of 'ooooohs' – fearful, giggly, apprehensive – and those of us who had previously shown no interest at all bustled to the front of the gallery to have a look.

Then the question, coming from three or four mouths. 'Sir, sir' – we always called Brian 'sir' – 'is there anyone in it?'

Before Brian could do any more than roll his eyes I was aware of Father Shearing at the top of the gallery stairs, blinking and half-smiling at the commotion.

His small hands, as always, were clasped in front of him.

'Boys ... *boys* ...' The calming tone brought near-silence almost immediately to the gallery. 'There is a person lying in rest here ...' He raised a finger.

Brian nodded across, saying nothing, and we trooped back to our pews. There was a certain amount of whispering.

'Martin,' Brian called across to me. 'We need some books from the vestry. The Howells.'

From the vestry. Lee Waldron looked at me and nodded. He knew what I was thinking. He whispered something to a boy next to him.

The vestry was at the back of the church, down a flight of steps and in the real, closed, haunted part of the church where really we went only in the bright morning daylight of the Sunday service to change into our cassocks. Getting to the vestry – and this is what Lee had immediately and gleefully twigged – would involve walking past the coffin.

Father Shearing, the half-smile still flickering on his face, said: 'I'll come down with you. I need to fetch something myself.'

Relief flooded through me. I walked down behind him from the gallery, watching the black cassock slip across the light-coloured steps.

I stayed behind him until about halfway down the left-hand aisle. This was St Leonard's chapel, where the relics of that saint were, supposedly, locked in a small box. Sometimes in the midwinter, if it was freezing in the gallery, or if we were doing a more modern recital such as the Britten and Brian needed to use the piano rather than the organ, we would rehearse down here.

Father Shearing paused, turned and let me catch up. I was watching, from the corner of my eye, for the coffin to come into sight, but it was difficult to make it out in the darkness and the pillars kept obscuring my view.

He smiled. The breath came from his little red mouth in steam and I could smell gin, faintly, on it. He didn't say anything but walked beside me as we came to the end of the aisle. To our right here, the floor opened out onto the altar. In the middle, clearly visible now, lay the coffin. It seemed enormous. A cloth – red, purple, I can't now remember – was certainly draped over the top but it had ridden up on the near side, so that I could see one of the big brass handles. I swallowed hard. It was the first time I had seen a coffin. I had never been this close to a dead person.

'It's the husband of one of the parishioners,' Father Shearing said matter-of-factly. He turned the light on outside the vestry door and I hesitated, waiting to follow him in, but he just nodded for me to enter. It didn't occur to me until later that there hadn't been anything he needed to 'fetch'.

When I came back out with the books and closed the door he turned off the light. He touched my shoulder. I felt no fear because I had no fear of him, none whatsoever.

'Martin,' he said, 'let me tell you something.'

I looked down, trying to be polite, to indicate attentiveness in the dark.

'Everything in the darkness is the same as it is in the light. Nothing changes.'

I nodded.

'And so,' he said, 'there is nothing to be afraid of.'

I nodded again. I waited. I thought he was going to say more but all I heard was the faintest whisper as he gathered up his cassock over his shoes and began to climb back up the steps.

He touched my shoulder again as we walked past the coffin. 'Not afraid?' he said.

I shook my head. 'No.'

In the spring of 1973, one cold Wednesday evening, my brother and I got our bikes out of the shed as usual to cycle up to choir practice.

Dad came to the back door as we wheeled them by. 'Say hello to Brian for me,' he said, and came out in his slippers to open the back gate and see us off.

It was unusually quiet as we reached the top of St Leonard's Avenue and the main doors of the church. But I could hear some noise from the other side, near the belltower. There was a strange light in the trees, too – something yellow flashing . . . flashing.

I looked at Ian and he shook his head at a question I hadn't asked. 'Dunno,' he said.

We bumped our bikes down the steps at the side of the church, walked along the little path bordered on one side by the memorial garden, the other by the church wall, and out into the wide square in front of the tower.

An ambulance was on the square, and two police cars. Seven or eight of the choir were standing nearby in a group with Brian. I saw Steve Carter and Lee Waldron.

Brian looked grim-faced. Spotting me, he said something to Steve and walked across. Lee and Steve started to follow him but then Steve stopped and held Lee back too. I saw him put his finger on his lips.

I thought Brian must either have been crying or was close to tears. He put his hands on my shoulders and swallowed hard. 'There's no nice way to put this. They've found Father Shearing dead up in the tower. It looks like a heart attack.'

'Oh, you're joking,' I said instinctively. Brian let it go. I glanced up at the tower, then across at Lee. He shook his head. 'What was he doing up there?' I said.

'Shooting bloody squirrels, apparently.'

I thought of Father Shearing: small, kindly, his pointed face blurred, as ever, by blue traces of stubble. I couldn't imagine him even holding a rifle, let alone raising it, aiming it, shooting. I imagined the weapon as tall as he was.

'The squirrels have been a real problem,' Brian said almost matter-of-factly. He rubbed his eyes. 'Chewing through all the wood and the rafters up there.' His gaze flickered up to the belltower.

Father Shearing *dead*. The little man who had guided me through catechism; who'd let us all play in his beautiful garden, knocking our football about among his plants and flowers – 'Oh, please, be a *bit* careful, boys.' I felt the tears welling up.

'I think you should go home, anyway,' said Brian. He looked across at Steve Carter. 'I think you all should. We'll see how things stand on Friday.'

I looked back up at the tower. Through the tall slits of windows I could see figures moving around.

Father Shearing had taken us up to the top of the tower a couple of times. He and Brian had thought it a real hoot. Access was by a winding staircase so old, narrow and steep that each anxious step seemed to take you round 180 degrees and up another three or four feet. It was a nerve-shredding climb. At the top was a small viewing gallery with a high wall round it. It was just possible to peer over and see Kenton spread out below. The flagstones up there, I remembered, were mossy and had weeds growing between them.

On the way back down I peeked into the belltower. One or two of the more daring boys stepped in. It was just a square of uneven stone flags with a very low, narrow wall round it. Too low for me. I had no head for heights and didn't fancy tripping over the edge. I stayed at the top of the stone steps, looking in. Father Shearing had taken us all up there but I couldn't place where he stood when I was looking in. I remember gazing, for a long time, at the huge bell and thinking how grotesque it seemed.

'He's still up there,' Brian was saying.

'He's right under the bell,' said Lee quietly.

'Lee!' Brian looked annoyed.

'Well, he is.' Lee shrugged.

I imagined his small, black-cassocked figure stretched out on the flags. Death changed everything. The stones of the church, the trees, even the pavement: everything presented itself differently. Shapes and colours changed. Nobody close to me had ever died before.

My brother and I trailed around with some of the others who had locked their bikes in Father Shearing's garden as usual. But what was 'usual' now? There was a light on in the vicarage and I wondered if Father Shearing had turned it on before he left to go to the tower. I still couldn't imagine him with a rifle. I tried to think of it tucked under his arm: the burnished wooden stock that it might have. Father Shearing would find nothing beautiful or admirable in that. Where had he kept it anyway?

I had a thought. 'We'd better ring Mum,' I said to Ian. I was already wondering how to handle all this with Dad.

We went to the telephone box on the main road and, above the roar of the early-evening traffic, I told Mum what had happened.

'Don't say anything to him at the moment,' she said. 'All right? Leave it to me.'

A small group of us cycled back down the hill from the church and then meandered along Kingshill Avenue. Televisions were on in people's houses. They didn't know about Father Shearing and they wouldn't care anyway. The old vicar. The old vicar at the church.

I wondered if I might have a really good cry, but the time had passed. Now I'd be crying for myself – for what was and what had gone.

Ian had taken his hands off the handlebars and was cycling along with his hands in his pockets. I thought how funny he looked pedalling away with cycle clips clamping his big flares above the clumpy platform shoes Mum had got him.

'Poor bloke,' he said suddenly.

The notice of Father Shearing's death formed the basis of a special edition of St Mary's parish magazine. It had a glossy cover and more pages than were usually photo-copied together. There was a small box of them at the back of the church two weeks after he was found in the belltower. On the cover was a cut-out picture of him in his cassock, raising his hand in blessing like a pope. It had the dates of his birth and death underneath. I wondered if Brian had sorted it out. It smelled expensive and looked very posh.

Florrie, the white-haired old lady who had arranged

the flowers in the church for as long as anyone could remember, took it upon herself to sell them. As she handed one over she looked at the cover as if saying goodbye each time. I cycled back from church with the magazine flapping on my handlebars. Dad was mowing the lawn – had been, according to my mum, 'for the last couple of hours: up and down, up and down'.

She shook her head over Father Shearing's picture. 'Oh, that's a shame.' But she handed it quickly back to me. 'Put it away somewhere upstairs,' she said. 'I don't need any more aggravation.'

Mum still hadn't told Dad about the vicar's demise. The death of anyone – not just family members but distant acquaintances, celebrities – could trigger a mood change in my dad. John Lennon's murder six years later, for instance, would prove a disastrous catalyst.

At the various funerals we were to attend during the following decade – first for my uncle Ron, then each of my grandparents – he tended to be flippant, mischievous even. He made silly jokes. At one of them there was a number plate on one of the hearses that almost spelled out a rude word – fart or shit or something – and Dad had giggled helplessly, lifting his glasses to wipe his eyes.

But his laughter was the weakest of defences. Hunched up in his funeral outfit – that same sports jacket but with a thin and rather dusty black tie – he would be fine until there was a particularly moving tribute or hymn sung. Then he'd sink back into the collar of his shirt, his hands clasped in front, and blink back the tears by examining the ceiling. For weeks after he'd brood secretly on the death, moping himself, slowly and inevitably, into a depression or high.

It was a fortnight since Father Shearing's body had been found in the belltower. His funeral had come and gone; it was on a school day so I hadn't even thought about going. I was still puzzled, though, about what had actually happened to him.

At choir practice, Steve Carter, who was a good year and a half older than the rest of us, mentioned something called 'Mandrax'. Brian's face was like thunder. He had whispered to him angrily to be quiet, raising a hand over his head as if he was going to strike him. I'd never seen him do anything like that before.

There was talk of Father Shearing having handfuls of 'Mandrax' pills in his pocket. I imagined them bouncing and spilling down the steps behind him as he walked round to the tower. And a *gun*, though?

When I got home I dug out the ten-year-old copy of *Black's Medical Dictionary* that my mum liked to pore over for Dad's symptoms or to see if any of us had cancer. I looked up Mandrax. A sleeping pill, an anti-depressant. So Father Shearing, perhaps, had been depressed? It wouldn't have surprised me. He could be sombre – and he liked to drink gin-and-orange, which, my mother had warned me, could make you very 'fed up'. It is only now, thirty-odd years later, that I realize Father Shearing climbed to the belltower and swallowed the pills to kill himself. There was no gun. The only squirrels were the little grey ones which used to run up and down the two big horse-chestnut trees at the front of his garden. He used to feed them with Ritz crackers from a box.

21

WOLD

The drinkin' I did on my last big gig
It made my voice go low
They said that they like the young sound
When they let me go . . .

Harry Chapin, W.O.L.D.

There is a photograph of Dad, my brother and me taken at Easter in 1974 at a place called Harrow Weald Lodge. My dad and brother are sitting on a brick wall, and I am standing on the wall between them. Harry Chapin's sad tale of an ageing disc jockey had been playing on the radio around the place all day. It was playing in my head when Mum took this picture.

My brother has his right foot up on the wall, the left dangling down – a semi-ironic pose for the camera (and, at eleven years old, Ian was more than capable of mischievous irony). My dad has his hands clutched in front of him and looks straight into the camera, his face set in the same half-apologetic smile that he always had in photographs. He looks exactly like I do now: thick-set but paunchy, bespectacled, willing. I know exactly what he was thinking, too. He was thinking, *I'm happy here but it isn't going to last*.

And me? I have my hands on my hips, my shoulders slightly hunched. I was worried because I was supposed to be somewhere else. It was Good Friday, arguably the holiest day of obligation, and I should have been in church, singing with the rest of the choir.

All afternoon and well into that early evening, when my mum came up and took this picture of us, I was asking Dad to tell me the time. You can just see his watch in the picture, worn on the inside of his wrist. He'd flick his hand round and say 'five thirty', 'six o'clock', 'six fifteen'. In my head I'd be clambering onto my bike, riding away, reaching St Mary's, climbing to the choir gallery . . .

But my bike stayed where it was, locked up round the back of the lodge somewhere, and I stayed where I was too. There were too few days like these. I clung onto them.

Dad had left Kodak earlier in the year. In the centre of Harrow, close to The Railway Hotel, where The Who had played some of their earliest gigs, a massive new civic centre had been built. It was modern, concrete, handsome in its way. There were fountains at the front and long, low water channels for them to spout into. Rows of trees were planted; a vast car park built. It looked like progress.

To the right of the main building, as you looked from Harrow's main highway, Station Road, was the brand-new civic-centre library, a lower, narrowish building with a ramp leading up to it. It was here, finally, that Dad was to find a job in which he was happy and a boss – Mr Ball – whom he liked.

Dad had always loved libraries. He was a connoisseur of them. Though the Kenton library was handiest, he would often cycle the mile or so to Wealdstone Library, head up into Harrow to visit the more modern Gayton, or even out to West Harrow and Pinner, where the small libraries had a rather more snobbish air about them. It was all the same to Dad: he delighted in them all. His library tickets had pride of place in the little plastic wallet he carried.

Dad's official title at the civic-centre library was 'library porter' but he had soon widened it out to 'general handyman'. Not since Edgware had he been so popular among his fellow staff – or so keen to take me in with him. 'You'll love it there, Mart,' he insisted to me one evening: 'it's a beautiful library.' 'Beautiful' was one of my dad's greatest acclamations.

I cycled up to meet him one evening in the early spring of 1974. It had been raining, and the damp, sitting on the pocked concrete skin of the civic centre, was drying out in a blaze of golden, late-evening sun.

Dad had told me to pedal through the car park and then 'wheel round' to the back of his building. He emerged from a smart, blond-wood door at the back, shielding his face with his hand and smiling. 'It's glorious, Mart, isn't it? Bloody glorious.' He was talking about the sunshine, but he could have been discussing his job, his prospects now. He had on his trusty green pullover, with shirt-sleeves, as ever, rolled up.

The part in which Dad worked was not a 'library' in the sense that I knew it – tall rows of bookcases and a stamping-in desk; that all must have lain elsewhere, if it was there at all. His area was a confusion of smaller rooms, the largest of which had microfiche machines, great binders full of cuttings from the *Harrow Observer* and local history books.

He took me down into a little office. 'I'm building them some more shelves,' he said, 'and making suggestions about how they can store some of the stuff they've got lying around.' He indicated some lengths of wood in the corner and I recognized them as ones he'd had squirrelled away at home.

'Your dad is bloody marvellous.' This was a tall, plump blonde woman who had bustled in, carrying arm-fuls of folders. 'He's really got us organized here.'

My dad, sitting on a child's stool he must have salvaged and taken into his little space – Dad was the ultimate collector of useful items – laughed, embarrassed. 'Well . . .'

'No, he is, he's brilliant.'

This was a word I'd never heard about my dad before. It hung in the air between the three of us unfamiliarly, like a balloon that had floated in.

'Anyway . . .' said the woman, and she was gone.

'Oh. One thing I *don't* like . . .' my dad said, and he took me by the arm. There was a small pile of large-sized art books on a table in an adjoining room. He picked one of them up and opened it. The first few pages had been torn out, including the one where the borrowing label would normally be glued. He held it as you might an injured animal. 'Terrible,' he said. 'See?'

I thought children, vandals, must have been to blame.

'I have to do this,' he said. 'I have to tear the first few pages out and then chuck 'em.'

This was how all libraries, I subsequently found out, dealt with books deemed irreparable or too shabby for continued lending. They were not allowed, apparently, to sell them or give them away: they had to be destroyed.

'Anyway,' said my dad. 'I'm not chucking them all.'

We went back into his room and he fished out his duffel bag and pulled open the top. Inside were two big volumes – *Picasso's Graphic Works* – illustrated with full-page reproductions of sketches, etchings and prints.

'Dad!' I was alarmed.

He shook his head. 'You can't throw stuff like this away. It's all bloody wrong.'

Of course I agreed with him (and the books are still on

my shelf today) but why, I thought, put the best job he'd ever had on the line for this?

He pushed the books back into his bag and leant down to put his arms round my head. 'Don't worry, eh? Don't worry.' I felt the cold skin of his cheek against my forehead.

A big part of Dad's job was to travel out to the different libraries in the borough to carry out routine maintenance. Sometimes he'd stand in for a caretaker who was ill or on holiday.

He'd always dreamed of working outdoors, of having a creative role – and here it was. He began to use the same language in relation to the libraries and their staff as he used towards hospitals and doctors: 'See, I can help these people. I can do things for them, make things for them.' He was a man of responsibility.

Dad always cycled – and often I'd go with him, listening to his stentorian wheezing as we pedalled up to Wealdstone or West Harrow. He had short brown overalls, and would carry the big set of keys for each building. When we arrived, Dad let himself into various rooms, offices and cubby-holes and I was thrilled by the idea of being somewhere the public didn't usually go. It felt important to be, as I thought of it, 'backstage' or 'behind the scenes' in these places. When Dad finally located the big panel of switches and brought the lights up on the ranks of empty study tables and chairs, the serried rows of bookshelves, it was as exciting as the curtain going up in a theatre. 'Tell you what, Mart,' he'd say, 'you sit yourself down over there with some books and I'll get on and get finished. I'll see you back here in half an hour.'

Then he'd disappear. After ten or fifteen minutes, hearing no sound from elsewhere in the building, I'd become curious. Inevitably I'd find him standing between the big tall shelves, a couple of overflowing waste-paper bins at his side, leaning his right elbow against a row of books and flicking through a novel or a volume on aquarium fish. 'All right, son? I was just on my way to empty these.'

That's how we ended up at Harrow Weald Lodge that Easter. A tall, square, formal house with sandy rendering, it was set back from the main road by a wide sweep of green and shielded by a couple of very old, very bent trees. I was pleased it couldn't really be seen by passing cars. There were large, neat terraced gardens at the back, divided by old walls of different heights on which my brother and I 'tightrope-walked' and chased.

We had never seen lawns so green and immaculately cut and Dad said his own grass would look like that soon. He crouched down and stroked the little blades gently, as if the lawn were a cat.

The people at the civic-centre library had asked him to 'look after' the lodge over Easter, but I never really knew what that meant. He emptied waste-paper bins, he moved some boxes of documents around and shifted a bit of furniture: but the whole place was immaculate. It reeked of polish and expensive wooden surfaces. It had a couple of offices in it, but it didn't look like anyone worked in them. The typewriters were shrouded in grey plastic covered with dust. There were no teacups or pictures of relatives on the walls. There were a few, larger empty rooms with felt-covered tables and strange old carved sideboards with nothing in them.

Looking back, I suppose it was a conference centre of some sort. But to us it was a mystery, an enigma: a house waiting for something to happen.

Why were those three days so memorable? Why, all these years later, do I think of them so often? I suppose that for me, a child of the generation who had read *The Phoenix and the Carpet* or *The Lion, the Witch and the Wardrobe* – those Edwardian books where the families lived in houses with servants – Harrow Weald Lodge fulfilled some sort of longing. But it was more than that. By casting us away, alone, in that beautiful old house, it felt, strangely, as though the outside world had woken up to us at last. I was a snob in that I felt our family – and my dad, in particular – deserved more attention and respect from those who might think we were poor and uneducated. We'd been trusted with the house because we were a family who could appreciate it – and someone had recognized that. Who that 'someone' was, I didn't know.

* * *

Dad's new-found vigour lifted Mum's spirits – and ours. Out on the wall that spring my mum and the neighbours buzzed with it.

Reg, ex-GPO, former navy man, liked jobs with responsibility – and, ideally, a uniform attached to it. Dad's overalls impressed him. He liked, too, the idea that one of us from the street was working at the new civic centre. 'It's good, Ron, it's good.'

My dad had his bike leaning on the wall at the front. He'd just cycled back from work and he still had his bicycle clips on above the brand-new Dr Marten shoes he'd bought. The new job filled Dad with confidence. He must have been earning a bit more money. As well as the shoes, he bought himself a new sports jacket and gave Mum some cash 'to treat herself'.

He was also eagerly planning a brand-new pond in the garden – 'something a bit deeper' – and some big goldfish to go in it: 'breeders', as he called them. Dad was an accomplished spender. Money slipped through his fingers. It had no value to him in itself. But Mum did not discourage him: we were nearly always short of the stuff, but when we had a little extra it was spent.

A few weeks after he started work at the civic centre, he splashed out on tickets for us to see Michael Crawford in a musical called *Billy*, based on *Billy Liar*, at the Drury Lane Theatre in Covent Garden. Dad liked Michael Crawford, who had become a big star as a result of the TV series *Some Mothers Do 'Ave 'Em*, which made my dad roar with laughter, but he also remembered him from the Sixties and films such as *Here We Go Round the Mulberry Bush*. 'He's a good actor. A very serious man,' Dad told me one night, as we were watching Crawford dangling over a cliff from the end of an exhaust pipe.

I had not been to a proper London theatre before. Most Christmases we'd shiver through an ice show at the Empire Pool, Wembley, always promising ourselves we'd bring a rug to put across our knees the following year. There had also been travelling players who came to our school and performed embarrassing plays with a moral or social message. But Drury Lane . . .

It was a very warm day, sunny and bright. As we approached the theatre I remember shielding my eyes in the glare. There was a large crowd of people round the door of the theatre, but there didn't seem to be many children among them. I tightened my grip on my dad's hand.

We were a long way from the stage and everyone on it seemed very small. There was a bedroom and, below it, reached by a ladder, a lounge, which also doubled as the funeral parlour where Billy worked. Whenever Michael Crawford appeared, Dad would touch me on the arm and nod, and, if the actor said something funny or broke into song, he would laugh quietly or make little remarks to himself that were loud enough, just, for others to hear – 'Marvellous', 'Oh, that's good' – until Mum poked him and told him to keep quiet. He was showing everyone around that he had a relationship with the star: he was taking proprietorship of Michael Crawford.

About thirty minutes into the show, and just as a big song-and-dance number had finished, one of the co-stars, George Sewell, stepped onto the stage. 'I'm sorry, ladies and gentlemen, but I am going to have to ask you all to leave, very slowly and calmly please, by the nearest available exit. We have had a bomb scare.'

There was some muttering around the audience.

I glanced at Mum, who looked anxious, and then started to get up. Dad was fiddling, absent-mindedly, with the usual array of carrier-bags, pullovers, and so on, under the seat. But he was still staring at the stage. The curtain was closing, rather cleverly I thought, on the chorus boys and girls frozen in place where they'd finished their routine.

Finally Dad blew out his cheeks and glanced at me. 'He's good, isn't he?' he said. 'What's his name again?' He flapped his hand at my mum, who was standing up and fidgeting to leave. 'What's that bloke's name, Peg? From *Special Branch*.'

'Oh, I don't know, Ron.' Mum sounded exasperated. 'I just don't want us to get blown up.'

'Yes, you're right,' my dad said, as if she'd asked him if he thought a choc-ice was a good idea. 'Your mum's right.'

We were made to stand across the road from the

theatre. I was amazed, when I looked across at the few knots of stewards and programme-sellers and officious-looking men in suits still gathered at the front of the theatre, to see George Sewell there again. He seemed to be supervising something.

'Ooh, exciting – we're all going to be blown up,' my brother joked, wide-eyed with mock horror.

'Shut up, Ian,' my mum said, thumping his arm. She drew her coat round her. 'Do you think we ought to just go, Ron?'

'No, no, we'll be all right,' my dad said. He had his arms behind his back, his wrists together, fully at ease with the situation. 'Anyway,' he said, loud enough for those around us to hear, 'Special Branch is in charge so we'll be OK.'

A few people looked round, with smiles, hearing my dad say this, and he smiled back, glad of the attention.

'Did you hear what I said, Peg?' He nudged my mum in the hope of repeating his joke, but she just tutted – and the 'tut' was meant for the crowd too.

In the end it was George Sewell who called us back in. He came to the edge of the opposite kerb, very smartly dressed in his silvery-grey suit, and yelled across, 'Ladies and gentlemen, the fire brigade inform me we can get started again.'

I noticed that one or two of the audience headed for Sewell now they'd been given the all-clear, no doubt hunting for autographs, or to repeat a version of my dad's joke about the Special Branch. But now the drama was over, the wind seemed to have been taken out of my dad's sails and neither he nor my mum seemed to be in a rush to return.

'Have you got everything, Peg?' he said, and made a big deal of sorting through all the jumpers and bags again as the crowd rushed past us. Dad liked disruptions. He liked a break from the ordinary. Now it was over he seemed disappointed. It was just a show again, not the Show That Had the Bomb.

As we were filing back in, someone in the orchestra hit the timpani – bang! – and most of the audience, including my mum and me, jumped out of our seats. My dad, though, was laughing even before the noise had echoed away. A voice on a microphone from the back of the stage said, 'Sorry about that,' over the PA system – and Dad thought he recognized Michael Crawford's voice.

This really set him off. 'Oh, he's brilliant, Michael Crawford. He's got such a great sense of humour, hasn't he, Peg?'

My mum, who didn't seem at all happy to be back in the theatre – let alone the victim of a silly prank – nodded unenthusiastically. 'Yes, he's very good.'

Dad was very quiet on the way home. We got some fish and chips. When he'd finished his, Dad rubbed the stubble on his cheek, like he always did when he was planning something. He said he thought the music in

Billy was very good. He'd been saying it all day. He leant back in his chair. 'I think I'll go up,' he said to my mum.

'But it's only seven o'clock.'

'Yeah,' Dad pushed his chair back, 'but I've had it, Peg – I'm worn out.' He leant across and gave my mum a kiss, then Ian and me. I heard him stomping, slowly and heavily, up the stairs.

My mum was leaning across. 'Thank him, Mart. Have you thanked him?'

I ran to the bottom of the stairs. 'Thanks, Dad.'

He peered over the banisters on the top landing. He looked pale and odd. 'Did you enjoy it?' he said.

'It was great, Dad, really great.'

Dad nodded and went to bed.

On Monday Dad came home with the soundtrack to *Billy* and put it on. Then he sat on the sofa, nodding along and laughing at some of the words. There was one song, 'Some of Us Belong to the Stars', which he played again and again. I thought it was odd because I could hear Michael Crawford's camp Frank Spencer voice in his singing tone, but Dad shook his head: 'This is a brilliant song. Brilliant.'

After a while he took the record off and disappeared upstairs.

Mum walked in on him up there about half an hour later. He was sitting on the edge of his bed, but had twisted round so that his left elbow was resting on the eiderdown, his right hand writing, in ballpoint, on the sleeve of *Billy*. 'What are you doing, Ron?' my mum asked him.

'I'm doing a bit of work.'

Mum wanted to see what he was writing but, she told me later, she didn't dare: she didn't know what sort of mood he was in.

Dad hid the sleeve, but the next day, when he cycled off to work, she found it. She showed it to me when I came in from school. It was covered in words which were printed in block capitals and arranged in vertical and horizontal lines so that they intermingled with one another like portions of a crossword puzzle. In one place he had written MICHAEL CRAWFORD across, then my name MARTIN down, using the 'A' in Michael. Through the word CRAWFORD he'd threaded the name ALF RAMSEY. He had written 'all geniuses' and 'God bless them'.

'Here we go again,' said Mum.

22

Some of Us Belong to the Stars

Dad had always scrawled on things when he was 'high': newspapers, magazines, photographs. He would revisit the same subjects: God, Alf Ramsey, Frank Sinatra. The process would be desperate, feverish, the pen pushed into the paper as if he was carving the words.

He would print declarations – 'A Very Clever Man' – or asides that seemed like diary entries – 'He Was Always Good To Us'. Sometimes there'd be messages – 'Peg does not understand' – with the 'not' double or triple underlined; he was very fond of underlining things. He didn't hide these jottings, but neither did he actually show them to any of us. They were like ancient inscriptions, just left to be found. We didn't ask him about them, either. Like many of the things he did when he was high, it would have felt wrong, even dangerous, to have mentioned them: like waking up a sleepwalker.

It shamed us but my brother and I often laughed at

these pictures. We were *Monty Python* fans and they appealed to our zany sense of humour. Nobody wrote on photographs, did they? But here was Dad, taking some of his best shots of us as babies – beautifully composed in black and white – and writing across our foreheads. Once he'd selected a photo of me, aged five or six, crouched in the back garden with a football, and carefully made his comment curve round the ball. 'Pick him, Sir Alf.'

Years later, during a terrible time for him, physically and mentally – when the world really did seem to have slipped away – he wrote and drew in indelible black directly on the walls of my old bedroom at Cullington Close. I'd moved out by then.

Mum had not been well. She'd had some problems with her right wrist and was suffering a lot of pain with it. The last thing she needed was Dad to be high again, but it seemed inevitable.

He took the *Billy* sleeve up to Drury Lane one Saturday afternoon in the hope of getting Michael Crawford to sign it, but, for reasons I never discovered, his quest failed. At some point during that day he rode in the back of a black cab, fell into conversation with the driver, and ended up buying a ticket for Frank Sinatra's concert at the Albert Hall.

Mum was furious. The ticket cost £50, an unthinkable amount to spend, even on Frank. For a day or two her anger was such that Dad's ascent into mania was checked. He stopped scribbling, his restlessness appeared to abate. Somehow her long sulk seemed to be sobering him up.

Mum went to the hospital about her wrist and was referred to a clinic. They plastered it tightly, binding a little metal support into the bandages. She had no energy now to keep up the argument over Sinatra. Dad began to slip off into long silences after tea; then, as we watched TV in the front room, he would pace in from the kitchen, then back out into the kitchen; into the front room and then out into the garden; up the stairs, round his bedroom, then back down into the kitchen.

Mum sat in her chair, her wrist leaning on the armrest, and shook her head in dismay. 'He's driving me bloody mad.'

Dad appeared in the front room again.

'Sit down, Ron.'

He looked at her blankly. 'Yeah,' he said, 'yeah' – and walked out again. We heard him pick up some teacups in the kitchen, then put them down.

When he wasn't pacing, he was playing records: Frank Sinatra, Dean Martin and the *Billy* album. 'Some of Us Belong to the Stars' rang constantly in our ears.

My mum intercepted a soft, bulky envelope he had left on the side to post. It was addressed to Michael Crawford, Drury Lane Theatre. She carefully eased open the gummed flap, wincing at the pain from her wrist. She didn't trust me to do it without tearing it. Inside was a pair of men's underpants. On the material, in ink, it said: 'Best of luck, Michael – from Ron.'

Later, she challenged my dad about it. He'd perched himself briefly on the sofa, his sad, dead eyes on the TV.

'What you got in that envelope, Ron?'

'Eh, what?'

'That envelope out there,' my mum said. 'What is it?'

He turned and looked at the door into the hall, then looked at Mum.

He waved the question away. 'Oh, it's nothing.'

'You're not going to send it, are you?'

I drew my legs up a little in my chair. Mum was on dangerous ground.

'Yeah . . . yeah, I'm going to send it.' He licked his lips. He was looking at the television again. 'It's for, er . . . it's for Michael Crawford.'

My mum glanced at me. She folded her arms. She wasn't going to risk saying anything else.

He put his thumb and forefinger either side of his nose and used them to push up his glasses and rub his eyes slowly. It was something I'd seen him do a hundred, a thousand, times and it always, somehow, moved me. Why do you love someone more for a little foible like that?

He seemed, then, to think of something. 'Peg,' he said. 'Do you think my sports jacket'll be all right for Sinatra?'

Mum frowned. 'What, to send him?'

It was not like my mum to be flippant and it was a silly thing to say. She knew as well as I that when Dad was high his concentration levels fluctuated widely. If he'd suddenly become focused enough to ask her a question, surely her answer had given away that she'd sneaked open his envelope?

Dad's red-rimmed eyes rested on her for a second but he simply seemed puzzled. 'No, no,' he said. 'To *wear*, for the Albert Hall.'

I breathed out again.

'Oh, yeah.' My mum sniffed. 'It's a lovely jacket, that. Very nice.'

'You've got to dress up for him, haven't you?' he said. He looked across at me. 'You've got to dress nice for Frank, eh, Mart?'

I nodded.

The envelope disappeared. Mum bit her bottom lip and tutted. 'Something like that turning up for him at the stage door. We'll have the police round.'

In the evening, after he'd cycled home from work, and listened, unhearing, to what my brother and I had been up to at school, Dad continued his restless wandering from room to room. He'd begun 'planning out' his new pond, so when he wandered into the back room he would pause, stand with his hands on the edge of the dining table and stare at some drawings he'd made.

Later, when we were alone, I asked Mum what she planned to do about Dad's illness.

Still in pain with her wrist, Mum was irritated. 'Martin, it's up to him. I do it every time. Then he finds out I'm doing it and there's rows – shouting and yelling. He can sort himself out this time.' The light from the TV flickered on her face. I knew she didn't mean any of this, that she would do what was necessary. But she suddenly looked quite drawn and old. 'I don't want him getting nasty,' she said quietly.

'Oh well, at least he's going to work OK,' I said.

She shook her head. 'Oh, I've had a call from *them*. From Mr Ball. They said they were worried about Dad, that he seemed a bit distracted.'

'He's not going to lose his job, is he?' I was genuinely anxious about this.

Mum shook her head. 'I don't think so. Mr Ball knows all about him.'

What an idiot Dad is, I thought, and then realized how hopeless that notion sounded in my head.

A couple of days later Dad started digging out the pond. He wore one of his old nylon work shirts, and big, floppy shorts. I went out to watch him. There were still wisps of spider-web on his wellington boots. I noticed he'd put on weight. His face was red.

He was digging quite manically and I thought of going back indoors. In the end I picked up a smaller shovel and helped him start banking some of the earth round the sides.

'I'm going to build a rockery,' he gasped. He rubbed the dirt and sweat on his cheeks.

I wondered where he was going to get the rocks.

Reg had come down to the fence.

'Oh, shit,' my dad said under his breath, which pleased me. Maybe he wasn't as ill as I thought.

'New pond, Ron?'

My dad was too polite not to straighten up and smile. 'Yeah, I thought I would.' He blew out his cheeks and gave a little laugh.

'If you need any tools . . .' Reg said, but he was already moving away to his shed, opening the door, switching on the weak little light inside.

'Oh, thanks, mate.' Dad was pleased to see Reg had something to do. 'He's not a bad old stick,' Dad said to me, stealing a phrase of my mum's, and jabbed his heavy shovel back into the hard yellow clay.

I heard the rattle, two gardens away, of Neville Brown's peanut tin as he called his racing pigeons down from the roof.

Just as my mum's disdain could 'sober' him for a while, so hard work levelled out his moods. If he was high it re-anchored him to earth. He must have been aware of this because he would often over-exert himself: work too long or too hard on a project. Sometimes, also too late. Once, when building shelves in the front room, he'd hammered and sawed wood long into the small hours. The tendency was to assume he was as high as a kite. The reality, perhaps, was that he was trying not to be.

Dad carried on digging for a couple of hours and then went into the back room for a smoke. He didn't pull his wellies off, but laid some sheets of newspaper under his armchair and rested his booted feet on those. He didn't really want to stop. He blew some smoke rings for me.

'The pond's going to be fantastic, Dad.'

'It is, son, it is.' He leant back in his chair and savoured his cigarette, his eyes resting, seemingly, on the polystyrene coving at the top of our walls. 'Should have done it years ago. Get some really big fish and let 'em grow.'

'How deep you going to make it?'

No answer.

'How deep, Dad?'

He looked at me blankly. 'Oh, yeah. Deep,' he said. He looked sad for a moment. Then he began pulling off his wellies.

It rained for three or four days. Dad sat sullenly inside, peering out of the back-room window. He was desperate to get at his pond, 'get the bloody thing finished'. The rain had made it all a chore.

He stood up, flexed the fingers of his hands, paced, blew his cheeks, put another record on. 'Some of Us Belong to the Stars'.

Returning from school a few afternoons later, I let myself in through the back door. The rain had stopped that morning but it had been drizzling again steadily since lunch-time. The sky, bruised and black, with a few, pale veins of sick-looking yellow, pressed down. My blazer was soaked through and my neck was red where I'd turned the collar up and it had chafed my skin.

Mum was in the kitchen. She put her finger to her lips and pointed out of the window. 'He's knocking down the shed.'

'Knocking it *down*?' I pulled a tea-cloth out of one of the drawers and went into the back room, towelling my hair.

There was a ferocious banging and knocking coming from the shed and then Dad, in his vest, backed out of the shed door. He had a sledgehammer in his hands. He leant back in and heaved out a couple of lumps of jagged-looking concrete.

My mum had come to stand beside me at the window. 'He said he needs a rockery, so he's knocking down the wall inside.'

'He's only in his vest,' I said.

'Well, he's a bloody fool, isn't he?'

The banging started up again and then came a yelled 'Fuck!' I ducked away from the window as he sprang back out of the shed again, clutching his foot. I couldn't help laughing, but Mum was not in a humorous mood.

'Serves him bloody right,' she said.

'Mum!'

'Well, it does. Reg told him, Mr Chapman told him: "If you knock down that wall, the whole bloody lot will come down on you." Well, I hope it does. I hope it comes down on his head.'

'Oh, come on . . .'

But she was furious. 'Well, I've had enough of it, Mart – ponds, rockeries, his bloody moods. I don't know whether I'm coming or going.' And then, quite suddenly, and so quickly – I'd barely been in the house a few minutes – Mum was crying. Great big tears coursed down her cheeks.

'Oh, Mum.' I tried to hug her, but she slipped out of my grasp and back into the kitchen.

'Don't mind me,' she said. 'I'm just a silly old fool.'

Dad came in about twenty minutes later. He sat on the step and pulled off his boots. He stripped off his vest in the kitchen, popped the top off a pint of milk with a muddy fingernail, then drained it, straight off, from the bottle. He belched and went upstairs. He hadn't said a word.

I was in the back room making a display of laying out my homework things. It was, I thought, an easy way to avoid getting into a row with him. I heard the bath running upstairs.

'Well, at least he's *having* a bloody bath.' My mum came down as he went up. 'He's going to see Frank

323

Sinatra tonight. Perhaps Frank'll take him home with him.' She made herself laugh with that.

Mum put her hands behind her back and looked out into the rainy garden. The lawn was covered with massive pieces of stone. It stood off the lawn like torn paper in the yellow light.

'He could make three bloody rockeries with that,' she said.

'Well, perhaps he will,' I said.

Mum had crushed up some tablets in his tea, she said, to try to calm him down on his return from the Albert Hall. Sinatra had been 'no bloody good', Dad said.

My mum pulled a face in sympathy.

'He mumbled,' Dad said, 'mumbled through it.'

I felt disappointed for my dad. I imagined the old man, Frank Sinatra, meandering about the stage. I'd seen him a few times on television. He carried the microphone under his nose, like it was a candle to light him off to bed, and spoke over the top of it.

Dad had been the only one who was not in evening dress. 'Everyone had bow-ties on. Bloody bow-ties.' He wrenched at his own skinny brown felt tie. He pulled undone the laces on his Dr Marten shoes but kept them on, leaning back on the sofa. 'Get us a cup of tea, Peg.'

Mum didn't look at me.

23

Goodbye Yellow Brick Road

We got the bus up to Harrow town centre to buy the new fish for our pond. We strolled up to 'Bessborough Bridge'. It was one of our favourite places: a steep hill that sloped up away from the cutting where the main railway line ran out of Harrow-on-the-Hill station. A little row of shops clung to the slope: old-established and, up until a few years later, when the council homogenized the town with building societies and chain stores, permanent.

We loved this street, my dad and I, because it had the aquarium shop and a model shop with one of those windows full to bursting with plastic aeroplane kits, working steam engines and other delights. We hardly ever bought anything in either of these places, but Dad was a great one for regular visits to 'have a look'. As he gazed round, he would rattle the change in his pocket as if his desire to buy might transmit some sort of alchemy into his fingers.

The aquarium shop was painted white and there were tanks all round the wall, flickering and glittering with fish. Dad was so excited that the remarks he made for my benefit were really for his own. 'Calm down, Mart, we've got to get the right one. Some beautiful fish here, *beautiful*.' The soft, diffused light from the tanks reflected on his face, making his hunger look beatific. 'Look at those!' He pointed at some marine fish in vivid yellows and blues. He straightened up a little and looked back towards the counter, wanting his compliments to be heard. 'Gorgeous. They're absolutely gorgeous. Take some keeping though, Mart.'

He held a warning hand up to me and again glanced back to the man at the till. 'That's right, isn't it, mate?'

The man, who was about fifty, tanned, with neat grey hair and the satisfied look of a regular golfer, took his cue. He swung over, nodding. 'Are you interested in marines, young man?'

I looked at him, trying to translate the cost of these fish into the quality of his clothes. He had a grey jumper with a zipped neck and a button-down check shirt.

'Not really. I'm more into cold-water.'

Dad immediately took my side: who did this man think he was? 'We like cold-water,' said my dad, with a slightly condescending tone. 'I've just built a pond, you see.'

The man nodded and pursed his lips. He didn't have us down as marine people. 'Got some beautiful cold-water specimens,' he said, becoming the salesman.

Specimens. I was hoping for a microscope for my birthday. I imagined a fat fish wriggling on the slide.

'Oh, in'eresting, in'eresting,' said my dad, finding no better equivalent for 'specimens'.

The man guided us round a series of larger tanks in which goldfish and orfe and little tench were jabbing and nosing at the glass. 'Some beautiful fish here,' he said, but he said it over the top of the tanks: it was my dad and I who crouched down to look.

The goldfish we chose were £1.50 each. A king's ransom. A male and a female, plump and bright orange: Dad didn't favour the fancy, multicoloured ones, or 'shubumpkins' as he called them. He counted out the coins from a little red plastic zip-up purse. We brought them home in a plastic bag inside a cardboard box.

Dad insisted that we lower the fish into the pond in their bags so that the temperature of the water they were in would match that of the pond, 'and they won't die of shock'. He straightened up. 'We'll give them an hour,' he said doubtfully.

But twenty minutes later he was out there undoing the bags. He couldn't resist. 'Get us some scissors, Peg,' he said irritably. The knot wouldn't give under his big, excited fingers.

She stuck her tongue out at him. She was feeding him tablets now, morning and night: had him more or less under control. She smiled at me.

'They're big bastards,' Dad said, as they swam out into their new home. It was one of his greatest compliments. It was used for footballers, boxers, people he worked with or met at bus stops. He had great admiration for 'big bastards'.

Dad's new pond was kidney-shaped and enormous – seven or eight feet long and eighteen inches deep in the middle. It sat behind the far wall of his shed, a few feet from Mrs Herbert's garden fence, and it had a shallow shelf at either end on which he stood water lilies. He'd fixed up a little waterfall into it – a section of plastic pipe that spilled water into a little gully made of the same rubber lining he'd used for the pond. It was very impressive. He'd used all the stone, the whole wall of the shed, to build a rockery around it.

The Herberts, Tom and Elsie, came out. Their gloomy, elderly dog, Tensing, limped round the lawn behind them, sniffing half-heartedly at the lawn. I had no idea, then, that Tensing was named after Sir Edmund Hillary's famous Sherpa and so I associated it with the dog's permanently anxious state of mind. It had a coat of tight wiry black curls and smelled horrible. The Herberts' plain, untidy house smelled of the dog too and so I hated going in there.

'All right, Ron? You've done a lovely job there,' said Mr Herbert. He was a small, friendly, professional man with a beautifully kept greenhouse.

Mrs Herbert nodded at his side. She had badly fitting

dentures, which pushed her chin forward and made her look slightly simian. She was a lovely woman and had always been very kind to my mum.

Dad folded his arms and nodded. He *had* done a good job. 'Pop round and have a proper look if you like,' he said.

But the Herberts were already shaking their heads. '*Oh no*, we can see it from here.'

They had never been in our garden, and would never come, as my father well knew. They were old-fashioned, suburban people with an almost religious respect for fences, hedges, boundaries. Once I had opened their front gate to try to see where the old crow had gone and Tom Herbert had almost immediately opened his front door. 'Anything I can help you with, Martin?'

The Herberts shared a roof with the Browns but Neville Brown's pigeons never strayed onto their half.

Dad's invitation was Mrs Herbert's cue to shiver in her apron. 'We'll have to go in now, Tom.'

Tom took her arm. 'Lovely pond, Ron. Really lovely.' The pair of them edged away along the path, the dog sniffing the back of Mr Herbert's slippers.

'My shed's "open-plan" now,' Dad suddenly said one dinner-time, a couple of nights later, testing the unfamiliar phrase rather nervously.

I laughed, thinking what a clever joke it was, but he was back concentrating on his food. It hadn't been a joke, it had just been an observation.

Mum frowned and rolled her eyes. All those pills and his mind was still racing.

My dad looked up again, chewing. 'I thought we'd go see Elton John, Mart,' he said. 'Fancy it?'

Elton John was another of my dad's favourites. Dad had come home one evening with the LP of *Don't Shoot Me I'm Only the Piano Player*. Inside the sleeve it had a sort of poster with the lyrics on and Dad had pulled this out and stuck it on the back wall of his shed. Sometimes, when I went in there to fetch the fish food, I'd study the words to his songs and read the musicians' names. I liked a song called 'Blues for Baby and Me' about escaping across America on a Greyhound bus – though I wasn't sure what a Greyhound bus was.

I didn't really want to see Elton John. I liked to go out but not to do anything definite: I just enjoyed meandering round shops or changing my library books or kicking a ball. I didn't want to sit or stand in a big crowd, particularly. Decades later I'd have to manufacture irritation that my own children were exactly the same.

I knew my dad didn't really want to go either, but he wanted to take me. He wanted to show me the concert, to present Elton to me – to watch my face as I experienced something new. I know now what a strong and irresistible instinct this is in a father: I know how much vicarious pleasure there is in it. Back then I rather sourly agreed with myself that I would 'go along with it', smile and make him smile. What nasty, cold, logical people we can be when we are fourteen years old!

The concert was at Watford football ground. I was not afraid or even apprehensive – I couldn't see how a pop concert was anything like a football match – but I was curious to go back to the place, years before, where I had felt so small and young and frightened.

We got the train up to Watford Junction – Dad, Ian and me – then followed the throngs of other fans. It was hard to get my bearings. Where was the road where the cars had been rocked over? Where had we been standing on the terraces? The only thing that appeared to be the same was the broken glass along the top of one of the walls near the turnstiles to deter fans from clambering in. Ian kept asking me if I remembered anything and I nodded.

The sky, a deep, bruised grey, hung low over the vast crowds milling around, so that their noise and chatter was clamped down, lidded. Flurries of rain blew across. I remembered the acrid, over-heated smell of hot dogs from those years before.

I was not ashamed to hold my dad's hand – never would be – but now I looked older boys in the eye. They were a different sort of mob anyway: long-haired, affable. Once or twice someone would turn and I'd think he was going to talk to me, tell me a joke. A few furry, yellow-and-black scarves were tied round wrists.

My brother bowled along in front, his hands in his pockets. His trousers were too short and his big platforms gave him a vaguely menacing air. My dad kept singing the same line, '*I'm a rocket maan*,' and then interrupting himself by pointing something out to us. He made hard work of walking in those days – had done since the printing job – his shoulders slumped, his feet pounding. I could hear his sides wheezing.

Elton was dressed as a hornet – the symbol of Watford – in yellow-and-black furry top and trousers. Dad threw his head back and laughed, shaking his head. He touched my shoulder. 'Look at 'im!'

I was watching the crowd. I was fascinated by the range of ages and types of people. Where did they all come from? How had they first heard Elton John?

My brother did a little dance in his platform shoes, scratching and scraping on the terrace steps. I frowned at him, mouthed 'Stupid boy,' and he pulled a face. I was wearing a brand-new zip-fronted jumper from my mum's Peter Craig catalogue: beige with a Fair Isle design across the top of the chest. It had a big collar that lay flat along each shoulder like the ears of a dog. First of all I kept my coat buttoned over it, not wanting to show off or to have the smell of smoke or hot dogs permeate the wool – I was becoming very vain – but then I unbuttoned my coat and puffed my chest out a bit to put the jersey on show.

We stood there for a couple of hours. Tears rolled down my dad's face when Elton played 'Candle in the Wind'.

'Oh, what a lovely song,' he said to me, and looked across to make sure the man next to me had heard. 'Beautiful.' He took a hanky out of his trouser pocket and blew his nose flamboyantly.

I quite wanted to go home by then. I needed a wee and didn't dare wander away. Then it started to rain. I pulled up my hood. The rain blew across and Dad buttoned his coat too. My brother's plastic hood was so big that he had to raise his head to look out. A few people backed under the canopy of the stand. One or two umbrellas went up.

On the stage, on his piano stool, Elton John swivelled round and shouted something across to one of his band members. Then, suddenly, unforgettably: '*Doo-pe-do-do-doopy-doopy-doop . . .*' Elton meandered, almost apologetically, into 'Singin' in the Rain'.

I looked up at my dad. He'd clamped his lower lip up over his upper one and big tears were rolling down. He shook his head speechlessly. I knew what he was think-ing: *It's what I would have done. If I could have been up there like he is, it's what I would have done.* I could see it written in his face, and I could see, too, the regret, the years of regret, for all the things he hadn't done, would never do.

There were rows and rows of swaying umbrellas now, and Elton was jigging around, conducting the crowd.

My dad looked down. 'And he's from up the road, too. From Pinner.' This, I knew, was not for the benefit of the man next to me or anyone else: this was for me to know.

* * *

Dad couldn't stop spending money. I'd long wanted a racing bike and now he was determined to get me one. He scanned the 'For Sale' columns in the *Harrow Observer* and found an ad offering a bike – 5 gears, VGC – for £14 o.n.o. He picked up his pen and put a ring round the address.

'We'll go round tomorrow night.'

My mum was at the kitchen door. 'You sure, Ron? You're spending a lot of money at the moment.'

My dad spread his arms. 'If you've got it, spend it,' he said. 'What else am I going to do? You'll 'ave your 'oliday.'

But I didn't think it was holidays that Mum was bothered about; her worry was the day when Dad twigged that she'd been feeding him his drugs – the day when the row would break out and in the misery and chaos and weariness of manic depression his job would once more be on the line . . .

After he'd disappeared into the front room to watch telly I picked up the newspaper he'd abandoned. I read the ad for the bike again, picturing it in my mind: sleek, fast, beautifully chromed. I imagined hurtling down Dennis Lane. Then I noticed that he'd marked a second ad. This was definitely not for a bike. I thought about showing it to Mum but changed my mind. I slipped it into the rack under the little coffee table.

I said nothing to Dad and he said nothing to me. It

would be an adventure. I'd have liked a thousand of those. After tea the following evening he pulled on his donkey-jacket, tucked the red purse into the big flap pocket, and steered me out of the front door. 'Wealdstone,' he said.

Wealdstone was one of the villages of the great Harrow conurbation. But if Kenton and Pinner had a haughty suburban neatness about them – certainly back then in the early Seventies – Wealdstone was the shabbier relation. I had always looked down on it a bit. In the labyrinth of small streets near the high street, it was a place of two-up, two-down houses like Coronation Street: narrow, mean and poor-looking. There never seemed to be much street lighting, or people walking around. It was as if the terrible train crash at Harrow & Wealdstone had left the place so stunned that it had withdrawn into itself.

When I was much younger there was a fishmonger at the top of the high street, opposite the station, who sold eels from a wooden box full of water, set on a low table outside. It fascinated me that the water stayed inside the wood. There were always two or three eels in it, thick and squirming, the colour of car tyres. As their backs broke the surface of the water, the moisture disappeared into droplets. Dad and I would stop and look at them, crouching down on the pavement, and then the man would come out and Dad would chat to him.

We did not, that evening, walk as far as the high

street. We turned into one of the bigger residential roads in Wealdstone – Mason's Avenue – and then off into a side-street that turned out to be a cul-de-sac. Dad pulled a piece of paper out of his wallet, studied it and then peered along the house numbers. We entered a garden through a little rickety gate and edged past a moped covered in tarpaulin.

The house was tiny. The staircase came almost to the front door. There seemed to be a lot of chairs with washing on them. I was aware of a woman at the back of the house. The man who brought us in looked very pale and tired. His T-shirt hung over his trousers. He had slippers on. 'About the crab?' he said.

Dad nodded. I was always amazed at his gall. He had no intention of buying it.

The man led us into a front room dominated by a vast tank, which, rather grotesquely, was higher than it was long. It was very brightly lit. The Japanese spider-crab ('*Suit marine enthusiast. Complete with tank and all fittings*') seemed to fill the aquarium. It had a small head and long spindly arms, which it constantly flexed, stirring up motes and specks and clouds of dancing larvae in the water.

The man stood back a little to let us admire it. I wondered how he'd come to obtain it – how a Japanese spider-crab had ended up here, among the washing and copies of *Woman's Realm*. But I kept quiet. I thought it would probably be a long story and I was keen to get on and buy my bike.

'Sixty pounds including the tank and fittings,' he said. 'My wife is . . .' He spread his hands.

'Not keen?' said Dad.

The man frowned and shook his head.

'Sixty pounds, eh?'

'I'll listen to offers,' the man said. He moved across and put his hands on the lid of the tank.

I thought, for one awful moment, that he was going to lift the thing out. I imagined watching it scuttle, dripping, across the carpet. But he was just adjusting some wires on the lights.

It was our cue to retreat. 'I'll have to have a think,' Dad said, scratching his head. 'Can I give you a ring?'

Outside, Dad clapped his hands together and said: 'That was good,' as if we'd just been to an exhibition or show. He put his arm round my shoulder. 'Now let's get your bike.'

24

Father MacCullough

It was the beginning of 1975. I was nearly fifteen years old now. I had long hair that was beginning to grow into a sort of unruly 'Afro'. I wore high-waisted baggy flares with platform boots or shoes and my favourite item of clothing was a bright-yellow sweatshirt with Marilyn Monroe's face screen-printed on the front that I'd bought through a small ad in the back of *Melody Maker*.

I was working in the library on Saturdays and, on Sundays, cycling out with my friend Stephen to go car-washing. We had regular 'clients' now, including a well-to-do man in Stanmore who paid us to wash and polish his Daimler every week and, once a month, saddle-soap the leather upholstery. He had a beautiful house in a road that, we were told, had once numbered Roger Moore among its residents. He had a large tank of tropical fish and, in his back garden, a small swimming pool.

I'd like to recall that I was a rebel, but I hadn't anything to rebel against. At Harrow County I was in the fourth form, moving, inevitably, towards getting a small handful of O levels in the only subjects I'd ever been good at – English and Art.

The 'brutal' school I had entered four years earlier, with its broken and graffiti-covered desks and chairs, had been transformed by a simple, and probably now illegal, method. Groups of boys were corralled into gangs, given wood-working tools, and ordered to repair and sand all the furniture. It should have provoked a riot: thirty years on, it probably would. Instead, gangs of small boys strutting around in oversized goggles and wielding power-sanders became a new school elite. Like Santa's army of helpers, they dragged splintered and pen-stained items down into rooms off the subterranean 'A' corridor and returned them, newly intact, cleaned, planed and varnished.

When my mum and dad came up to the school for the 'open evening' at the end of the summer term, the whole place seemed to sparkle. I can see my dad sitting on a chair up in our English room overlooking the evening traffic on Sheepcote Road. He looked very big in that room, and his brand-new C&A grey jacket looked immaculate among the wood and polish. My English master, Mr Golland – a man I had come to love – stood in familiar chalky black gown, talking and laughing with him.

There is always one very special teacher in your life and 'Jim' Golland was mine. He is the reason I am writing these words. I had been asked, in an exam, to take a famous short story by Ted Hughes – 'The Horses' – and explain its poetic quality. I decided to rewrite it as prose. It was a bit awkward and clunky in places. At the end of the exam I had the sinking feeling that I should have just answered the question and not tried to do anything 'clever'. But Jim Golland had loved it. On that open evening, my mum said later – as my dad looked on, nodding and smiling – he had told them it was 'brilliant' and that I *had* to be a writer. I felt embarrassed, overwhelmed – but I never forgot that imperative. It was a blessing. It was also vindication for my mum and dad. They had never pushed me to do anything – had neither the inclination nor the education, to be honest, to interfere – and so I had just tried to do my best. Unwittingly, perhaps, they had given me independence of mind, the greatest blessing of all.

Dad was starting to put on a lot of weight – and it was beginning to get to him. He had never eaten sensibly – packets of crisps, cakes and biscuits were wolfed down with abandon – and his breathlessness meant he wasn't getting as much exercise as he used to. Years later we would discover that the lithium, too, played its own part in making him fat. Neither the breathlessness nor the weight gain seemed to bother his doctors, and they would turn out to be side-issues in the long-term, but the extra bulk bothered him.

Granddad hadn't helped. Early that spring he and Gran had returned, tanned and healthy, from another stay at posh Dora's villa in Portugal. They drove round to see us one Sunday, bringing some ornaments for my mum and dad, and some sweets for us.

Elb stood back from my dad, cocked his head to one side and said: 'You're getting a size, son.'

My dad just looked embarrassed, pulling at his short-sleeve shirt to try to disguise the ring of fat round his waist. They settled down to play some cribbage but Dad stayed subdued for most of the evening.

Dad was never one to sulk for long. By the following day, having had his self-consciousness about his weight publicly confirmed, he started trying to turn it into a joke.

Dad had always been vain, in an affable, self-deprecatory sort of way. Often when I was around he would glance into the mirror, flick an invisible strand of hair, raise an eyebrow and purr: 'God, Ron, you're a good-looking bloke.'

He had hung a full-length mirror on the landing – banging in the screws with a hammer, naturally – so that whenever he or Mum came out of their bedroom the first thing they saw was themselves. This didn't suit my mum – it wouldn't have impressed any woman, certainly not first thing in the morning – but my dad loved it. He would stand there, in his pants, scratching his balls and casting his head from side to side. Sometimes he'd get up close and examine his teeth. He was very proud of his teeth.

Now he was in front of that mirror again. He lifted the bottom of his green tank-top and pulled in his stomach over the waistband of his old, slate-grey trousers. He was in his socks and his big toe poked out of one. I loved being around Dad when he was in self-critical mood because he was always so funny. He pulled a face in the mirror, sticking his tongue out of the corner of his mouth and twisting his lip up. He kept the pose and the expression and said: 'I'm not too bad, am I, Peg? I don't think I'm particularly fat.'

'No.' Mum was dismissive. She clapped him on the back, quite hard, I thought. 'Your old man's a bloody nuisance,' she hissed – and she wasn't smiling as she said it.

'How do *you* think I look, Mart?' and he twisted his nose and lips round to the right and stuck out his tongue in an impressive gurn.

I laughed and crawled across to the mirror, pulling a similar face for my reflection. Two mad faces, top and bottom of the glass, gawked back.

'We're both lovely,' I said. We held the expression for a few seconds and then started laughing. He kissed me on the top of my head.

As I was walking down the stairs I looked up and saw

my dad turn to the side and let his stomach out again. He looked, suddenly, miserable.

He *had* put on a lot of weight. His breathlessness since taking the printing job had curtailed a lot of his walking and now when he cycled he did so slowly, the bike swaying from side to side as he laboured on the pedals. (He could be quick when he wanted to, though. One night, cycling back from the civic centre, he was passing the block of flats next to the Harrow ABC cinema, which backed onto the Wealdstone FC football ground. The yellow light in the sky over the cinema roof and the familiar chattering hum of a nearby crowd indicated a home game was in progress. Suddenly a football – ghostly white in the sodium yellow of the street lamps – arced through the sky and landed in the service road to my dad's right. In a flash, he dismounted, scooped it up, stuffed it in his duffel bag and pedalled away at high speed. A professional-looking-size Mitre ball graced all our Kenton Park kick-abouts for months afterwards.)

The weight situation wasn't helped by his dressing habits. Dad had never been particularly inclined to wear many clothes about the house. Sometimes he'd have his pyjamas on, sometimes a vest and trousers. Occasionally (when Mum would protest as my brother, inevitably, hooted with laughter) he'd sit down to watch the telly in a pair of underpants from which his testicles and/or penis were making a dramatic escape.

'For God's sake, Ron.' My mum would wrinkle her nose and cross her arms in disgust.

My dad would laugh and look across to my brother for support. 'You've seen it all before!'

'Well, I don't want to bloody see it now.'

As spring turned to summer and the weather became warmer, Dad dragged his old deck-chair out of the shed one Sunday afternoon and set it up on the crazy-paving.

The sunshine, and general activity in the garden, had already brought Reg to the fence. Mum, my brother and I were also on the crazy-paving, drinking tea at the pub-style bench table that Dad had bought the year before. The scene was set, quite literally. Having unfolded the deck-chair to face his beloved lawn, Dad took up his cup and saucer, reversed and sat down in it. There was an absolutely sickening tearing sound – one of those loud, stage rips – and Dad was straight through it, his backside coming to rest neatly on the stone, cushioned only by tattered remains of the thin fabric. He'd had the good sense, somehow, to keep the cup of tea raised high as he made his sudden descent, but inertia is inertia: the tea slopped up in his cup and, a split second after he'd hit the ground, splashed down neatly on his vest.

'Oh, *bugger*!'

My brother, never one to hold back at moments like this, simply exploded into laughter, spraying his own tea out of nose and mouth. Reg, delighted as ever by the sudden arrival of his beloved slapstick, howled. Even Mum, who knew the consequences of such accidents could often be unpleasant, clapped her hand over her mouth.

But it just got better. Now, Dad bellowed, he was 'stuck in the fucking deck-chair'. He simply couldn't get up. He couldn't wriggle free – his backside was jammed in the wooden frame – and if he had gained purchase on the spindly wooden arm-rests the whole lot would have tipped over. So he just sat there, puffing and blowing, trapped and helpless.

Reg was beside himself now. The tears rolled down his face. Auntie Ellen, hearing the commotion from her kitchen, came out too, with her youngest son, Nigel. He stood, rocking with laughter, his hands in his trouser pockets like his dad.

We had to let Dad rest there for a few moments while we all recovered, but then Ian was across – 'Come on, Dad' – and I was there too, taking his arms, helping him up.

Reg shook his head, wiping his eyes. 'Oh, Ron, Ron.' He'd been given an indelible memory, one to be relived, time and again, on the wall.

Dad, bless him, looked across at Reg and shook his head, smiling and puffing, eyes wide – keen not to let Reg think it was any less hilarious to the victim.

And Reg, perhaps remembering, as we all did, the chimney-sweeping incident, was suddenly full of gushing sympathy. 'See, they don't make those bloody things properly any more. I've got one . . .' and he waved his hand vaguely towards his own shed, which was a mirror-image of ours, except more untidy, and with all its walls still standing.

Amid all the laughter, though, the damage was done. For the next ten years, on and off, Dad would be fighting his weight, ultimately with the most tragic of consequences.

The deck-chair incident immediately spurred Dad into action. 'It's fucking ridiculous. I've got to get some weight off me.'

Over the next few days he walked over to my nan's, to Auntie Jean's and even talked about cycling back up to Shenley 'just to have a look'. He thought of all sorts of excuses to cycle down to the corner shop. He even got out his old tennis racket.

I felt sorry for him. I couldn't have cared less what size he was – and neither could my brother. Years later when I put on a bit of weight myself I found it difficult to care unless someone remarked on it, but perhaps that's the case with most people.

Dad was simply not equipped to lose weight. He loved his food, then he liked lying down, full-length, on the sofa to watch TV: no dietician would ever recommend that as a fitness regime. Then there was the problem of the drugs he was taking. Years of lithium were hardly likely to have been beneficial to his body shape.

But he had to do something. In the preceding few weeks – and with a resounding ping! – Dad had snapped two of the rubber bands supporting the sofa cushions and then broken similar supports in his favourite armchair. With his usual resourcefulness he had found a sheet of wood from somewhere and slid it under the chair cushion.

His weight was also beginning to depress him. 'Dark Side of the Moon' would go on the record-player and I'd find him, perched on the broken sofa, staring into space again.

Although our voices had broken long before, Ian and I were still singing in the choir at St Mary's. A new priest, Father John MacCullough, had arrived at our smaller, 'sister' church, The Holy Spirit, and he had started a Friday night youth club. It mainly consisted of the choir, but some boys – and, joyfully for us – girls from the local area had also joined. We brought our singles, in vinyl Woolworths record boxes, and danced to them; we played ping-pong; and then a lad called David Hughes would make us all chips in the church-hall kitchen.

Father MacCullough would look in during the evening and, sometimes, dance to the records, hoisting his cassock up over his elastic-sided slip-ons and dark priest's socks. He was in his early thirties, tall, thin, with bunches of dark curly hair clinging to the sides of a small, prematurely bald head. A man of huge contrasts in mood, he was very serious about his spirituality and inclined to be impatient and ferociously bad-tempered, yet he was also gentle, easily amused and self-confessedly lonely. He told me how little he earned. He was an illustration of the sadness of a priest's life.

Like Brian Apperson, he would invite groups of us round on a Sunday afternoon to play records. He liked Sir John Betjeman's albums with the Jim Parker orchestra and it was in his very formal little back room with its side-tables and upright, 'granny' armchairs that I first heard classical music that I loved: Vaughan Williams' 'Lark Ascending' and – Father MacCullough's favourite – Elgar's 'Dream of Gerontius'.

That summer, as Dad brooded on his weight, Father MacCullough paid a visit to Cullington Close. My mum and dad had met him before, and both liked him – he was not a man who demanded ceremony or fuss – but there was still the frenzied round of vacuuming and polishing before he arrived.

He had organized for us to go on a pilgrimage to the Shrine of our Lady in Walsingham, Norfolk, but he'd come to talk about a much more ambitious trip, a visit to Lourdes, which he was planning in a year or so's time.

I had never been abroad. I had not flown on an aeroplane. (My mum and dad had only flown once and that was to Jersey for their honeymoon. That would be the only time in their lives they left England.)

My parents rarely argued about anything that anyone

in authority wanted my brother and me to do and Father MacCullough, I knew, was only using Lourdes as an excuse to get round and meet some families at home. My mum worried a bit about the cost but my dad, in his customary fashion, waved her query away.

'It doesn't matter, Peg – it'll get 'em out to see some new things, meet some new people.'

Father MacCullough explained about Lourdes itself, about Bernadette and the vision of Mary she had seen in the famous grotto.

'Oh, yes, we saw the film,' my mum said. 'Who was in that, Ron?'

My dad scratched his chin. I knew he hadn't been listening. 'Do you want to have a look at my pond, Father?' he said.

Father MacCullough followed Dad out through the back door. Ducking under the washing line, holding his cassock up over the crazy-paving, he moved daintily, like a ballet dancer.

Dad brought the fish food from the shed and handed it to Father MacCullough, who sprinkled it, jokingly, as if it was holy water. Then he blessed the pond.

My dad's face lit up. 'Oh,' he said, 'oh. That's very kind of you. Isn't that nice of him, Mart? Peg!' he called to my mum in the kitchen and she came down the path. 'He's blessed the pond for us.' He glanced across to the fence to see if Reg had heard the commotion but I thought they must have gone out.

Father MacCullough was enjoying himself. 'You know what this pond really needs, Ron?'

My dad put his hand on his hip and looked intently at Father MacCullough. He had always loved to be engaged in this way. 'Tell me.'

'A gnome.' Father MacCullough sniffed.

My dad's expression didn't change for a moment. Then he straightened and looked at Father MacCullough. 'Yes,' he said, laughing, 'yes, you're right.'

'Come on, then,' said Father MacCullough, and he touched my dad's arm. 'Find me a hat and a rod.'

And so that is how one of my favourite photographs from my childhood came to be taken. There are others – holiday snaps, a wonderful picture of my mum and dad, shivering but happy in the back garden – but Father MacCullough, at the edge of my dad's pond, in a pointy woollen hat that we found somewhere, clutching a little rod of bamboo: that is a photograph that meant so much to my dad.

All his life, those who presumed more authority, education, money – all of these clever people – passed by and paid lip service, not unkindly, to someone who yearned to be among them, working, creating. Father MacCullough, by conspiring, for the simple fun of it, in a joke he knew my father would love, connected instantly with that yearning.

We watched Father MacCullough as he bobbed back up Cullington Close, an unlikely, black-cassocked figure in our road of squalling children and stray dogs.

My dad was still shaking his head. 'Ah, funny,' he said. '*Bloody* funny.'

When, a few weeks later, my brother and I left on our 'pilgrimage' to Walsingham, we were quite relieved to get away. Dad had sunk back into staring silences again.

'I'll be fine,' my mum said: 'you enjoy yourselves.'

Granddad had offered to pick us up. We were meeting the coach at St Mary's but we had a large suitcase between us.

My mum was out on the wall with the neighbours when he drew up. He got out of the car, swinging his keys. He loved an audience.

Reg strolled out of his gate, hands in pockets, attracted by the car. Granddad had a Ford Consul now. 'Elb.'

'Reg.'

Reg nodded at it. 'Running all right?'

'Yeah,' said my granddad. 'Like a dream. Decent car, as it 'appens.'

I wondered where Dad was. As they chatted, I glanced back towards the porch windows but it was dark in there. Ian sat on the wall.

'I'll go and see Ron,' Granddad said. My mum walked with him down the path.

Reg lingered round Granddad's car, leaning in to peer through the windows and crouching to examine the wheel arches.

Granddad came out ten minutes later. He shook his head at me. 'Not well, is he, Martin?' he said quietly.

I shrugged. I didn't really know.

'Bring me back some holy water,' called Reg, laughing. He was standing by his gatepost. 'I'll give it to her and see if she's cured.'

Ellen, on the wall to his left, thumped him on the knee. 'Bloody cheek. Take no notice,' she said to us. 'He's a bloody fool.'

We kissed Mum. Then I saw Dad at the porch window. I thought he'd wave to us, but he was looking the other way, picking his teeth with a matchstick.

25

To Go or to Stay

There was a concrete mixer in our front garden. It had been set down on a couple of old boards and stood, at a rakish angle on the sloping lawn, as if lifting one leg to dance.

I looked at Ian and he attempted a casual shrug. He seemed very young at that moment. His long hair was lighter than mine and curled up at the sides over the big ears that Mum had once, half-heartedly, tried to 'tape down'. She was always worried that he'd be teased about them at school, but Ian was so popular, even with older boys at Harrow County, that it was never even an issue.

'Barney,' he said and gave a low laugh. Mindful of the way Dad careered around causing chaos, Ian had taken to nicknaming him 'Barney Rubble' after the stout little character in *The Flintstones*. He prodded the gate open with the wheel of his bike.

I suppose I knew that something would happen while

we were away. Dad was bored – and he was always at his most dangerous when he was bored. He was also frustrated, because he was getting fat and couldn't get the weight off quickly enough. Life with Dad was a balance of trying not to expose him to anything too dramatic, while making sure he always had something to do: some sort of project. But losing weight couldn't be it. To lose weight he had to keep looking for physical things to do.

Mum came to the door. 'He's in the back garden. He's mending the path.'

'The path?' I looked in her face to try to read his mood.

'He's a bit up and down,' she said, seeing my expression. 'How was your holiday?'

'What do you mean "up and down"? What's he been up to?'

Mum shook her head. 'I don't know, Mart, I really don't – he's all over the bloody place.'

Ian was fishing some little gifts and postcards out of his rucksack. He was already blocking it all out, ignoring it, getting on with things. I couldn't blame him for that, but my stomach was churning.

'How was your holiday?' Mum was asking us both.

'Yeah, yeah, it was good.' I was eager to get in the back room and see what was going on outside.

Dad was crouched on the path by the shed door. He

had a board next to him with wet cement on it, and was trowelling it into the paving.

I went back out through the hall and fetched my bike from the front garden, where I had leant it with Ian's on the hedge. It was my new racer and I wanted to put it away.

I wheeled it down through the back gate.

'Hi, Dad – how's it going?'

He looked up. He didn't have his glasses on – always a terrible sign – and he hadn't shaved.

He straightened up, without saying anything. He seemed to be working something over in his mind. Then, almost as if a wheel had turned, or a switch clicked on, he said: 'Well, while you've been on holiday, I've been getting on with it. Too much to ask for any fucking help from my sons.'

The words hung in the air. I opened my mouth and quickly closed it again. His tone was almost robotic but there was a spiteful edge to it. He didn't look at me. He hadn't looked at me since I'd entered the back garden. He just stared down at his work. The trowel was dangling in his hand and I noticed it was leaving a little ridge of cement on the leg of his trousers. I couldn't move. I felt that, if I did, he would start speaking again and I was worried what he might say.

'Mind your trousers,' I said, finally.

'What?' He looked at me angrily.

'Your trousers, Dad.' I pointed at the mark on them.

He looked down and then tugged at the material. 'I'm not *fucking* bothered about that.' He seemed outraged. 'Only you and Ian worry about things like that. I've got bloody work to do.' But he didn't move. 'I mean,' and his voice had now taken on an edge of wheedling sarcasm, 'if you're worried about things like that . . .' He picked up the board of cement. He was getting worked up. I could see it in his face. He was pursing his lips, breathing hard through his nose. He gritted his teeth.

'It's like *her*, it's like *her* . . .' He waved his hand towards the kitchen window. 'Always worried about some fucking stupid thing. Eh? Eh?' He glared at me, leaning in close, and then he was away, stalking the few short strides towards the back door.

He had never hit Mum, but so often – *so often* – he had seemed as if he was about to. This was one of those moments. My heart leapt up but I couldn't move. I was terrified. I saw him, as he walked past the fence between us and Mrs Herbert's, snatch up a bucket that had been standing there, his arm jerking a bit with the weight of it. And then he was shouting, yelling: 'Peg! Peg!'

I saw my mum through the kitchen window, a flash of panic on her face, and as I followed my dad down the little alleyway to the back door I saw her standing in the doorway between the kitchen and the back room.

'He's come out here like a fucking idiot, eh? The posh boy. *"What are you doing? What are you doing?"*' He mocked me with a girlish whine. 'Well, I'll show you what I'm doing, eh? I'll show you.'

He snatched up the rug from the floor and tossed it to the side. I noticed – how the stupid detail cuts through at times like this – that the corner of it was now resting in the cat food. Then, with his big, dirty hands, he up-ended the bucket – the big, heavy metal bucket crusted with dried cement – and shook it over the kitchen floor.

An awful expression had set hard on his face: an unfamiliar mask of genuine meanness. Even the time he had smashed up the room, swept everything off the mantelpiece, he had not looked like that.

The heavy, gritty, grey cement dangled from the lip of the bucket for a second, then folded itself down over the red tiles: the red tiles that my mum scrubbed and wiped and polished, day in, day out.

'Oh, Ron! Ron!' My mum put her hands to her mouth.

I was at the back door. I shook my head at her.

'"*Ron, Ron*", eh?' he shouted at Mum. '*Eh?* If I want to mix it here, I'll fucking well . . .' He took his trowel. 'I'll fucking well . . .' He stabbed the trowel into the concrete several times, turning it over and over. Then he jammed it into the centre of the heap and stood up. 'None of you help me! *None of you!* Eh? Eh?' He was screaming now, like a teenager. He swivelled round, fists clenched at his sides, and glared at me again. He was wobbling his head, sarcastically now, and his teeth were bared. There were flecks of spittle on his bottom lip. 'Fucking useless, you are,' he said to me. 'No fucking help at all.'

And then he pushed roughly past Mum, thrusting her back against the stove, her elbow banging painfully against the edge.

We heard the front door slam behind him.

I stood there for a moment at the back door. Mum was rubbing her arm and looking from me to the cement on the floor, and the look of panic was still in her eyes, but she didn't cry. Everything seemed to have unravelled. I tried to work out where we were, and how we had got there, but every process seemed endlessly long: the slow winding up to the fury, the slow winding down to depression, and all of us, day after day, wound up in it. We were forever trudging backwards and forwards along the same dull roads.

For a second I was filled with unreasonable, un-reasoning teenage anger. 'Oh, why don't you just *bloody* leave him?'

Mum didn't answer. She put her hands on her hips, glanced down at the cement, up at the kitchen window and reset her shoulders. She looked numb. But she was getting on with it. She pushed past me, walked down to the shed and came back in with Dad's enormous shovel.

'Well, Mum?' I knew I was pushing it, that this was the wrong time to be demanding answers, but I was frightened and we were truly in this together. Dad had never, even when he threatened me with boiling water, turned on me verbally like that before.

'I can't leave him,' she said. 'You know I can't.'

'But *why not*?'

Even as I said it she had paused, both hands gripped on the handle of the shovel. She was half turned from me but I could see her shoulders shaking.

'Mum . . .' I put my arms round her neck and I could feel her tears on my hand.

'Oh, Mart,' she said. 'What are we going to do with him?'

He came in just after nine. I was playing records in the front room so I didn't hear his key scrape in the lock. When I heard the front door open and close, I froze.

He opened the door from the hall and poked his head in. He looked newly tall in the doorway and it occurred to me, afterwards, that I was seeing him now, almost for the first time, as a threatening character.

He didn't look at me. 'Turn it down.'

Then I heard him clump heavily up the stairs. I took the record off.

Auntie Jean had called earlier. He'd been over at her house complaining bitterly that everyone was against him, no one understood what he was trying to do. Then he'd fallen asleep, snoring, in an armchair. He didn't pace in other people's houses.

'We'll just have to keep out of his way,' Mum had said,

sighing, as if this was a new tactic, something we hadn't thought of before.

That summer, I think, was the first time I felt truly depressed about my dad's illness. I was going through the loneliness that afflicts everyone in their early teens – a sense that life is going on elsewhere – and the long, sunny days just seemed endless and dull. I tried to keep busy. I cycled for miles, to Bushey, Elstree, Watford. One afternoon I went all the way to St Albans and back.

On Sundays Stephen Collier and I carried on our car-washing routine. The weekend after the cement incident, when I'd been hoping our car-washing might keep me out of the house for a bit longer than usual, our rich customer asked us to empty and scrub the swimming pool in his back garden. He offered us £15 each to do it. It was an unbelievable sum.

There were only a few inches of green, stagnant water in the pool, but spread across a thirty- by twelve-foot space it was a lot of water. Stephen and I speculated on how many hours it might take: three? four? In the end it took us all afternoon. I kept thinking about Dad. This was the sort of job he'd relish. Suddenly, inexplicably, standing four or five feet down in that big white concrete trough in Stanmore, waiting for Stephen to hand me down buckets attached to pieces of string, I felt irretrievably sad and sick. Where had the years gone with Dad? How much of any of it had been any good?

The customer had given us some strong coffee earlier

– the sort that came as a liquid in a bottle. I pulled myself out of the pool, ran into the shrubs at the edge of his lawn and was spectacularly sick.

Stephen followed. He saw my panic as I straightened up. 'It's all right, mate – they're out at the front.' He handed me a tissue. 'You OK?'

I nodded.

Once the pool was empty the man broke open a cardboard box of Ajax tins and handed them to us. We poured the powder over the heads of a couple of stiff-bristled brooms and scoured the sides of the pool.

We finished at about seven o'clock. The man ran a hose down his lawn and all three of us stood for a while at the edge, watching the pool fill up. Then we were invited up into the dark house, with its heavy furniture and the aquarium murmuring away, and given fruit cake and cream. When the man handed us the three ten-pound notes and shook our hands, it seemed like a watershed: I suddenly felt I had entered the adult world of private transactions.

As we pedalled back down from Stanmore, feeling rich, cocky, our hands off the handlebars, Stephen chatted about what we'd buy with the money and speculated whether we'd be able to clean the man's pool again one day. 'Imagine how much dosh we'd get if it was full!' He almost wobbled off his bike with laughter, theatrically slapping his knee. But I wasn't listening. The sadness I had felt earlier had turned into a sort of ennui and a certain treacherous thought had, for the first time, entered my mind: wouldn't it be great if there was somewhere to go other than home? Wouldn't it be good to be on my own?

A day or so after I'd cycled back from Stanmore with all that unfamiliar money in my pocket and all those strange thoughts in my head, Dad attempted, for a second time, to take his own life.

After the kitchen incident, he had paced the house for a couple of days: lips working, hands flapping aimlessly at his sides. He was wearing his cursed Green Flashes, sockless, and with the laces loose or undone. He had not gone to work. It had not occurred to him to go. Mum had called the civic centre and, she said, 'explained'.

As much as possible, we had stayed out of his way. I, in particular, kept a low profile. For the time being I was hated, loathed: the boy at the grammar school who was 'fucking useless', 'no fucking help at all'.

He put records on – Frank Sinatra, Dean Martin – and as quickly took them off again. He was keen on a Dean Martin song called 'Gentle on my Mind'. *'Oh, it's knowing that your door is always open and your path is free to walk . . .'*

He sat on the edge of his armchair, hands clasped together, nose resting on the top of his thumbs, his big gut spread out, his skin, his hair unwashed. The air was filled with the stifling smell of his sweat and his restlessness. The man who generally liked to throw windows open kept them closed on his hot confusion. The sweet stench seemed to cling to everything. When he wandered into the garden, Mum would 'spray around' with the air freshener, hiding it at the bottom of the cupboard when he drifted back in. He had stopped eating. He drank half cups of tea or just let it go cold. Then, one afternoon, he marched off to the doctor's and got himself signed off work.

The surgery receptionist called to tell us. 'He seems very energetic,' she said. 'Is everything all right?' Poor mum had to start again. Didn't anyone keep records? Didn't anyone remember?

But at that point the rushing traffic in Dad's mind had finally slowed. He had taken to his bed every afternoon, one, two, three days in a row – was asleep, in fact, when I returned from my car-washing.

On the Monday afternoon, though, when Mum took him up a cup of tea – an offering that always calmed him – the big, long hump in the bed seemed once again supernaturally still.

'Ron? Ron?'

She shook him. He moaned. She shook him again. But instead of moaning and sitting up, he simply lay there, his greasy black hair splayed on the pillow above the candlewick.

Mum checked the side of the bed – and found the bottle with just two or three pills left. 'Oh, for God's sake.'

I was at school. Ian was at school. Thirty years later, Mum has all but blocked it out. 'So what did you do, Mum?' *I walked him round.* 'Round the bedroom?' *'Round somewhere – the bedroom, the box-room. I can't remember.' 'How did you feel?' 'I was so angry with him, so angry. That he would try to do it a second time . . . I was bloody furious.'*

Granddad came of course. He was there in minutes. Taking his son's shoulders, he walked him round, talking, talking. 'Silly sod, eh? Silly sod.' Dad moaned in his dad's arms.

How did Granddad feel, I wonder? How did he feel that his son kept trying to slip away?

But I knew the answer. I knew it every time I looked into Granddad's face. It was in the set of his jaw, the dull look in his eye. He would look at my dad, sometimes, on a Sunday evening, when he was talking – look at him in a way my nan never looked – and I knew he'd be thinking: *While I'm alive you're safe. While I'm alive, you're going nowhere.*

So he was back in Northwick Park again – 'poxy' Northwick Park, as my dad would, over the years, have it – back in the jumble of rain-stained concrete boxes, with the gloomy outlook – endless, noisy traffic on one side, dead parkland on the other. I remember thinking that it was the perfect miserable place for a psychiatric unit if you wanted to make it part of a 'normal' hospital in a town. I was a bit of a snob about these things back then because I'd been to Shenley but I feel the same way about it now: if you were disturbed and unhappy in the first place, what chance would you have in those surroundings?

My mum dutifully stocked her big shopping bag most days and caught the bus to visit him. My brother went with her, but I stayed away: the sulky teenager. He obviously hated me so I didn't want to see him. I went to school, to choir, to youth club. I pretended to get on with my life without him and missed him every moment he was away.

But I *was* him, of course. In my bedroom I had a big gilt mirror that Dad had rescued from a charity shop somewhere along the way and I was constantly looking into it. The face that looked back, I now saw, was my dad's: the roundish set of the jaw, the high forehead. My hair was long and wild, whereas his had always been short and neatly parted, but on every plane of my face – and I examined every plane, as he did, as he always would – my dad's features were beginning to imprint themselves. I walked like him, too: a heavy, forward motion, working the shoulders, leaning into the wind.

Dad started coming home in the afternoons. He had been put on heavy doses of lithium and, though the restlessness remained, the aggression, thankfully, had been quickly smoothed away. He worked his lips as the drug coursed through, forever pulling his mouth this way and that — a side-effect he would always hate. His knee jerked constantly too, shaking the whole of one side of his body when he sat down to watch the television or listen to a record.

He had to go back to the hospital in the evenings. At the front door, my mum would kiss him and stroke his face and his hair as if she'd never see him again, was amazed that he was still there.

Mum did not discuss this second overdose with my brother and me. There were no suggestions this time that he was merely trying to get some sleep. The second time around, that theory might have seemed all too appallingly true. I still couldn't accept it as a suicide attempt, though. I was not suffering from naivety or hopeless self-delusion: it was an instinct far worse than either. It was a feeling that the act of suicide was far too complex and selfish for someone as simple and straight-forward as my dad to contemplate. It was like finding him at the wheel of a car or playing golf: it was simply *not* him.

I'd like to recall that the overdose plunged me into a deep gloom for days, that I had tried to imagine his funeral, burying him, life without his all-pervading presence, but I'd be lying: none of it touched me. It was just another accidental overdose. Just another untidy episode in a shambolic drama.

Mum was in tearful mood. The man who had dumped cement in her kitchen just weeks before was being 'humiliated', she felt, at Northwick Park. 'They queue up for the medication, and I see him standing there, waiting, waiting . . .' She wiped a tear.

I wondered then whether the pressure of Dad's illness was making my mum unwell. I remember mulling that over in my head for a day, digging out her wretched old *Black's Medical Dictionary* to see if there was any mention of the stress manic depression puts on those around the sufferer. But there was nothing. The entry was very short. There was more information about ear infections.

26

The Cuckoo's Nest

Dad was in Northwick Park for a long time. The doctors seemed reluctant to discharge him. As his moods began to balance out and he took up the reins, once more, of normal life – mowing the lawn, reading books, watching TV from his favourite place on the settee – he pleaded to extend his home visits overnight. But the doctors were adamant: if he stays overnight without permission he'll be put back in pyjamas.

Dad risked their wrath by returning at ever later hours, marching up through Harrow town centre long after dark. Unusually for him, he would sometimes spend the last couple of hours of his 'freedom' sitting out on the wall with the neighbours. When the time came, eventually, for him to return, they would applaud his departure, Auntie Ellen and Mrs Herbert yelling encouraging words to him as he marched to the end of the street, turning every few yards or so to wave back.

* * *

I had a much longed-for distraction now: my first proper girlfriend. That summer, cycling aimlessly round town late one Sunday afternoon, I'd got off my bike and wheeled it into a recreation ground known as Headstone Manor. This was the site every year of the Harrow Show, a celebration of the borough with fairground rides, side-shows, parachute displays. The show was coming to an end, but as I plodded up past the big barn that was Headstone Manor's centrepiece I spotted a girl sitting on a swing in a children's play area nearby. She was about my age, or perhaps a year younger, small and slim, with dark brown hair and even darker, almost gypsyish eyes. She wore white high-heeled sandals and a light-green summer dress.

It was the outfit that seemed incongruous: why would you wear all that to sit in a dusty playground? I felt my heart beat a little faster. I wheeled my bike across, propped it next to a bench about twenty yards from the swings, sat down and pretended to enjoy the late-afternoon sunshine.

After a while she got up and walked, slowly and very deliberately, in my direction. My mouth went dry. She sauntered past – I thought I even detected a little wiggle to her hips – and over to the park exit.

I knew I had to follow her. I just knew. I let her get a few yards ahead and then I stood up and casually moved off after her, wheeling my bike slowly along and turning an interested gaze to the left and right as if Headstone Manor was the most fascinating spot I had ever visited.

She went out of the park and into the little lane that led down to the main road. There had been some hustle and bustle in the manor grounds where workmen were dismantling the show, but along here it was very quiet. She walked about fifty yards down the lane and then stopped. She turned, put her hands on her hips and cocked her head to one side.

'Are you following me?' she said. Her voice was tiny and nasal but with an endearing little catch, a huskiness about it.

I heard bells clanging in my head as the blood rushed to my temples. I didn't know what to say. I opened my mouth to speak but nothing appropriate would spring to my lips. I thought she was so beautiful, so beautiful. She was a real, live grown-up girl I had never seen before and she was speaking to me.

Thankfully, she barely waited for an answer. With a tinkling laugh, she said: 'You *are*, aren't you?' and walked up towards me, the little smile still on her face. Her skin was very pale but very clear. I was wearing my Marilyn Monroe sweatshirt. 'I like your shirt,' she said. I pulled at it pathetically with my fingers, trying to balance the bike with my other hand. And then she said, unforgettably, immortally, 'Come on, then. Walk with me.'

God bless you, Elaine Slowe, God bless you.

I didn't fall in love with Elaine Slowe – I didn't fall in love until years later – but I loved so much about her. She was witty and sarcastic and clever. It was impossible to lie to her, to fool her in any way, and so I think she knew, almost from the first moment we sat down in her mum's front room with glasses of orange juice, that I didn't love her and never would. She knew it because she knew she couldn't ever love me. We were going to be mates and that was it; and when she eventually fell in love I would be a delighted onlooker.

If my memory is right, only her mum was still alive. My recollection is that this was why we ended up talking about my dad – and that hearing of her loss, at such a young age, prompted me to explain that, although I still had a dad, he was often very ill. I felt we had to be even, that I couldn't completely have something she didn't.

This was the first time I realized that my dad, and his story, had a value to me. It made me seem vulnerable and interesting. At fifteen years old, with my testosterone in overdrive, it was a startlingly important discovery.

Elaine fished through a metal rack of torn-sleeved singles and pulled out the risqué 'Spiders and Snakes' by Jim Stafford. It immediately became the sexiest record I'd ever heard. The tale of the boy at the water-hole teasing the girl by waving creepy-crawlies at her seemed peculiarly relevant to us: two strangers who had circled each other, on a hot summer's day, with nothing on their minds other than to meet someone.

When I said goodbye to Elaine that afternoon, I felt light-headed and dislocated; I had to keep checking my watch. But I knew that she'd suggest we meet again the following day and I knew there would be years and years of such days.

Over the next few weeks it became clear that Elaine was not quite the 'stranger' I'd first thought. A pupil at Harrow County Girls' school, she already knew a number of my friends at the boys' school from taking the same unruly home-bound bus through Harrow town centre. I took her home to meet my parents and she declared that my dad was a 'real character'. This interpretation had never occurred to me before.

I would never bring friends in when Dad was ill. If they called I would keep them at the door and then go out somewhere with them. But when he was well he loved being around them and they enjoyed his company too. He would neither talk down to them, nor moderate what he said. Once, during one of my teenage winters, when a group of my friends were gathered in the front room, I'd asked my dad very casually where the cat was. It was an elderly animal and the weather was freezing.

Dad, who hated the cat, replied, 'Out in the frozen wastes, thank fuck,' a reply so bluntly amusing that it was repeated by my friends for years afterwards.

That was the Christmas of *One Flew Over the Cuckoo's Nest*. When Dad returned to work, he heard about the book and the film from one of the girls in the library.

There was a long waiting list to borrow the book. He brought it home and read it in two days.

'It's brilliant, Peg. Brilliant.'

My mum nodded but said nothing. It had been a long haul back from the illness this time: she wasn't ready to let herself be entertained by some American writer's view of it.

'He's going to want to go and see the film,' she said to me, 'and I don't bloody well want to go and see it with him.' She was wagging her head in the annoying, self-righteous way she sometimes had, but I was in no mood to argue with her. If one thing was likely to trigger my dad again it was this film.

Oddly, though – and it was very odd – my dad hadn't quite made the connection between the book and his illness, the book and his life. I assumed at first that he had, but, when he talked about it, it was as if the film was a madcap comedy – made for Jack Nicholson's devilish talents – and that he wanted to see it for no other reason than that it would be funny. He always distanced himself from his illness when he was well again, but could he have distanced himself this far?

He certainly loved the cinema, had always loved it. As soon as a good children's film came out – *Mary Poppins, Chitty Chitty Bang Bang* – Dad took us to see it. He had loved every minute of *Jungle Book* years before and had taken us back to see it three times.

I remember sitting next to him the first time we'd seen

the famous sequence 'I Want to Be Like You', with the gorilla dancing across the throne in his crown. Dad had been helpless with laughter, the tears glittering on his face in the light from the screen.

I found it much harder to laugh, harder to enjoy anything much in those crowded auditoriums, because, ironically – and unwittingly – Dad had ruined the cinema for me years before.

At some point during an earlier illness, when he was trying to make me a 'man' – sending me to Cub Scouts; corralling me into the Cullington football team – he had also insisted that I join the other children in the road at Saturday morning pictures. Under sufferance, and apologizing every step of the way – 'It'll be over in a couple of hours; you'll enjoy it' – Mum had walked me up to the big ABC cinema in Harrow town centre.

There were two big ragged queues of children, one either side of the entrance. They were mostly boys, leaping and dodging and running round, and every one of them seemed to my shy, fussy, eight-year-old mind a savage. They had the brutal, wind-tanned, red-pinched faces of boys who spent all their time outside breaking milk bottles, throwing fireworks, getting into trouble. I have never felt, at any point in my life or career, more like someone about to be cast to the wolves.

Inside and alone, momentarily baffled by the semi-darkness and the screaming and noise around me, I edged gingerly to a seat. I was in a little jacket, my face washed, my hair brushed. I felt very self-conscious. The boys had crowded in. Very few of them had sat down, and the ones who had done so had immediately put their feet on the back of the seat in front. I glanced at the luminous hands on my Timex and then hastily covered it again with the sleeve of my jersey, pulling it down where it had been folded up at the wrist. I was, surely, among thieves.

They kicked the back of my seat. They pushed past, leapt around, climbed and clambered, fought and spat and shouted. There was a smell of farts and grubby hands.

I sat still, my eyes fixed on the silken curtains covering the big screen, willing, *willing*, the film to start so there'd be a distraction. I felt that everyone in the cinema knew I was an outsider: that I shouldn't be there. Summoning an enormous force of will, because I was terrified, truly terrified, in that atmosphere, I turned my head stiffly, trying not to catch anyone's eyes but scanning the semi-darkened rows behind to see if I could spot a familiar face from my school. Someone, anyone. Perhaps Rambridge is here, I thought – or Norris! Norris might go to Saturday morning pictures, I thought. I imagined his big honest face and his kind manner: *'Nothing to worry about, Martin, it's a laugh.'* But there was no Norris. There were no familiar faces at all, just a confusion of arms and legs and scowls and that horrible, honking laughter of children who had shouted so much their voices were already semi-broken.

Suddenly I felt something snatch at my pocket and something else flash away from me. My handkerchief – my nice, white, folded handkerchief poked neatly into my jacket pocket that morning by my mother's fingers – had been stolen away by an unseen hand. I swallowed hard and kept looking ahead. *It's not mine, it's not mine.* I was aware of it flashing up in the darkness to my right and of the howls of laughter that accompanied each throw.

The boy next to me laughed into the side of my face, and I turned in horror to see his big, pink, stupid mouth wide open. All down the row the others picked up on his sneering mockery. '*It's his! It's his!*'

I felt the tears well in my eyes. What did they know about handkerchiefs, or any nice things? My mum, who never had much, had given it to me and now it was lost. I just stared at the screen, my face a furious, frightened, embarrassed red – *oh, where was the film?* – while my hanky was flung from filthy hand to fithy hand, and along the row to my right, everyone was screaming, shouting, honking, coughing.

It took an age for it to happen but then suddenly the house lights began to dim. I was no longer aware of the flashing white of my tossed handkerchief: it had been lost for ever on the floor or down the side of a seat. Lost and immediately forgotten – at least by them.

I remember nothing of the films I watched except one image: a pirate balanced on the edge of a ship, waving his cutlass around. For the most part I went into a sort of trance, imagining that this would make the horror pass more quickly. I couldn't wait to get out of that cinema and to this day, even with my own children, I have never gone back into one without nursing a secret dread of the audience. A row of three or four young men with feet up on the seat-backs in front, a single, unprompted yell or shout towards the screen, the lighting of an illicit cigarette – even, now, the dread ring of a mobile – and I am paralysed with fear.

So Dad went to see *One Flew Over the Cuckoo's Nest*, and Mum, of course, went with him. My brother and I stayed at home and had put ourselves to bed by the time they came back.

I had the whole story from my mum the next day. She described how Dad had sat stock-still throughout as the plot unfolded – Jack Nicholson, the reluctant mental patient, facing the prospect and, eventually, the terrible, literally mind-destroying reality, of frontal lobotomy. When it was over Dad could barely speak. His eyes brimmed with tears. He took my mum by the arm and steered her along the row and out through the foyer and it was only when they were right away, in the cold night air, the glow at the front of the cinema receding behind them, that he turned to her and said: 'It was Shenley.'

Mum was worried that the film would 'tip Dad over', but it didn't. He talked about it for months, years, afterwards: he embraced it absolutely, and finally, as a very accurate reflection of what he'd been through. Mum, in her turn, told me – not him – what she had felt: how she'd shivered when she saw Nicholson's dead gaze, that she'd sighed with recognition at the way, like Dad, he'd hide pills under his tongue and then spit them out later. To my dad she said only: 'It's very sad.'

27

Beaches and Backchat

It was raining. It had been raining constantly for the last two days. There had been sporadic deluges that drove us back into our little guest-house just off the sea front at Bournemouth, but for the most part, as now, it was just drizzling.

Dad, shopping bag in hand, kept declaring that we 'must make the best of it' – marching us up to the shops or into fuggy little fish-and-chip shops with wet footprints on the tiled floor and the sea a blur of condensation through the big front windows.

This was to be our last family holiday together. I can see us, still, 'bowling' along that promenade, Dad leaning forward into his stride, almost toppling off his toes, his face set, serious – as it always was when he was walking – the breath coming in stentorian blasts; Ian and I in preposterous, wind-flapped flares and clumpy platform shoes: a mixture of still-youthful keenness and the compulsory reluctance of mid-adolescence. I was sixteen, nearly seventeen, and on the point of leaving school to go to sixth-form college; my brother had suddenly 'shot up', as Mum put it, to become a tall and gangly fourteen-year-old.

Dad was not going to be beaten by the rain that whipped across his cheeks and brought a dewdrop to the end of his nose. He kept his casual C&A jacket open as we struggled along the promenade, as if the wind and the wet were just an illusion, while Mum hurried along at his side, her face red and screwed up against the sharp sand flying up off the beach.

Suddenly, and on an irresistible impulse, the decision was made: 'Let's go down there, kids, come on' – we would be the 'kids' for another few years yet – and Dad plunged off down the steps, steadying himself against one of the big, slime-covered groynes.

'Oh, Ron!' Mum wrapped her coat round her and stayed put in a half-hearted protest as we bounced down the uneven steps behind him, but she was soon following too. 'Let's not go too far anyway,' she called.

'No, that's all right, Peg, we'll stop here.' Dad was always keen to set up 'camp' as quickly as possible. He pulled a couple of towels out of the bag and spread them out down near the concrete wall of the promenade. There were a few surprised glances from passers-by: apart from a skinny boy struggling along the shoreline with his dog, we were the only souls on the beach.

Dad sniffed against the cold wind; he screwed open his big new aluminium vacuum flask – the history of our holidays was a history of flasks – and poured some tea into the plastic cup lid for Mum.

She wrinkled her nose against the rim: 'Never quite tastes the same.'

'This is nice,' said my dad hopefully and glanced back up at the prom to see if anyone was following us down.

Beaches made Dad young again. Holidays in general took years off him. Although he and Mum never left Britain after that one time honeymooning in Jersey, after Ian and I left home, ten or twelve years later, they embarked on a series of more 'adventurous' trips round the coast, eschewing Bournemouth and Brighton for Portsmouth and Plymouth: 'There's not what you'd call *beaches* there but it's very, very in'eresting. Lot of 'istory.' On one or two occasions he'd be ill and Mum would come back with tales of signing up for 'excursions', only to have Dad walking along, dead-eyed and unhearing, while she had to pretend an interest in whatever guided tour he'd roped her into. Most of the time, though, they both came back renewed.

The wind had dropped a bit, there was the faintest crayon-yellow of sun somewhere up in the dark clouds and Dad was lying back on his towel, cradling his head in his hands.

'What you gonna do when you leave school, then, Mart? You gonna do that journalism, are you?'

MARTIN TOWNSEND

I was embarrassed, and a little bit superstitious, about discussing it, but Mr Golland, my English master, had found a place called The London College of Printing at Elephant & Castle in south London, which had a one-year course in magazine journalism. It seemed almost too good to be true.

'I worked at the Elephant, didn't I, Peg?' my dad was saying – and I wish now I'd been less reticent about talking and discussed that with him too, but I didn't. 'I think you'll enjoy it up there, mate,' he said. 'It's an in'eresting place.'

'I hope so,' I said. 'But I've got to get the right grades first.'

He sat up, slapping the sand off the knee of his trousers. He put his arm round my shoulder. 'Oh, you'll do that, son. You're a bloody genius!' and he laughed and pulled a funny face, looking at Mum.

I shook my head at my brother.

'He's mad, mad,' said Ian, in a Monty Python voice. 'He'll have to be shot.'

All families set themselves, one way or another, against the world – at least, until the 'world' proves itself friendly. Usually Dad was willing to make the first move to establish peaceful relations, but sometimes, detecting that the people involved would never be his 'sort' (chatty, outgoing, not afraid to swear or tell off-colour stories), he'd restrict communication to a few polite 'hellos' and 'see ya laters'.

The latter had been the case, most of the week, at our guest-house. There were two other families staying there and, in the evenings, and sometimes in the afternoons – the weather being bad and these souls not as courageous as Dad wanted us to be – they would gather to play cards or chat in the 'communal' room at the front. This was a very small room, into which was crammed a television, complete with doily and pot plant on top, a coffee table with two more doilies and some old magazines on it, and at least eight hard and uncomfortable chairs. As a result the two families had become quite close, sharing jokes and stories together and playing baffling card games that were neither of the two we knew – gin rummy or whist.

Dad, a bit reticent about them all to begin with, was not that keen to intrude on this cosy gathering, but Mum, Ian and I found ourselves among them one afternoon while we waited for Dad to come down. We planned another sortie on the pier.

One of the families included two sour-faced girls. They were about ten and twelve years old. I'd disliked them on sight because they didn't say hello when you spoke to them, they just smiled half-sarcastically and then whispered among themselves as you passed by. We were too old, Ian and I decided, for this sort of thing. We'd concluded, in fact, that we were too old for the holiday, full stop, and had switched into a sort of automatic pilot, following our parents around and being polite, but desperate to be back home among our records and friends. These girls, anyhow, were in the room when we settled ourselves down, and immediately began nudging and whispering to each other.

My mum, to make conversation, asked the 'where you up from?' question and other platitudes. After a while, as Mum got into her stride, enjoying a very pleasant conversation with one of the women, I was aware that the girls were adding 'asides' that seemed to be part of the conversation but were actually little jibes at my mum's cockney accent and habit of repeating herself.

In the middle of all this, my dad came in. 'Hullo,' he said. The girls giggled. I was furious.

'Having a nice chat, we are,' my mum said.

'Nice chat,' repeated one of the girls.

My dad smiled across at them.

'They're down from Preston,' said my mum.

'Preston?' said my dad.

'Sixty-six,' stage-whispered the older girl.

'Ninety-nine,' said the younger one.

My mum seemed oblivious to any of this, but I saw my dad's face harden slightly. The conversation went on for a few minutes longer, the girls sixty-sixing and ninety-nining all the repetitions, so that even their own mother was shooting them angry glances. Their father, over by the television, was having a separate conversation with the other family.

'We'd better go, Peg,' said Dad and moved off towards the door.

'OK, well, we're going,' said Mum.

I leant down to pick up my bag, listening out for and vaguely detecting the beginning of a whispered 'sixty-six', when suddenly one of the girls gave out a piercing 'ow!'

Dad was full of apologies.

'Big feet!' moaned the older girl, and there were tears in her eyes as she clutched the flip-flopped foot Dad had just crushed with his Dr Marten shoe.

'I'm so sorry: my fault,' said my dad, addressing his apologies to the girl's father on the other side of the room.

'Oh, don't worry,' he said: 'she's always getting 'em trod on. I tell her: put some bloody decent shoes on.'

I saw the girl's mother look from her daughter to my dad and then exchange a glance with my mum: a slow nod and the very trace of a smile.

Aside from the holidays we'd organized as a family over the years, there were, during the late Seventies and early Eighties, various 'street excursions' from Cullington Close, all of them arranged by the small and bustling figure of Fred Herbert. They were infamous events, inevitably ending in some sort of row and, occasionally, fight, as old rivalries and divisions between our neighbours were reopened by a surfeit of cheap lager.

Fred took it all in his stride. 'They do get a bit boisterous, these things,' he'd tell us, out on the wall. 'But it's soon forgotten.'

Fred had made, and erected in his front garden, a little notice-board on a pole that advertised these events to passing residents. As 1976 turned to Jubilee Year 1977, it began to fill up with various appeals for on-the-day helpers, makers of bunting and cakes for a 'new Cullington Close project'.

Ellen and, in particular, Reg were delighted. 'Gonna have a street party, Ron – what do you think?' they'd told my dad one evening as he wheeled his bike up the road. He was coming home from work and hungry for his tea, so I knew they wouldn't get much out of him. I'd come up to meet him at the gate.

'Yeah, that'll be good. All right, son?' He nodded across to me.

'What are you gonna do, eh, Ron – sing a song?' said Reg, promptly dissolving into laughter.

Dad gave an unenthusiastic little laugh. 'Oh, I'll probably keep me head down.'

'No,' said old Mrs Herbert, and she tugged at Dad's jumper, her expression dark and fierce: 'you can get the kids together – get 'em doing something, a show.'

'Yeah, OK,' said my dad. He scratched his head, which was always a sign of his reluctance. 'We better go in. Tea's getting cold.'

There had obviously been a time, four, five, years previously, when Dad would have leapt at the chance to organize Cullington Close's raggle-taggle of tearaways for a street party. But he'd quietened down, drawn back among us, his family. The street had begun to change, anyhow, in small ways. One of the Browns – I forget which now – had gone to prison for his part in a robbery. There were new faces in the houses opposite us. The Close had got its first Indian families – and its first owner-occupiers as the 'right to buy' got into full swing.

Perhaps in acknowledgement of the money likely to be spent on the new 'private' homes, the council had arranged, a few months before, for the outsides of all the homes still being rented to be resprayed. Within a week the familiar grey exteriors of my youth had been changed to a strictly regimented vanilla, pink and green.

Ellen flew into a fury when one of the painting teams tested out his spray-gun on her fence. 'Bloody cheek,' she told my mum in the back garden while Reg bounced about at her side, ready with a joke. He got it in, in the end: 'The whole street looks like a bloody tutti-frutti!'

Reg was still repeating his tutti-frutti joke weeks later when the Jubilee street party got under way. He was planning to perform a 'sand dance' in the style of Wilson, Kepple & Betty, the old music-hall entertainers. He'd found a faded old fez from somewhere and a white bed-sheet, which would be tied up with the cord from his dressing-gown.

Dad had disappeared for the day – 'gone out'. He'd cycled over to Granddad's, I think.

'He'll miss my dance. I'm not doing it again just for

him!' Reg declared, and flapped his hand camply like Dick Emery.

Mum did not seem overly bothered by Dad's absence: 'Street parties are not his sort of thing, Reg.' But it hadn't been that long ago, I thought, when they had.

There was red, white and blue bunting of various sorts hung from window to window, across the road, and from window to telegraph pole. In the morning there were regular curses hurled at visiting motorists who bravely tried to 'interrupt' the process of stringing it across. 'Bugger off!'

Trestle tables were erected on the verge at the far 'rough' end of the street and Ellen, who rarely cooked for her own family – they ate take-aways, or biscuits – supervised the catering. There were plates and plates of white sandwiches filled with the sort of ancient fish pastes that only made their appearance on such occasions.

It started to rain at about three o'clock.

Dad had cycled back and, apparently, gone straight to bed. 'I hope he's not having another bloody turn,' my mum said to Ellen. I thought he was just staying out of the way.

Some of the children, including my brother, had put on their dads' old shirts, fixed safety-pins on them, daubed various strange markings on their faces with their mums' mascara, and come along as 'punks'. The Sex Pistols' seditious 'God Save the Queen' – which Dad thought was 'fantastic' – was lodged at number 1 in the charts, though, in deference to Her Majesty, many record shops had crossed it out or refused to mark it on the charts they hung up in their windows.

A little kerfuffle over by one of the trestle tables had distracted many of those of an age likely to remember Wilson, Kepple & Betty (it turned out later that a woman had been caught loading fruit and sandwiches into the pockets of her 'shoplifter's coat'). So the chattering mob of junior 'Johnny Rottens' was the bulk of the audience Reg attracted when he finally came strolling along, swathed in his sheet, fez in hand, to perform his sand dance. He had a little tape-recorder with him. He gathered up his sheet around him, rather primly, to lay the machine on the wet grass, then looked up to see if anyone else was coming.

My mum, Ellen, Ellen's son Nigel and Mrs Herbert came over, arms crossed against the wet.

Reg punched the little button and the unlikely strains of 'The Sheik of Araby' drifted tinnily through the steady drizzle. He plonked the fez on his head and flicked the little tassle out of his eyes. Then he began to dip and scoop his left hand forward, like the head of a snake, in time with the music. He swivelled to repeat the action with his right, grinning from ear to ear. The 'punks' giggled, a little uncertainly.

Encouraged, Reg attempted to shuffle forward a bit, but the sheet was too long, the ground too slippery. He caught his ankle in the material and simply splayed forward, flat out on the long grass. The punks exploded with laughter.

Ellen ran across to take his hand as Reg struggled to his feet, his legs whirling around in the swathes of bedsheet. It was the ultimate act of slapstick from a man who adored the genre, but I didn't really think he'd be happy – and he wasn't.

'Just fuck off,' he shouted at the punks, and they turned away, frowning and muttering. You didn't expect to hear that sort of language in our street from someone else's dad.

'Very good, Reg, honestly,' Mum was saying, but our neighbour was inconsolable.

'You try to set up something properly . . .' He was still almost shouting.

Ellen was consoling. 'It was good, though, it was.'

But Reg was finished for the day. He lifted up his skirts, revealing black ankle socks and hairy, bony ankles, and clumped off up the street.

Dad listened to the story later. He had, he said, cycled over to his dad's, then come back and gone to bed for a read. He was adamant that the street party wasn't his thing at all.

I was sad he missed it, and I was puzzled. I remember wondering at the time if he was jealous of Fred, who had taken the things he, Dad, used to do spontaneously in the street and made them all 'official' – pinning notices up and calling from house to house to collect money for the excursions. I had never really seen my dad as a jealous person, though.

It was only when I read again my diaries of that period that I gained some clue, perhaps, to his lack of enthusiasm. There are various entries relating to Granddad being drunk and not coming home; to my nan having to stay the night with us.

At the time, I'd taken Granddad's drinking to be one of those jokey, blokey things that he did. He also went up to the West End sometimes, to the Victoria sporting club to watch boxing matches. It was part of Granddad's personality, like the Sunday-night cribbage, and the two bob and the little pin-up of a busty woman he kept hanging from his shaving glass at Gran's house and which so disturbed me at that age.

But perhaps Granddad's drinking was beginning to worry Dad. You don't think, at that age, that your father will worry about his dad the way you worry about your own. Dad was always cursing Elb – for the shoddy electrical work he did; his surliness, sometimes, around my gran (who gave as good as she got, to be honest); but it never occurred to me that he might be worried about him. It never crossed my mind. I wish, now, that it had, that I could have offered him some comfort. But, for a family whose problems were laid so bare for the world to see, there were many things, still, that were not discussed.

* * *

And now I wonder if one of those 'secrets' was Dad's third overdose. The first was an 'accident'; the second I was left to make my own mind up about; the third . . . I didn't know about the third. Or perhaps I did and just blocked it out? No, I didn't know.

My mum tells me now that she visited Dad – who was back, trapped, in Northwick Park again; Northwick Park from which, ultimately, there would be no escape – and told him: 'You'll push the self-destruct button once too often.' But when was that? Was I too busy, too pre-occupied with my own affairs, to notice that my dad had tried to commit suicide?

Was I still at sixth-form college – luxuriating, at last, in the presence of girls after the spit and dirt of grammar school – or had I started commuting up to the London College of Printing?

My mum can't put a year on that third attempt. She just shakes her head.

We had become, my brother and I, an irritant to our dad, I knew that. He'd left school at fourteen: why were we still at home?

He hadn't stopped loving us, nor we him, but we were taking up too much room: the man who had made everything in the house and garden for us now wanted to live there in peace. He was not old-fashioned – he had all the time in the world for us still if we wanted to call upon his time; he did not look down on our clothes, or music or our friends – but I thought I saw his elbows lift slightly when he was around us, as if we were squeezing him, making him feel closed-in. He'd had enough, I think, of being the subject of our attention and our worry; he wanted just to live his life now. Open the windows and breathe. Or not.

He had settled into a comfortable late middle age, this manic-depressive, occasional would-be suicide.

We flew out on that long-anticipated pilgrimage to Lourdes, my brother and I. We drank beer and went to Confession for the first time; bought screw-top Virgin Mary figures to fill with Holy Water; and we prayed hard for Dad. Prayed that he would be 'well'. It was asking too much, perhaps, even of Lourdes, where a lady in the previous few months had apparently dipped her ailing limbs in the waters of the grotto and had subsequently had a cancer-gnawed bone grow back.

28

Do It Yourself

I left Lowlands College and entered the London College of Printing. I sleep-walked through a year there, learning about law, photography and magazine design. I was on my way to the World of Work and it all seemed to have happened too fast.

At nineteen years of age I found myself out of college and in a warehouse in Wembley, typing up order forms for office equipment. Armed with my typing skills and a nominal 100 words-per-minute shorthand, I had signed up with a temp agency and been sent out to the warehouse as 'holiday relief' for one of the secretaries.

The men in the warehouse – rangy young men like the Browns – were disappointed not to be sent a girl replacement and one or two eyed me disdainfully the entire fortnight I was there. I didn't care. The job paid £73 a week, in a proper brown pay-packet with a Cellophane window and holes punched in it. I was rich.

I tried to give some of it to my mum, knowing that it would please my dad, but of course she wouldn't take it.

Part of the arrangement with the London College of Printing was that every student who left without a job in journalism to go to would be entered on a list by the NCTJ (National Council for the Training of Journalists). The NCTJ took it upon themselves to line up interviews for those individuals: an extraordinary luxury.

Thus I found myself one afternoon, a few weeks after I'd left the warehouse, on a train to East Croydon en route to *Do It Yourself* magazine. They needed a 'Staff Writer'.

It wasn't the sort of place I'd ever imagined I'd start my career: I had dreams of working on some high-minded organ like *Architect's Journal*. But I thought there was so little chance of getting the DIY job that I might as well go along just to get some practice in being interviewed.

The two men who met me were Tony Wilkins, the editor, and Ron Grace, the 'technical editor'. They were both fascinating characters, but it was inexplicable how they could have ended up together.

Wilkins was probably then in his late thirties or early forties. He had blond hair of a baby-like fluffiness and hue, parted severely on the left. He was a committed Christian and everything about his pale, open features and unquenchable enthusiasm screamed out his religious zest. He spoke in a high-pitched, piping voice that would break, slightly, into a sort of exasperated yodel when he was upset or excited.

A year or so later I would hear stories about his determination to pursue a straight and narrow path that would stay with me my whole life.

He insisted that he, and only he, wrote the 'cover lines' which advertised the contents of a particular month's issue. But unfortunately he had a habit of coming up with screaming double entendres. When they were pointed out to him by the deputy, John McGowan – brother of *Ready Steady Go!* star Cathy – he would appear to have no idea what John was talking about. I will relate them here because my dad, in particular, found them hilarious and repeated them time and again through the years.

An annual delight was Tony's appeal to the women readers of the magazine: '*Ladies, get your husband a new tool for Christmas*'. Another, which, astonishingly, was read out on *That's Life*, was an attempt to encapsulate a project that combined a child's bed and playhouse. Tony's line, read deathlessly by the legendary Cyril Fletcher, was: '*Bunk up on a Wendy house*'. My favourite, and the one my dad would never tire of hearing, was the dog's shelter built out of a barrel: '*Build a firkin dog kennel*'.

When John, a dark-featured, rather morose-looking

man who actually had a wonderful sense of humour, was handed these lines to read he would shake his head, his shoulders, seemingly slumping even more. Then he would stand up slowly from his desk, plod across, like a condemned man, to Tony's boxed-off cubicle of an office in the corner and close the door. Tony's reaction was always, so John told us, the same: 'Look, mate' – he called everybody 'mate' when he was irritated – 'look, mate, it's your *mind*. Our readers don't think like you do.'

Even after his cover line's star turn on the BBC, he refused to see anything odd in what he'd written. 'What's wrong with everybody? These are *perfectly good* words.'

Ron Grace, in contrast, was quite happy, when Tony wasn't around, to crack ribald jokes at which he would laugh with his head thrown exuberantly back. A small man with big, bulging eyes, he was constantly at war with his contact lenses. He would try to wash them in his mouth after eating his morning biscuit and suddenly peer up at you, sorely, with half a Lincoln Cream wedged in his eyelid.

Kind and intelligent, Ron had, nevertheless, made himself a figure of fun in the office because he was ever so slightly pompous. He cultivated an active dislike, not so much of John McGowan, but of John's baby-faced partner-in-crime, Roger DuBern, the office joker. John and Roger, with the almost tacit approval of Tony

Wilkins, pursued a hyperactive and lucrative sideline in freelance work. At one point they were even editing another magazine in a different publishing group, meeting the designer 'halfway' at Clapham Junction station to read proofs and make corrections.

Tony Wilkins, who was no fool, tolerated this activity – though he never acknowledged it – because McGowan and DuBern were, back then, the doyens of Do-It-Yourself journalism. The magazine would have been barely half as good without them – and Tony knew it. Also they never let their work on *DIY* suffer.

But Ron Grace was not so generous. He existed in a state of open warfare with John and Roger, paying overly polite lip service to John's position and general attitude of seriousness but losing no opportunity to throw barbs at 'that clown' DuBern. He would attempt to score technical points by scrutinizing the photographs Roger had taken of, say, erecting a fence and then pointing out minor errors, if he could find any, either to the editor or his long-suffering secretary, Debbie.

Roger, in his turn, would play practical jokes on Ron, leaving telephone messages on his desk asking him to ring 'Mr G. Rarf', together with the number of London Zoo, or Mr Fogg at the weather office. Ron would fall for these every time, immediately declaring, 'Oh, *that* old chestnut!' loud enough for Roger to hear, as if the fact that it was an old chestnut made his lapse completely understandable.

* * *

So this was the office in which I found myself that August day nearly thirty years ago, waiting for my interview. I had made such a good job of convincing myself that the position was way beyond my abilities that I hadn't even bothered looking at the magazine before I came along – a naïve and stupid error, which Wilkins soon picked up on.

'So you don't really *know* the sort of things we do,' he said – and my imagination added a weary 'tch'. He was sitting at his desk with my skeletal CV – date of birth; couple of hobbies; poems printed in the local paper – in front of him. To his side, sitting on a very upright wooden chair, was Ron Grace, the ankle of his right leg propped up on his left knee. He was sucking on an unlit pipe, rocking slightly, his big glassy eyes gazing at me.

The exact details of the next ten minutes or so have faded in my recollection, although I do remember that only Wilkins spoke – Grace adding merely a few nods and grunts – and that there were various questions about my journalism college and what I thought I'd achieved there (Tony Wilkins was a big supporter of the NCTJ). It took an age, anyhow, for the question that I'd been dreading to come around.

'Have you ever done any DIY?' asked Tony, and he was smiling quite sweetly and sincerely, clearly expecting an able-bodied teenager like myself to have pitched in around the house with all sorts of complicated projects. Ron Grace added an inquisitive 'hmm?' and leant forward a bit, not wanting to miss any detail of any lathe and wood-turning work I might have indulged in.

I couldn't lie. I didn't want to lie. 'Not really,' I said.

Wilkins sighed.

'What about with your dad?' said Ron Grace. It was the first time, really, that he'd spoken.

I couldn't help it. I laughed. Not a guffaw, but just a little exhalation of air.

Ron Grace smiled. 'What's funny?' he asked.

I shook my head. I was in a quandary. The memory of the interview years before with Mr Marchant at school, where I'd unknowingly belittled my dad's job, still burned in my mind. I clamped my lips shut.

'Does your dad not do any work around the house, then?' said Tony, and he said it, once again, in such a friendly, wide-eyed way that the answer 'no', though it might have disappointed him, would not have been the end of the world.

But I didn't say 'no'. I could have done, I *should* have done, but it wouldn't have been the truth, would it?

'He does,' I said, 'but he doesn't really know what he's doing: he bangs in screws with a hammer.'

I'd betrayed my dad again. I could say now, being wise long after the event, that the desire to answer truthfully somehow outweighed my guilt, but that wasn't the case. If there was a genuine explanation it was that I'd been in the room too long, the job had slipped away, and I was never going to see these people ever again, so why not just give them an honest answer?

The effect, though, was astonishing. Starved of any sort of DIY chatter for half an hour – and, believe me, that was an issue with him – Ron Grace burst into life. 'Ah, but you *can* bang some screws in with a hammer, can't you, Tony?'

Tony, who seemed a little more doubtful, nodded. 'I believe so.'

'Yes, yes, you *can*.' Ron was insistent. 'I think your old man knows a bit more about DIY than you think.'

I couldn't believe it.

'And you help him, do you?' said Tony. He had stood up and was shuffling and gathering together his papers now.

'I do,' I said, rather stunned, but he had his back turned to me and didn't seem to hear.

At the door, Tony shook my hand and Ron gave me copies of the magazine and of the annual 'specials' that they produced. I dropped the whole lot in a bin on the way back to East Croydon station.

My dad was waiting for me when the train pulled in at Northwick Park Tube station. I could see him at the end of the little approach road, pacing up and down by the bus stop, slapping an evening paper against his thigh. It was a warm evening and he was in a short-sleeved shirt.

I can't put down in words how much I loved him at

that moment. He had never met me from the train before, and he was meeting me, today, on the second occasion when I had publicly bad-mouthed him. The tears welled up in my eyes.

'You all right, son?' He put his arms on my shoulders.

I shook my head. 'Yeah, I'm fine. I didn't get it.'

He seemed almost relieved. How many knock-backs had he had from job interviews over the years? 'Never mind,' he said. 'There's always another one.'

I wanted to tell him about the conversation – about the way Ron Grace had jumped on a silly story about banging in screws and tried to legitimize it – I wanted to see if Dad would see the funny side. But I didn't, because a stronger impulse, to forget about it all, took over. He was off chattering about something else, anyway – football or music: something – and I was just pleased to be by his side.

We turned off the Kenton Road and walked up to Kenton Park, and I was glad, suddenly, that earlier it had gone so wrong, because every day I'd be leaving all this – all these glorious spaces where I'd had such adventures as a child: the tree where I'd once lost a toy parachute and Mum and Dad had come across with the washing-line prop to retrieve it; the little hollow in the corner of the lower football field that had always filled with water after heavy rain and become our 'lake'; the top field where I'd played football with the Kenton Martyrs. I belonged in Harrow, I didn't belong in Croydon.

We cut up to the big top field, along the perimeter fence of Elmgrove School and down to the area of wasteland – the 'dump'. It was a truly glorious evening, with soft, warm sunshine and a breeze flattening the grass all across to the cricket pavilion and the allotments beyond. Dad had once had one of those – had tried to grow vegetables on it.

From this, the top field, the tower of St Mary's, Kenton, dominates the middle distance and I thought then, as I always did when I saw it, of poor, lost Father Shearing gulping down tablets in the fussy little parlour of his vicarage.

Dad was talking, though, about the boy from our road who had come up here and launched an enormous model glider. He had swung it up on high on a line and a hook, but by the time the hook dropped down – scattering the urchins from our road who'd come to watch – the plane was already too high. He and his dad followed it briefly in their car, but they never saw it again.

'Shame,' Dad said. 'It had taken him weeks to build, you know.'

We picked our way through the rubble and broken bottles overgrown with mounds of nettle and dock and found our way to the wide path, worn down by the feet of generations of Cullington Close children, and back to our street.

* * *

A letter came from the publishers, two days later, offering me the job. I read it through several times, convinced it was a poorly expressed invitation to a second interview or that it had come to the wrong person. I was excited of course – I was delirious with excitement – but I couldn't understand how it had happened.

'That's fantastic, Martin. Well done.' My mum was all over me, stroking my hair, kissing my face.

Dad was in the background, nodding and grinning. 'I knew you'd do it. I just knew.'

Five thousand, two hundred pounds a year. It was an inconceivable sum. How could I possibly be worth any of it?

'You'll be able to move out now,' said my dad.

'If he wants to,' said my mum.

My dad pursed his lips. 'Of course, yeah; no hurry.' But I thought I could see the elbows lift once again.

I turned the interview over in my mind, trying to unearth some clue to my success, but the only information I had imparted that could be of any use at all was the nonsense about my dad and the screws. There had, literally, been nothing else.

And suddenly I thought: all these years of worry, all these years of fretting about what other people think, of what other people do that my father doesn't do – stay well; avoid smashing up their own front room; own their own house; drive a car; have two telephones; put on a suit for the office; know exactly the right thing to say;

dress for dinner – that is, change out of their pyjamas before they sit down – and keep their elbows off the table ... All those years of worrying what people might think and, in the end, it doesn't matter at all because here I am with £5,200 and no earthly idea how it happened.

I looked at my dad. He was in his usual armchair in the back room. He'd just lit his evening cigarette and was mulling over a newspaper spread open on the carpet between his slippers. 'Dad ... ?'

He glanced up. 'Son?'

'Dad, in the interview ...' and I told him the whole story.

He smiled all the way through, laughing as I described the strange little character that was Ron Grace. For the next three or four years, as I beavered away on the magazine, he would nag me for fresh stories about Ron.

'Well,' he said, 'actually I *did* know what I was doing.'

'What, you used the right sort of screws?'

'*No.*' He looked at me askance. 'But I knew you could bang screws in like nails and that they'd stay in.'

'You didn't know,' I began to say. 'You just hit 'em and hoped for the best.'

'No, I *knew*,' he said with a yawn. 'I knew, because my old man told me.'

There was something about the simplicity with which he said this. I looked at him for a long time. Those big blue-grey eyes, the sticky-up black hair now beginning to go silvery at the temples.

He caught my stare and his face broke into a broad grin. 'What's up?'

'Dad,' I said, 'I really love you, you know.'

He nodded. 'Yeah. Yeah. I know you do.'

29

Not Fade Away

It was June 1996. I had been married for seven years to Jane O'Gorman, a beautiful, generous, loving woman I'd met during eighteen torrid and confused months at Eddie Shah's *Today* newspaper.

We had a one-year-old son, Benedict, and Jane was pregnant with our second child. I'd named Benedict after reading a newspaper article about the extraordinary kindness of some Benedictine monks, one Christmas, to a homeless man. I wasn't usually touched by stories of charity – in fact I ran a mile from them – but that one appealed somehow. I loved the name. It had weight and authority and a certain ecclesiastical charm about it. It was only much later that I realized St Benedict's saints day – 11 July – falls on my birthday.

My wife Jane was – is – an amazing girl, and she came from a similar background to my own: a council house dominated by a strong, if deeply loving, father and a quietly ambitious mother.

At home my father was becoming ill again – 'drifting away', as my poor mum put it.

Jane and I had moved to Chiswick in west London, but we'd popped over to Cullington Close that Sunday afternoon en route to see the Rolling Stones at Wembley Stadium, Mum having agreed to look after Benedict.

I was in the kitchen. That poor old kitchen. It had measured out its history in lino and mats and, after that, as a bit more money came our way, cushion-flooring; then in the succession of cats that had come and gone, their various bowls set out in front of the fridge. It had measured out its history, too, in quarrels and fights.

My mum looked quite small and lonely in it now. She had not aged but she had seemed, as most parents do, to shrink a little. The family, most of them, had gone. Both grandmothers and my granddad had died a few years before – my granddad's funeral tipping my dad over into a long period of illness; my Nana Pattrick's death pitching him into a strange, silent mood that was neither illness nor normality. He had stayed away from her funeral. As the cortège left the street – all the neighbours, as usual, at their gates – he had leant on his shed door, the omnipresent tin of fish food in his hand, scattering flakes into the pond. How deeply hurt had he been by the fall-out from that row with Nan all those years ago? What was the row really about? I will never know now.

Yet for years he had cycled across to see her, to unburden his problems on her as she sat, her fingers flickering on the arms of her chair, her small gold watch embedded deep in her plump wrist; the tick, tick, of Granddad's clock echoing round the room.

My mother's sister Joy had gone too, and her husband Bill. My uncle Ron, Jean's husband – a hopeless, lifelong manic-depressive like my dad – had died suddenly in his fifties.

Earlier that afternoon, my dad had sat in his pants in the back room, blowing up a paddling pool draped across his knees. He was now very overweight; his skin pasty, his flabby jowls forcing his broad features into an involuntary frown.

Over the following few weeks, as he became 'high', he would embark on a regime of jogging and exercise in a desperate attempt to shed a few pounds. He wheeled the inflated paddling pool through the kitchen, out onto the lawn, and ran the hose down to it. My brother had come down from his home in Milton Keynes with his little daughter Lauren and she and Benedict plonked themselves in, then immediately sprang back up, flapping their hands for someone to bring hot water and warm it up a bit. My dad, unsure whether he should fetch it, dithered on the lawn, his feet dancing, his mouth working, his eyes glazed, then eventually called: 'Peg, Peg – the kids need some hot water!'

In the back room, where she was watching from the window with us, my mum rolled her eyes at me. 'He's going to be as high as a bloody kite in this lovely weather, Mart – marvellous, isn't it?'

After lunch, we all sat out there in the afternoon sunshine, my mum and Jane in some plastic lawn-chairs Dad had salvaged from somewhere or other, Dad lying on the grass at the side of the paddling pool, dabbling his fingers in the water and handing the children various toys.

He had built a little patio of flagstones on the lawn, ten or twelve of them in an oblong, and – in a nod towards the grandiosity he was always, in small ways, trying to achieve in his garden – placed at either end a large stone stallion's head. The pair had flared nostrils and wind-blown manes. He had always loved stone ornaments. He'd even moulded a figure himself a few years back: a concrete head, seemingly bearded and long-haired like Christ, though he'd never actually said it was Him. Cemented to the back wall of his shed, it had long since lost its nose and now brooded over the pond like an ageing boxer.

Dad, though proud of my achievements, had long got into his head that the jobs I did were too stressful, and that they were 'no good' for me. He clung onto the notion that life should be led more slowly and that the anxieties of work should never occupy your free time. In all of this, of course, he was right. In his mind, always, Frank Sinatra's 'Nice 'n' Easy' was the wisest song he'd ever heard – and I'd hear it playing at the back of mine, sometimes, when he took me aside or, bringing me a cup of tea, leant in close, his warm breath on my face, his beautiful grey-blue eyes bright with concern.

'Is everything all right at work?' he'd always say to me quietly at some point. 'You look very tired.'

'No, everything's fine,' I'd reply, but of course it wasn't. I was with *You* magazine at *The Mail on Sunday* at the time and not enjoying myself very much at all.

On this day, though, there was no such conversation. For most of the afternoon, Dad was sunk in his own thoughts, or, perhaps, in no thoughts at all: who knew what was going on in his mind at times like this?

Eventually it was time for us to start getting ready to see the Stones. Jane stayed in her chair and theatrically 'hid' behind her newspaper.

'You don't really want to go, do you?' I said.

My mum laughed: 'Oh, Jane!'

I wasn't that keen myself, to be honest – the Stones had never been my favourite group – but the tickets were free, it was a big show – their Voodoo Lounge tour – and I felt guilty about not using them.

Dad scratched his head. 'I'll go, mate. I'd like to go.' He looked up at me, shielding his eyes with the palm of his hand: 'We could go together.'

* * *

411

If I'm honest, I'd grown apart from my dad over the previous decade. I had bought my first house in the
mid-Eighties with some redundancy money I'd got
when a magazine I'd devised – *The Hit* – folded. But I
hadn't moved into it. I co-owned it with a friend, who
had no real intention of living there, and the idea of rattling around a big house over in South Harrow on my
own did not appeal. I was happy – most of the time anyway – living with Mum and Dad.

But my brother was living away from home and my
dad was keen to get me out too. Was it for his sake, I
wonder now, or mine? I'd like to believe it was for mine.

One afternoon he came back from the civic centre and
announced that he wanted me out that evening. 'You've
got your own bloody house now. Go and live in it.'

He was right. I rounded up some mates who, as luck
would have it, were labouring temporarily for a
removals company and that evening an enormous van
took me away from Cullington Close. I was twenty-six.

A couple of years after this my dad was finally retired
from the civic centre, 'on sickness grounds'. During the
years that followed it was my brother who acted as
Mum's main support when Dad was ill; it was my
brother, indeed, who took Dad in for a few days when he
was high, to give Mum a rest; to give his wandering feet
somewhere to go. The last years of my father's life are
my brother's story rather than mine.

To an extent, I'd deliberately dropped out of the main

story. I was weary of my dad's illness. The ups and downs of his moods that I'd tolerated when I was a child, and even into my late teens, now tried my patience very often. I had become successful and a little self-important: suddenly his problems – the problems of my family – seemed small compared with the other things I'd convinced myself I had to worry about. I'm not proud of any of this.

So that afternoon, anyhow, I took my dad to see the Rolling Stones.

I went up to his bedroom as he was getting dressed. He had put on one of his famous 'sports jackets' and a tie. It was hard to get him out of a tie if he was going somewhere 'nice' – a habit I had happily inherited from him. He smoothed the front flaps of the jacket down over his girth and turned, rather self-consciously, this way and that, glancing in the mirror, his vanity filtering awkwardly through the ticks and twitching of his illness.

'Do I look,' he said hesitatingly, 'all right, Mart?'

'You look great.'

He nodded, then he looked straight in my eyes. 'Thanks for taking me. I'm really grateful.'

We took the train from Northwick Park: the little grey Metropolitan-line carriages that had threaded all through the early years of my life.

Dad had taken me on my first Tube journeys: to Trafalgar Square to see the lions and the fountains; to the museums and the National Gallery. There was a painting in there that he'd always loved: a Dutch rendering of Christ facing his inquisitor, the inquisitor leaning across his desk, his finger raised, and Christ standing before him, looking down, the candlelight illuminating his face.

The train rolled in to Wembley Park and we joined the throng heading towards the stadium: middle-aged people mostly, dressed, it seemed, for an afternoon picnic or an excursion to the sea. Dad stumbled along beside me, his body, as ever, jutting forward, his eyes fixed on the ground.

We had seats high up at the side of the stadium near the royal box. Privileged seats. The press facility. I nodded to one or two people I knew and introduced my dad. He sat with his hands clasped together under his belly, the way Granddad used to. Down below on the football pitch people jostled for position in front of the vast stage with its flapping side-curtains and towers of speakers.

We talked about the time we'd seen Bruce Springsteen together. Dad loved Bruce. In his vinyl record case at home he had the singles 'Dancing in the Dark' and 'Born to Run'. The concert had been just across the car park from here, at the smaller Wembley Arena. At the end, Bruce had had the house lights turned brighter so that he could see everyone's faces. Dad's eyes had filled with tears. He loved showmen. He loved anything or anyone larger than life.

I asked Dad if he wanted a beer from the bar and it struck me suddenly that I'd never bought him one before. Never bought my old man a drink. I had never even drunk one with him. All that, somehow, had passed us by.

'Ooh, yeah. Yeah, that'd be lovely.'

There was a roar from the crowd and a hard, familiar tattoo of drums around the stadium: 'Not Fade Away'. Dad beat out the rhythm on the metal rail in front of him. He'd only had one pint but he'd immediately livened up.

When a familiar figure in a vibrant blue shirt danced onto the stage, Dad gave a low laugh of recognition: a little choked chuckle. 'Mick Jagger,' he said, and looked at me with a nod. I thought of all those years before when he'd 'presented' me with Rodney Marsh.

That was to be the last time I went out with him. All those miles we walked, ponds and lakes we visited, the disjointed, perfunctory, breathless conversations we had as we laboured to pedal our bicycles up a hill. The little red plastic purse in his back pocket. Thirty bob in it for a bike that must be somewhere out there. Come on, Mart, let's go look.

And all of those trips – taken in hope, taken in despair, taken, mostly, in the spirit of adventure – all of these to end on a strange, hard echoey afternoon in a vast, soulless stadium. Gone itself, now.

30

Endgames

It was 7 November 1995, and it was raining – one of those freezing squalls that seem to pierce the skin.

I was working on a national newspaper magazine in Kensington and ran out to lunch with a colleague, my jacket over my head. It was a bright-red designer jacket that I'd bought in a sale the previous Christmas and I can't think of any earthly reason why I wore it for work that day. I never had before.

We stayed out until just before 3 p.m., then strolled back. As we approached the entrance to our building I saw a red BMW parked out front. It was a little way out from the kerb and at an odd angle, as if it had been left in a hurry. Then I noticed the number-plate. I had the tiniest little lurch in my stomach. It was Jane's car.

How quickly events move from comedy to tragedy. In the weeks before that wet afternoon in Kensington my mum had been calling me every other day about Dad.

He had been up to Hyde Park a few months earlier and been tremendously – and, from our point of view, dangerously – moved by the celebrations for the fiftieth anniversary of the end of the war. He had sunk, gradually, into long periods of morose silence, then, without any appreciable final trigger, had lurched up into the most horrendous 'high'.

Now that Dad was retired my mum couldn't even cling onto the brief interlude of guilt and confusion that compelled him to struggle on at work for a week or two until the illness took hold. She was stuck under the same small roof with him as his behaviour became ever more wild and erratic.

He began attending Sunday morning services at a Baptist church in Wealdstone; he would take a train to Hyde Park and wander round aimlessly. Above all, he exercised.

He had never eaten 'sensibly'. He was from a generation that had been through the deprivations of war and ate whatever was put in front of them, but he also loved to eat in front of the TV. He'd lie on the sofa, the plate on the cushion next to him, and wolf down snacks as he watched *Porridge* or *The Two Ronnies*.

Then, around 1991, he'd been diagnosed as a diabetic – an optician had spotted the symptoms, quite by accident, during a routine eye examination – and was forced to give up sugary things. Within a month or two his weight dropped from fifteen stone to thirteen. He dug out suits he hadn't worn in years and went shopping in them, enjoying the feeling.

But a stubborn ring of blubber remained round his stomach. He would slap it and pinch it and punch at it. He blamed the lithium, which gave him another reason, from time to time, to stop taking the drug – and when he stopped taking it, as he had just done, the determination to lose weight, combined with the churning restlessness of his mind, resulted in a rush of activity.

He bought some weights, he found 'on the boards' a clanking old rowing machine of uncertain age and origin, and, at sixty-three, he took up jogging. Dad had never been a runner. He'd cycled, played tennis and football, and walked endlessly, but I had never seen him run. Even when he was refereeing the Cullington Close football matches he'd keep abreast of the action with a series of lolloping sideways jerks along the touch-line – never a sprint.

When he was well he would, I'm sure, see no reason to run; when he was ill his brain raced so quickly that every movement must have seemed like speeded-up film. Now, though, he wobbled and puffed and blew, his feet shuffling along the pavement, his poor, damaged lungs honking and wheezing in time with his slow-swinging arms.

My mum thought that, finally, he had gone 'mad'. It seems a strange conclusion to reach after so much madness had already preceded, but this was behaviour, in her view, that indicated his depression was occurring in a new and more acute form. 'He's not a bloody jogger. And what does he want with a rowing machine?'

Concerned for my mum's health, I went to visit on my own one Saturday afternoon.

She greeted me at the door with a huge grin on her face. 'Oh, I shouldn't,' she said, almost as soon as she'd got the front door open, 'I really *shouldn't* . . .' and she was flapping her hands at me.

'Shouldn't what?'

Mum lowered her voice to a whisper: 'Shouldn't bloody *laugh*. Come and look at this.'

She led me into the back room. Dad was out on the crazy-paving. He was in shorts and an old white vest, sitting in his rowing machine. Together, peering through the back curtains, we watched as he 'oared' so frenziedly that the battered contraption leapt and jumped all over the crazy-paving. At one point he clambered awkwardly out of his seat and glared at the ancient machine as if it was an errant child.

It *was* a funny sight, but it was also a disturbing one. Dad remained fat – the exercise, so far, making no appreciable impact on his gut – but he'd lost weight rapidly, and rather grotesquely, in the face. His skin hung in loose jowls and had taken on the colour of damp clay. He looked terrible.

* * *

One afternoon Dad set up a decorator's trestle table on the pavement at the front gate of the house and put fruit, a few ornaments and various pieces of bric-a-brac on it. The Queen, he said, was about to make a visit.

He stood out there for an hour or so, chatting to various neighbours, arranging and rearranging the objects in full and earnest anticipation of her arrival. Eventually, he sat down on the wall and ate one of the oranges from his table, twisting round to drop the peel into our front garden. He kept his gaze fixed, though, on the end of the road. Any minute now . . .

'What's up, Ron?' Reg came out of his house and loped up to the gate on his pipe-cleaner legs.

'I'm waiting for somebody,' he muttered. He wasn't going to involve the royal family with Reg.

But Reg already knew. My mum had been round to tell Ellen earlier.

'Oh, poor bloke,' Ellen had sighed. 'Still, it's a nice day. If there's anything you need . . .' Ellen had once been a nurse and virtually every conversation she had with you ended with her fingers fluttering round your back as if fluffing up an imaginary pillow.

My mum had nodded, rolling her eyes at the gate.

'Is all this for sale?' Reg was asking Dad. He sat down next to him behind the table, his keen eyes scanning the strange collection of objects.

My dad laughed. 'Yeah.'

'You'll make a few bob, then!' Reg's machine-gun laugh cannoned round the empty street.

Dad came in, cursing Reg, one keen eye still trained on the gate.

He stood up. He sat down. He wrung his hands, his mouth pursing and unpursing as he gazed out of the window.

'She'll be here, she's coming, she's coming . . .' he told my mum and, when she looked doubtful, he suddenly turned on her. 'Don't give me that *fucking look*. She's on her way.'

My mum phoned Northwick Park hospital and two doctors came out. One of them knew Dad very well because he had been treating him for a few years. The other, who might have been training or on secondment, seemed to be there to observe.

Dad talked to them in his smooth, reasonable way, the illness, as it always did, drawing out layers of craftiness that were never usually part of his personality. Mum wheeled in a trolley with a large pot of tea under a cosy and some biscuits. The doctors, practised in such situations, continued the conversation in a light, banterish way, asking Dad about the family, his garden, how he was enjoying his retirement . . .

It was an embarrassingly familiar ritual to the doctors and, more crucially, to my dad: the softening-up of the patient, the gentle cajoling words that would lead them, inevitably, to the suggestion that he might like to come into hospital for a while.

Perhaps they jumped in too soon. More likely my dad, a manic-depressive for over four decades of his life, was simply not willing to play the game any more. Whatever the explanation, barely had the more senior doctor broached the subject of his possible admission than Dad flew into a temper more quickly than he had ever done in his life.

He plucked the full teapot from the table and hurled it at the doctors sitting on the settee. They raised their hands in panic and threw themselves to the side, almost as one, as the pot crashed into the little display cabinet in the corner of the room, shattering the glass.

My mum, who had screamed as the pot flew, stood up and yelled, 'Ron!' – but Dad was out of the door. He didn't put a coat on, or even a cardigan: he went straight out of the house, face grimly set, and walked quickly up the road.

Mum was shaking. The ferocity of the movement and the sheer speed with which Dad had picked up the pot and thrown it had stunned her. Still more, the obvious intention. He had *meant* to hit the doctors; he had *meant* to do them harm. This was new.

The more senior of the pair was now on his feet, apologizing, offering to clear up, gabbling, gabbling: he, too, was in shock. His colleague made a gesture of trying to console my mum. There was steaming tea and shards of glass all over the place.

'I'm so sorry, doctor. I'm so sorry.'

'It doesn't matter.'

'No, no, it's awful. It's really awful.' And then my mum was trying to explain, trying to help them understand. 'He's never been like that. I've never known him like that. He's always had the utmost respect for you – for all doctors. This is ridiculous.'

They nodded. 'Yes, yes,' they said, wiping their sleeves, opening and shutting their mouths, still raising their eyes, every now and then, to the bay window.

Final indignities. The straw and the camel's back.

You think that all the little details that make up your life arm you against the big disasters. My dad rose early every morning, shaved in two inches of hot water in the washing-up bowl – an unchanging regime. He fed his goldfish and he plucked all the greenfly off the yellow roses that rambled over his little shed. He was steady and sensible and good, but he was ill.

The doctors came back, next day, with two policemen.

'What's this all about?' my dad said, but he'd barely got the sentence out before one of the policemen drew out a pair of handcuffs. In the small room with its swirling-patterned carpet and china ornaments they seemed enormous, clanking and alien.

'No,' said my mum absently, the word stripped of any meaning.

Dad looked at the policeman open-mouthed. The officer took and lifted his wrists as easily as if they were a baby's and snapped the cuffs round them.

Dad didn't say a word. Not a word.

As they took him up the path, Reg, standing on his pathway, cursed the copper loudly, crudely and bluntly.

My mum, on her chair in the front room, wept.

Jane's car was in the road outside the office and all I could think was: Benedict. Something's happened to Benedict.

I dashed into the building, punched the buttons on the lift, cursing, cursing, the slowness of that stupid glass box, and then I was in – in and up to my floor.

A woman there – I won't name her, but she has my undying hatred for her insensitivity and stupidity, clucked: 'There's been a death in your family, I think.'

A death in my family, she *thinks*. I looked at her. 'Who, for fuck's sake? *Who?*'

She flapped her hands. 'I'm not sure . . . I didn't take the message.' She was elderly, had been in the office too long, had no idea what she was saying or doing.

I was in a blind panic now. Our offices were open-plan and one or two of my friends came across. None of them knew about any message. *Where was Jane?*

Then the phone rang on my desk. Jane was calling up from reception. She'd searched the building for me, then every restaurant and wine bar in the area.

'Bub,' she said, 'prepare yourself for some bad news.'

I was thinking: *Not Benedict, please not Benedict.*

'Your dad has died.'

Dad. And then I thought – and, heaven help me, I said: 'Thank God.'

Forgive me, Dad. Forgive me.

Dad wheeled his bike out of the side entrance of the psychiatric unit and immediately felt the sharp sting of the wind and wet on his face. He'd been allowed to keep the bike at the hospital so he could cycle home and see Mum in the afternoons.

Don't mind the rain, son. Gets on Peg's nerves – how many times has she run off into doorways on holidays? Makes me roar. I'm all right with it. Pours down all the time anyway. Good for the garden. No point in letting it hold you up.

I'll be off home in a minute. Have a cup of tea, read the paper. Look at me fish. Something else to do first, though.

He put his right hand on the damp saddle and eased the bike along the path to the open ground, his other hand shoved in the left pocket of his trousers.

I should have got meself a tracksuit, Mart, but doesn't matter – only having a short jog round anyway.

No one in bloody Northwick Park. Not surprised. See a few nurses coming through here from time to time, on their way to their lodgings on the other side. One or two say hello.

Bloody plimsolls are wet, but here goes anyway. Stick the bike down on the ground and have a little turn round the field. Just a quick blow ...

Then home for a cup of tea. I could do with a cup of tea . . .

A dog-walker found my dad's body. Don't they always? Dog-walkers must go out every day half in anticipation of such an event.

He was how I'd imagined him to be all those years before when he was so late coming back from Stanmore ponds: face down in the field, the rain pounding down on his back.

Get up, Dad. He's not getting up.

His bike was propped against a hedge about a hundred yards away, the rain running off the pedals, the handlebars. *Oil up that chain, Mart, or it'll rust.*

Face down and getting wetter and wetter.

It was the same rain: the rain that had fallen across the shoulders of my red jacket and Jane's red car; the rain that had fallen all across London that afternoon.

I remembered a line from a song by The Only Ones. It played on through my numbed brain all day. '*I want to die in the same place I was born . . . miles from nowhere.*'

See you, Dad.

See you, son.

31

A Hill . . . and a Road

We all drank tea, cups and cups of tea, until the milk made me feel bloated and tired.

The tea mixed with the numbness I felt inside and it all melted, for two or three days, into one endless, overcast afternoon in the front room at Cullington Close with my mum, my brother and my wife. The room had grown suddenly – eternally – small in my dad's absence.

Grim-faced, trying to be helpful, people came and went, the gate swinging back against the hedge: Dad's sister, Jean; my cousin Linda and her son Alex; the neighbours.

'But it was so sudden,' they all said. 'He wasn't ill, was he, Peg? He didn't look ill, did he?' The rhetorical questions were no doubt an attempt to mitigate the pain, as if weaving a little mystery round his death might make us all feel better. But there was no mystery. He was gone.

My mum, red-eyed, all cried out for the time being, sat in heavy, brooding silence. She was immaculately dressed in neatly pressed skirt and cardigan. Death had visited, but it would not undo her. Not on your life. It hadn't undone her mother, had it? Never.

She ran her tongue round the inside of her cheek and across her teeth, then sighed. She shook her head slowly, once, twice, going over it all in a mind that had nothing else, at present, to occupy it. 'I must wash my face,' she said, but she didn't move.

Then, suddenly, came more tears. 'Oh, God.' Her right hand clutched her collapsing lower face. 'Oh, God, Mart, he's gone. He's *gone*.'

My brother was out of his seat and across, arm round her neck, stroking her hair. Such a strong lad, so strong: much stronger than I am. 'Don't cry, Mum, don't cry. It's all over for him now, isn't it? All the pain. He had a good life. A good life. We all loved him, didn't we?'

And that started me off again – the tears that, for the last forty-eight hours, had come and gone in waves of remembrance, when I tortured myself with the clichéd notion of things I might have forgotten to say or do, though safe in the knowledge, when the tears had dried, that I'd never held back. I remembered the last time I had kissed him, a few weekends before, his cold breath rising under the porch of Cullington Close. In the darkness, his face had been very pale.

Thirty-odd years of saying 'I love you' to each other –

and never any shame in that. Decades of kissing and hugging when we met – and no question of not doing so. The perfect father-and-son relationship. Almost.

I plodded upstairs to the loo and peeked into my old bedroom – the room Dad had latterly used as a sort of 'study'. Same green walls – 'Sea Spray', the paint was called. I did it with a roller while Dad clucked around with advice. Along the wall, a sofa bed, to which, after restlessly tossing and turning and keeping Mum awake, Dad had sometimes fled. His old glass-fronted bureau with some books ranged along the top. The old red encyclopaedia had long gone, and the *Reader's Digest DIY Manual* in its little grey case. Given away.

In another corner, his records: Johnny Mathis, Mario Lanza, Tom Jones. The Rat Pack – Frank, Dino, Sammy – had all scuttled away: gifts for patients; one or two left at my brother's house in Milton Keynes. It seemed extraordinary, now, that Sinatra's voice had once echoed through this house literally Night and Day. I'd hated it then. I'd have given anything to hear it now: Dad bouncing on his toes by the record-player, pulling his lips this way and that. Nice 'n' easy does it.

I turned to leave the room and saw, for the first time, the words scrawled hither and thither across the wall by the door. A shock. 'Oh,' I found myself saying, needing at that moment to hear a voice.

'Martin', 'Ian', 'All heroes'. 'Michael Crawford', 'Peace in the world', 'Winston'. Some of them were in straight lines; others were arranged like crosswords, or just crosses. There had always been something religious lurking in the background of these scrawls. I touched the letters. Black, blue.

Now I was upstairs I had to get it all out of the way. I looked in to my parents' bedroom, then crept across the rug and opened Dad's wardrobe door. His ties hung on the back of it, over a rail, thin strips of beige and blue and red. During the 'punk' years of 1976–78, I raided this stock of skinny neckwear on a regular basis, picking ties that he'd carefully chosen for weddings and christenings and precious dates with Mum and knotting them round 40p shirts I found in Oxfam shops. He always said, 'Oh, keep it, Mart' – found it impossible, in fact, to lend anything other than on a permanent basis – but I hung them back here anyway. I had my own selfish, child-like reasons: I wanted the wardrobe to stay as it was.

I looked at his suits. Why had he had that bottle-green one made? Mum had always hated it. And on the floor, on the dusty lino, his Dr Marten shoes and those dreaded Green Flash plimsolls. I couldn't bring myself to touch them. I closed the wardrobe door, choking back the sudden, welling saltiness in my eyes.

There was more. Downstairs, without ceremony or particular emotion, Mum showed me the things he'd had in his pocket when they found him: a little paper diary for 1996 – the year he'd never see – his precious

Omega wristwatch, his poor old black-framed glasses. I turned away. Unbearable.

'I don't think the watch is working,' she said.

I took it from her. 'I'll get it fixed.'

Outside, the downpour continued. '*More rain*,' as my long-dead nana would always chirp whenever any of us sneezed.

Escaping the silence, trembling with the tea, Jane and I drove out through the drizzle to God-knows-where in Sudbury or Greenford or Perivale to register my father's death. It was one of those in-between places, now bisected by A-roads, that make up the forgotten map of Middlesex.

I remembered, when I was five or six, my dad coming home with a big red book, the word 'Middlesex' inlaid in gothic type on the front. Inside, there were old photographs of Harrow: the imposing house at 'Grim's Dyke' where W. S. Gilbert had drowned in the lake trying to rescue a young lady he was teaching to swim; the old toll-gate on Harrow-on-the-Hill with Keystone Cop-type figures standing to attention; a view of Wealdstone High Street when all the women had parasols and the shops elegant awnings. I had walked in all these places with my dad, always – in my memory – in the winter, and in the soft light of 5.30 p.m. when the world, for a few moments before darkness, goes deathly quiet.

Jane and I waited in a drab council building I never

knew existed – the sort of building that might, overnight, turn into a drop-in centre or a dance studio. Meanwhile, downtrodden civil servants hung grimly on.

There, in a room drenched in sunlight that had vanquished the rain, we registered the passing, on 7 November 1995, of Ronald Norman Townsend, for the benefit of a gentle, tie-less young man. He wrote, with admirable care, in an enormous ledger. The marbled cover made me think of Dad's clogged veins. I shook my head to get rid of the thought.

He confirmed the cause of death as a massive heart attack. Then he added details that could only have come, quickly and mysteriously, from Northwick Park. Dad's internal organs, it seemed, had been hopelessly damaged by over forty years of lithium. A doctor told my mum, much later, that his kidneys were 'shot to pieces'. He had also contracted gangrene fom his diabetes.

The young man seemed so genuinely sorry at my father's death that I found myself feeling sorry for him, trapped in this place. Such establishments of old-fashioned, earnest officialdom, I thought, could only be temporary. Soon he'd be looking for another job, poor devil. I wasn't feeling very happy with the world. When he passed me the certificate I contrived to touch his hand. *It'll be all right*, I wanted to say.

My mother engaged Mr Putnam the undertaker, explaining that he had 'buried all our family'. My brother glanced at me with a half-smile when she said it. We were desperate to find some humour somewhere in all this.

Mr Putnam was tall and broad-shouldered – a man designed to carry coffins. His premises, at Streatfield Road, were just across from the old Sam Cook fruiterers where my nana, in spidery, fingerless gloves, had once worked. I remembered her holding up a handful of soily potatoes and grinning over the top of them at me.

When he passed her in the street, Nana had liked to joke with Mr Putnam that he wasn't 'getting hold of me yet a while'. His easy laugh at the familiar quip suggested that he knew he would and was not sentimental about the prospect. A very handsome, upright man, he had a twinkle in his black eyes. Certainly no lady who lived thereabouts would have wanted to be buried by anyone else.

Mr Putnam called my mother 'Peg'. He had known her since she was a child. My dad was lying in his chapel of rest at the back of his premises. We were in his small office at the front, sitting before its bare desk. He asked us if we'd like to see him one last time. Mum said she would. I shook my head. I wanted to remember what I remembered.

When she came out, a few minutes later, she was in tears again. 'He looked lovely,' she said. 'I gave him a kiss.' Mr Putnam nodded and handed her a tissue. He was standing behind his desk. I had never seen him seated. "Ere y'are: blow your nose, Peg. It's always hard,' he said. 'Always hard.' He traced his finger across the blotter on his desk and glanced out of the window.

Afterwards Mum told me she wished she hadn't seen him at all. 'He seemed so small,' she said. 'Not like himself at all.'

The funeral was held at St Mary's. There were still one or two people connected to the place that I knew, but I had never met the vicar and he seemed to have only a vague knowledge of his predecessors.

I can't remember when I had finally left the choir but I think it might have been at the end of the Seventies, just before I started at the London College of Printing. A man called Paul Everington had taken over from Brian as choirmaster. I liked him very much. He had his own upholstery and fabrics business in Wimbledon and was quite wealthy. Choral music was his hobby and he was an excellent organist. He also liked to bring in orchestras to perform at mass and had attempted some very complex settings. When Paul left, though, the vicar at the time had dithered over finding a replacement and many of the members had drifted away. Perhaps I'd been one of them.

The ceremony was very well attended. It was a low, sullen day, grey and cloudless. Outside on the courtyard where the choirboys used to gather, members of our family mixed with many of our neighbours from

Cullington Close: Reg and Ellen; the Browns; the Herberts. They seemed quiet and a little confused, as if the funeral was something that needed explaining and they were waiting for someone to speak. Roger Brown came over to me. 'Shame about your dad, Mart – we used to love 'im. Lovely geezer, weren't 'e?' Behind him, over by the vicarage fencing, his father Neville nervously smoked a cigarette, nodding across at me with a look of intense concentration on his face.

The elegant old vicarage had long gone, replaced by a dull, modern house. More houses had gone up at the back of Father Shearing's old garden, too, burying the orchard where we'd 'buzzed' cider-apples at one another. The Church gradually selling up.

The congregation began to move nervously into the church, dawdling a little at the doors as if there might be tigers within. Cigarettes were put out. My auntie Jean looked crushed. She was leaning on my cousin Linda. Uncle Ernie and Auntie Pat had driven up from Worthing with my various cousins, and my aunties Maureen and Sheila, uncle John and cousin David had come from as far away as Scotland to be there.

My brother and I were wearing the matching dark-blue double-breasted suits I'd had made up for us for my wedding. Ian was making people laugh – something he'd always been able to do, in any situation, since he was old enough to talk. A great gift. He had my father's ability, too, to shrug off the worst possible situations. Life had to go on.

I glanced back, from our pew at the front of the nave, towards the old font in the north-west corner of the church. I had a transparency of myself being christened at that font, the light coming in from the stained glass and just catching the face of the old priest as he cradled me in his arms. My dad had taken that picture.

Suddenly I missed him more than I'd ever missed anyone in my life and I wanted him back so badly. The tears welled up in my eyes. I felt myself sob. 'Oh, Dad.'

'Come on, mate.' My brother leant across and put his arm round my shoulder. I shook my head. Why, oh why, did he have to go? Why now, when Benedict was so small and they'd barely had the chance to get to know each other? I had the anger, then, the huge, surging, unreasonable anger of the ages felt by every son in every century at the loss – the unjust, unfair, cruel loss – of his father. Always too suddenly. Always too soon. I still feel it now, writing these words. Anger and sorrow.

Mum had had a wreath made in the shape of a koi carp and it sat on the altar at the foot of the coffin-trestle: the spot where, nearly forty years earlier, she and my dad had first knelt as man and wife.

She had asked me what music we should play and I suggested the hymn 'Dear Lord and Father of Mankind', even though it was the saddest I knew and would do none of us any good at all. But for the end I'd chosen Widor's Toccata, a surging, circular organ voluntary more usually played at weddings. It had rung in my ears and my brother's on many Saturdays as we scuttled back down the gallery steps clutching our hard-earned fifty-pence pieces.

I didn't think Dad would want people to be miserable as they left.

Dad was buried at Harrow Weald cemetery, a mile or so from his beloved Stanmore ponds. The grounds slope up steeply towards a ragged line of trees and I watched my mum plodding slowly up that hill ahead of me, her head down, her best brown coat buttoned up neck to knee.

Dad and I had walked and cycled past this place dozens of times – so alive, so alive.

As the coffin was lowered into the ground I couldn't stop thinking about his eyes. I had read a passage in a biography of someone or other a few years before in which the son had said that the worst thing about burying his father was the idea that his beautiful, clear blue eyes were now in the earth. That's how I felt.

The rain had been falling sporadically in brief showers all afternoon, but as we struggled for a footing in the slippery clay at Dad's graveside the sun broke through and a rainbow arced steeply down over Kenton. I know it sounds like the cheesiest and most unbelievable of clichés, but it happened. My mother, already in-consolable, broke into fresh tears.

* * *

I thought of writing to the hospital and asking why Dad had been allowed to go jogging at all, but in my mind's eye I could see him waving his arm dismissively: *Don't bother, son – no one was going to stop me*.

No one ever stopped my dad doing anything, really; not that he ever did anything terribly dishonest or bad. But his ferocious determination to get on – to have a family, to earn a living, to establish a home and a garden and a decent life – was forged and always affected by two things: a shamefully bad state education and the horror of his national service. Progress for him must have been like trying to walk along a road with a strong length of elastic attached to his back: he would get so far and then be pulled back. But he had to keep walking, he had to. However many times venturing forth seemed to get him nowhere, he had to continue putting one foot ahead of the other.

And so we get to the heart of the matter. I make no apologies for leaving this story – this explanation, perhaps – until the very end, because it did not inform every thought I ever had about my dad. It wasn't always in my mind when his moods began to fluctuate, the sweet turned to sour, the black to white. I had to find my own way through and I didn't want any easy answers.

My mother told me the story once. My father never discussed it. Ever. He had been doing his national service in Bielefeld in Germany in 1950 or 1951, so he would have been about nineteen – the same age I was when I started work.

He was walking down a country road with a couple of his colleagues, all three of them in uniform. They had been given the afternoon off, or were on some sort of patrol – I'm not sure of the exact circumstances.

In my mind's eye, though, I have them walking on a dry, roughly made road through a scrubby and arid landscape. I'm sure this is unlikely in that part of Germany but it's how I imagine it. I can see the dust coming up from their uncomfortable, unfamiliar boots.

I am watching the three men from behind, perhaps because, knowing what is about to happen, I am adopting the perspective of the driver who ploughed into them. I can imagine my father to the left of the group, his arms swinging, as they always did: his black, Silvikrined head bobbing along. He is wearing khaki trousers but no jacket and his sleeves are rolled up above his elbows. The other two are strolling slightly apart from him, hands in pockets. My dad is gesticulating with his hands, telling some yarn or other – and this is the dad I never had: the dad who had not yet been through what happened next.

I can hear my dad's voice and a burst of his laughter from a long way off, like when I am at the end of the garden and I hear him in the kitchen with my mum. He is telling a story or joke to his mates – some tale about his dad, perhaps. I can imagine him chatting a great deal about his 'old man', because Albert to my dad would have been like my dad to me: a much braver, bolder figure than I would ever be.

Either they hear the German car behind them and think it will simply pass, in the yawning gap between my dad and his friends, or they don't hear it at all.

I can imagine my dad half-turning, his jaw dropping, a few strings of talked-out spittle stretching between his lips, before his eyes widen and his mouth rounds in a shriek, a shout, a yell. But the sound is swallowed up by the vast, yawning roar of an engine.

The other sounds he hears, the crashing, shattering, smashing sounds of the impact, are beyond my imagination. As is the sight of the two crushed and broken bodies. I cannot conjure that up. When the hit-and-run driver has long gone, his vehicle swerving a little as he tries to make sense of his crazed and bloodied windscreen, the image I have in my mind is of my dad alone on the road. I cannot see his friends anywhere.

I can see no one for him to crouch over, to touch, to tend, to whisper those simple, soothing words that he could always bestow. I close my eyes tightly and try to find his friends, but they will not come; I try to move him across the dust to a ditch or a hollow where they have crawled or been scattered; but then memory becomes a film we've all seen a dozen times – some sort of action adventure – and that's not right at all.

So he just stands alone on the road, helpless, his hands flexing, his body swivelling, his mouth opening and closing in panic, while in his head everything is being rearranged: like stage-hands moving props, changing the background, the foreground, the very nature of the scene.

On that road where his friends died, the dad I never really knew slipped into the half-shadows and the dad I had was born. Imagine him walking back! Imagine how he must have felt: the loneliness; the helplessness; the confusion that never ended. Imagine how many times for years afterwards he made that walk. I am only glad that for dozens of those forlorn miles I was able to be at his side.

Let's go and tell someone now, Dad. It will all be fine. We'll do it together. Let's go and tell someone.

Afterword

More than eleven years have passed since my father's death. Shenley Hospital is long gone, the villas bulldozed to make way for housing. Other mental hospitals – and London was at one time ringed by them – have been converted into flats or hotels. Little wonder, then, that when I walk down the street, or travel by Tube or bus, I see men and women with manic-depressive symptoms all around me. They have nowhere else to go.

Northwick Park hospital carries on, its name destined to be linked for ever with the infamous 'elephant man' medical trials that took place there early in 2006.

The arguments about the 'correct' treatment of mental health problems rumble on too, only pricking the general public's consciousness when an assault, rape or murder is committed by a sufferer. The main debate seems to be about the rights of the patient weighed against the safety of the public at large. I hear very little discussion about the 'rights' of families who have a manic-depressive in their fold.

I bear no bitterness towards my father, or his doctors. I don't go in for bitterness, as a general rule, and I'm sure that the doctors were doing their best. My family climbed the walls in frustration when my father became 'high' and the medical authorities dithered over taking him into hospital, but at least there was a hospital for him to go to. Besides, if he'd gone into hospital sooner, or more frequently, might he have died ten years earlier? Given the damage that the lithium did to his insides, I wouldn't bet against it.

My greatest frustration is with the stigma still attached to all forms of mental illness. All of us are blessed with brains and so the statistical chance of some of them going wrong is indisputable, yet when that happens we turn away. We are ashamed of the sufferer, or embarrassed, or both. The treatment in the media of high-profile manic-depressives such as the boxer Frank Bruno has been scandalous; the suggestion, early on, that he might be 'getting well' an unforgivable statement of ignorance. Manic-depressives do not get well. At best, they cope.

It was a column I wrote in the *Sunday Express* about Frank's plight that led to my decision to write this book. I wanted to express, and present on paper, not only my feelings about my father but my feelings about the illness that overshadowed much of his life. I don't know whether my experiences will be of any help to anyone else, but they may be of some comfort. Lots of families go through what we went through. We are, none of us, alone.

As for me, I have raised a family, enjoyed a good career and, thank God, stayed healthy. It's tempting to say that my experiences with my father's illness gave me a determination to succeed, but that would be a lie. The illness was something neither of us wanted. It was an unwanted outsider in our relationship.

My mother and father gave me the determination to get on. Their encouragement and enthusiasm lies behind every word of this book – and everything else that I do. God bless them both.

BILLY'S HALO
Ruth Mckernan

'MOVING AND ENTHRALLING. THIS IS A WONDERFUL
BOOK'
Bill Bryson

When her father, Billy, succumbed to a mystery illness and slipped
from consciousness into coma, Ruth McKernan watched his life ebb
away with a mixture of love and terror. She struggled for control by
using her knowledge as a neuroscientist working at the forefront of
medical research to analyse his condition.

In this moving account of her father's last year, love, grief and hope
are intertwined with a crystal-clear scientific explanation of the way
our brains and bodies work. The result is an inspired blend where the
contrasting view of scientist and daughter ultimately unite.

'AN ILLUMINATING COMBINATION OF MEDICAL
SCIENCE AND PERSONAL FEELING'
Lewis Wolpert

'CHARTS THE ANATOMY OF LOVE AND LOSS . . . AN
ORIGINAL, ENLIGHTENING AND ULTIMATELY VERY
MOVING BOOK'
Paul Broks, author of *Into the Silent Land: Travels in Neuropsychology*

'AN INTRIGUING ORIGINAL VENTURE . . . THE
EXCURSIONS INTO SCIENCE GENUINELY
AUGMENT THE STORY-LINE'
Independent

9780552772822

BLACK SWAN

FOREVER TODAY
A memoir of never-ending love
By Deborah Wearing

'A REMARKABLE, RESILIENT AND RESOURCEFUL
WOMAN . . . YOU CAN'T READ THIS BOOK
WITHOUT CRYING'
Sunday Times

Forever Today is Deborah Wearing's astonishing account of her
husband Clive's devastating amnesia, which struck almost overnight
and wiped out Clive's entire past. Trapped in a frozen moment of the
present, he was left with only his talent as a musician intact, and his
profound love for Deborah. She fought single-mindedly for years – for
Clive, and for pioneering treatment, until a desperate need to save
herself made her flee to America, leaving Clive behind. But their bond
was too strong to be ignored and Deborah was drawn back to
England and to Clive, in a most moving demonstration of
enduring love.

'OVERWHELMINGLY MOVING . . . A DESCRIPTION OF
UTTERLY UNSELFISH LOVE'
Daily Mail

'A HARROWING, HAUNTING AND HEARTENING BOOK –
A LOSS-STORY WHICH IS ALSO A LOVE STORY'
Andrew Motion

'AN EXTRAORDINARY STORY OF CONSTANCY IN LOVE,
AND DEBORAH WEARING TELLS IT BRILLIANTLY'
Evening Standard

'DELIVERS A MESSAGE OF HOPE ABOUT
HUMAN IDENTITY'
Mail on Sunday

'LOVING, TERRIFYING AND OFTEN EXTREMELY
FUNNY . . . ASTONISHING'
Deborah Moggach

9780552771696

CORGI BOOKS

ALONE
By Pip Granger

In 1950s London, a little girl is busy being brave.

The only daughter of alcoholic parents, Pip Granger spent much of her childhood on the margins of society; on the outside of life, looking in.

Drink was the factor behind the series of crises, the furious rows and life-threatening accidents Pip had to contend with. It also explained why her home life was so very different from that of most other people she knew.

Bullied at school, neglected by her parents, and cared for, at times, by complete strangers, Pip realized that there was only one way to turn her life around. One day she would have to cut loose from her family, and have the courage to build her own life – alone.

Set in a world when sheets and blankets were washed by hand, bananas were considered a luxury, and separation and divorce were shameful events, *Alone* is a brave, original and totally authentic book about a young girl's courage in a trouble-filled world.

9780552155366

CORGI BOOKS

OUT OF THE DARK
One Woman's Harrowing Journey to Discover her Past
By Linda Caine & Dr Robin Royston

Life for Linda Caine should hold no fears. As a contented wife and
mother, she should have everything to live for. Yet a blackness has
started to leak into her thoughts. Images flash through her head
leaving her stunned and breathless. On the face of it, there is no
rational explanation for the way she feels.

But Linda believes there is something bad inside her. At the back
of her mind a voice tells her over and over again that everything
will be OK. When it finally gets too much, she can always simply
die. '*How shall I die if that time comes? I need to know these things.
They have to be planned.*' It must look like an accident. She will
drive off a cliff on her way home from her weekly shopping trip.
After all, who commits suicide with a load of groceries in their car?

The raw and powerful journey that Linda takes with her
psychiatrist Robin Royston to discover what lies at the heart of her
depression will leave you breathless. The secrets in her African
childhood and adolescence are buried so deep that to reveal them
may destroy her completely. Nothing is what it seems, no one is
above suspicion. Together Linda and Robin race to unravel the
clues, before it is too late . . .

'READS LIKE A PSYCHOLOGICAL DETECTIVE STORY
. . . LINDA'S PASSAGE BACK TO HEALTH AND SANITY
MAKES FOR COMPULSIVE READING'
Mail on Sunday

9780552148696

CORGI BOOKS